JOE CARR'S RECEIVING ANTENNA HANDBOOK

by

Joseph J. Carr, K4IPV

publications inc.

Solana Beach, California

Printed in the United States of America.

Cover design and illustrations: Brian McMurdo, Ventana Studio, Valley Center, CA

Developmental editing: Jose Onda-Corta, Tecate, BCN, Mexico

Production services: Sara Patton, Words of Wonder, Wailuku, HI

ISBN: 1–878707–07–8
Library of Congress catalog number: 92-074266

HighText is a registered trademark of HighText Publications, Inc.

Converting from English to Metric Measurements

This book was written by an American author and published in the United States for an American readership, so most measurements are made in English units—which, for all practical purposes, are America-only units these days. However, you may live in a nation that has succumbed to insidious French hegemony in weights and measures. For the benefit of those so afflicted, here are some conversion factors:

- To convert inches into centimeters, multiply the measurement in inches by 2.54.

- To convert feet into meters, multiply the measurement in feet by 0.3048.

- To convert yards into meters, multiply the measurement in yards by 0.9144.

- To convert miles into kilometers, multiply the measurement in miles by 1.61.

ANTLERS Software

Many of the antennas in this book can be designed using an executable BASIC program called ANTLERS. If you would like a copy, which will run on MS-DOS IBM compatible machines, then write me for information and price at:

Joe Carr
P.O. Box 1099
Falls Church, VA 22041

Please enclose a large self-addressed, stamped envelope (three stamps) for a free listing of the program.

Contents

Chapter 9:   119

VERTICAL ANTENNAS

Chapter 10:   131

DIRECTIONAL ANTENNAS

Chapter 11:   143

SMALL LOOP RECEIVING ANTENNAS

Chapter 12:   171

LOW FREQUENCY ANTENNAS

Double Dedication

This book is dedicated to two people who helped me learn to appreciate antennas. One is the late Johnnie Harper Throne, K4NFU/5: a dude what knew some smoke about antennas—and had the integrity and interest to teach others. The other is the late Hugh T. Collins, a Voice of America radio engineer, next door neighbor, surrogate father, and man of wisdom. He taught me a lot about transmitter and receiver antennas, the latter derived from showing U.S. embassy and military personnel how to receive VOA broadcasts in posts that were truly hardship locations. Besides his technical mentoring, Hugh also changed my life by kicking my butt into college back in 1966–67.

Read This Before Erecting Any Antenna!
(and don't forget it either!)

Erecting antennas can be a dangerous affair. Every year the radio community is saddened by stories of people who were killed or seriously injured by antennas that they were erecting. The most serious threat comes from foolishly attempting to erect a wire antenna by tossing it over the AC power lines coming into the house. While it may be tempting to do so, especially when the most convenient support structures are on opposite sides of the power line, this feat **MUST NEVER BE ATTEMPTED!** The argument that both antenna and power wires are insulated does not help, for insulation can and does deteriorate or cut through (and with remarkably little force). It is NEVER safe to do this trick, so **DON'T DO IT!** Please???

Also, keep in mind where the antenna will go if it breaks and plan your installation accordingly. Look around the yard and determine whether or not it will be capable of wind-whipping into a power line, or if it will become a hazard on a foot path or sidewalk, or if it will crash into a window or vehicle (and those insulators and balun coils WILL break glass when wind-whipped).

Use properly designed factory-made insulators, not ad hoc substitutes, for the end and center insulators. The rope should be sufficiently strong to hold the antenna (plus ice load if you live in a colder climate) under all wind conditions, and should be strain-relieved with a spring or counterweight. Use good quality wire in #12 or #14 size. A steel core, copperclad wire—like that available under the brand name of Copperweld—intended especially for antennas is recommended.

When erecting the antenna, especially if standing on a ladder, be aware of where the wire is at all times. It can easily become entangled in your feet or ladder support, and cause a serious fall. Always work with another person so that help is near at hand; if you're a young reader, work with a knowledgeable adult until you are experienced in the antenna erection process. Wire antennas are notoriously easy, or so it seems, to erect. . . but that's a fool's game from a safety perspective.

You also need to be careful when soldering connections, particularly if you're using a high-wattage iron. Such irons (and the molten solder) can cause painful burns if you're not careful. Allow plenty of time for soldered connections to cool before touching them.

Here's some legal-type stuff HighText is making me put in here:

"This book contains information that involves electricity and requires the use of tools and the possession of certain physical abilities. Neither the publisher nor the author can accept responsibility for your use of this information or for your safety. Although all information is believed to be correct, and efforts were made to ensure correctness, no warranty is made explicitly or implicitly as to its completeness, correctness, or fitness for any particular application."

Are you HighText people now satisfied???

I can't possibly foresee all possible situations, so please exercise some basic good sense when planning, erecting, or repairing antennas. The secret to successfully building and installing any antenna—and having fun doing it—is to plan your efforts, take your time, watch what you're doing, and double-check your work. Try it and see for yourself!

– Joe Carr, Falls Church, VA

CHAPTER 1

Some Preliminaries

Before we can get into the nuts and bolts of antenna design and construction, we need to review some important points about radio waves and signal propagation you'll need to know to understand the material in the rest of this book. Some of the following may be a review for you, so please feel free to skip ahead as appropriate…I won't be offended (I promise).

Wavelength and Frequency

Sure, we're all familiar with the relationship between the frequency and wavelength of a radio signal. But just in case you've forgotten…

$$\text{wavelength} = \left(\frac{300}{\text{frequency in MHz}} \right)$$

…gives the wavelength in meters for a signal of a given frequency. By the way, wavelength is often denoted by the symbol λ in various radio books and articles. We'll also use it in this book.

Radio Wave Polarization

The *polarization* of a radio wave is defined as the direction of the electric field (E-field). The E-field vector has a positive and negative end, which is measured by the effect the field has on any electrons that are within the E-field. The polarization of a wave sent from a transmitting antenna can be deduced by looking at the construction of the antenna. If the principal length of the antenna is horizontal (Figure 1-1A), as it is with many wire antennas, then the wave is horizontally polarized. Similarly, if the principal length is vertical (Figure 1-1B), as it is on AM broadcasting antenna towers, then the emitted electromagnetic wave is vertically polarized.

For some receiver owners, especially those using the VHF and UHF frequencies, the antenna polarization is important for maximizing the received signal. The principal length of the receiver antenna is ideally oriented to match the polarization of the incoming radio wave. *Cross-polarization*—a horizontal antenna picking up a vertically polarized wave (or vice versa)—causes a reduction of signal strength on the order of about 3 dB. Since we're interested in antennas for frequencies below 30 MHz, however, we have less need to consider polarization issues than VHF/UHF listeners. This is because sky wave signals below 30 MHz have scrambled polarization due to refraction off the ionosphere. Although there are general guidelines concerning "best" polarizations for given VHF/UHF frequencies, the situation over long, international shortwave paths is not so easily defined because

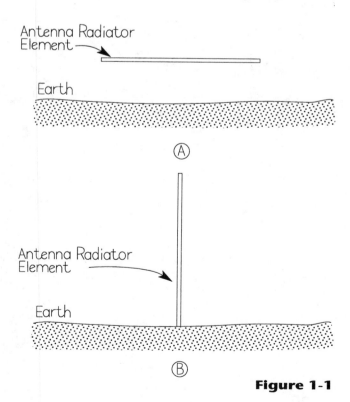

Figure 1-1

there are polarity shifts over the transmission path. Indeed, there may be multiple transmission paths between a transmitter and receiver, and the two waves may arrive out of phase with each other…and with differing polarities.

Angle of Arrival

A critical concept for antenna designers is the *angle of arrival* (AOA) of the desired signals. Ground wave signals are of little concern in this respect because the only angle of arrival that we must consider is the *azimuth*—from which direction does it come. Point the antenna in the right direction, or use an azimuthal omnidirectional antenna, and the signal is received. But sky wave signals refracted back to Earth in the ionosphere are different. They have not only an azimuthal angle of arrival, which is the "great circle" bearing between receiver and transmitter, but also an elevation angle of arrival. (A great circle is the shortest path between two points on

Earth. Since the Earth is round, a great circle path is a curved line instead of a true straight line. To determine the great circle bearing from your location to another, sit down with a globe and some string. The results can be surprising. For example, the shortest path from much of the United States to Asia is not to the west; it's to the *north*, over the North Pole.)

Figure 1-2 shows two ways that angle of arrival can change. In Figure 1-2A, we see that the angles of arrival of three signals, from three different locations, are different just by virtue of the respective skip distances. In Figure 1-2B, a different situation is seen. Here the ionosphere will change during reception of a signal, and the effective height will vary so the angle of arrival at the receiver also changes. When this occurs fast enough, a flutter is heard. It is common for ionospheric changes to occur over a period of several minutes, especially as the band fades for the evening.

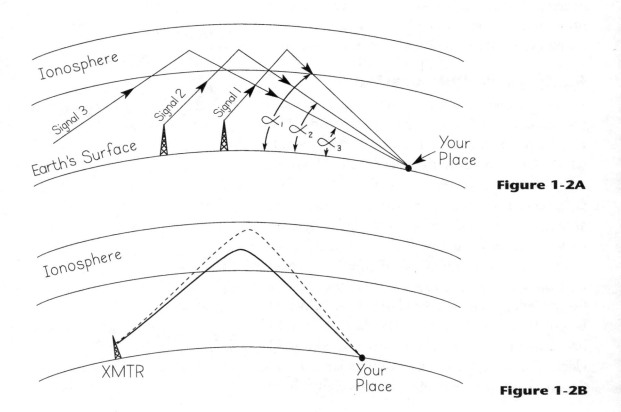

Figure 1-2A

Figure 1-2B

For some antennas, the mechanical position of the antenna can be used to compensate for the angle of arrival. Some small loops work well in this respect, as we'll see later in this book. Other antennas, however, either can't be moved or the angle of maximum response (called "angle of radiation" elsewhere) is insensitive to changes in mechanical position. It would waste a lot of time or money tilting a Yagi beam, for example, in order to compensate for angle of arrival problems. Only the design of the antenna and its installation height above ground can change the angle of maximum response.

Reciprocity

Most descriptions of radio antennas are written from the transmitting point of view. This approach is usually also sufficient for receiver owners because there is a law of reciprocity in effect for all known antennas. That is, an antenna functions in exactly the same manner on both transmit and receive. Describing an antenna for transmitting essentially describes it also for receiving. While technically true, the transmitter point of view loses something for receiver owners. I decided, therefore, to write this chapter on basic antenna theory from the receiver point of view.

One reason for adopting a receiver point of view is that reciprocity does not mean that you would wisely choose the same style of antenna for both receiving and transmitting at the same site. While practical matters often force such arrangements to be the case, the goals of receiving and transmitting are different, so rely on different characteristics of the antenna for optimum performance. Also, when selecting an antenna for a site that is purely for receiving, you would select the antenna based on those features that are optimal for reception. For example, a deep null might be more important to a receiver than the raw gain that appeals to transmitter operators.

Antenna Patterns and Bandwidth

An *antenna pattern* is a graph of the antenna response as a function of the angle of arrival of the radio signal. Two patterns are generally taken. We've already met the first: a horizontal, or bird's eye view, called the *azimuth* pattern. The other is a vertical, or side view, called the *elevation* pattern. Keep in mind, however, that these patterns are just two dimensional slices taken at certain locations. The entire pattern is a three dimensional form of azimuth and elevation patterns at all angles.

The *gain* of the antenna refers to the fact that some antennas seem to boost the signal strength compared to other antennas. When looking at gain, it's necessary to use a reference source for making a comparison. The usual practice is to compare an antenna to either a theoretical construct called an *isotropic* source (we'll look at this later; for now, just think of it as an antenna offering no gain or loss) or a standard reference antenna such as a half-wavelength dipole.

Gain and Decibels

Gain is typically measured using a system called *decibels* (abbreviated "dB"). The use of decibels for electrical measurements originated with the telephone industry, and was named after telephone inventor Alexander Graham Bell. The original unit was the "bel." The prefix "deci" means 1/10, so the "decibel" is one-tenth of a bel. The bel is too large for most common applications, so it is rarely, if ever, used.

The decibel is nothing more than a means of expressing a ratio between two signal levels, such as the relative strength of a received radio signal from two different antennas being compared. Because the decibel is only a ratio, it is also dimensionless; that is, it's not a fixed unit like the centimeter or inch. It doesn't make any sense to talk about a value like "6 dB" unless we know the signal levels being compared. The decibel can be used to express gains or losses between signal levels.

The decibel is based on the response of the human ear to changes in the loudness of a sound. This means it is a logarithmic rather than linear term. For example, suppose the power of a transmitter was increased from 100 watts to 200 watts. How much louder would the signal from the transmitter sound? Common sense (and "linear" thinking) might suggest that the signal would sound twice as loud. But that's wrong—in fact, there would be only a slight, barely noticeable increase in the loudness of the signal. The transmitter power would have to be increased ten times—from 100 watts to 1000 watts—before the signal would sound twice as loud. This is how a logarithmic response works.

One decibel is about equal to the smallest audible change in signal level—in other words, a difference that's just enough to be noticed. Since decibels are logarithmic, seemingly minor changes in the number of decibels used to measure gain or loss can express big differences in power levels. For example, a 10 dB gain in a signal is equivalent to increasing the power ten times. A 60 dB gain in a signal is not equal to increasing the power 60 times; instead, it is equal to increasing the power 1,000,000 times!

You can calculate the difference between two power levels in decibels by using the following formula:

$$dB = 10_{\log}\left(\frac{P1}{P2}\right)$$

However, most people just memorize some commonly used decibel levels and their equivalent gain or loss in power. Here are some of the most common ones:

     3 dB = gain or loss of 2
     6 dB = gain or loss of 4
    10 dB = gain or loss of 10
    20 dB = gain or loss of 100
    30 dB = gain or loss of 1000
    40 dB = gain or loss of 10,000
    50 dB = gain or loss of 100,000
    60 dB = gain or loss of 1,000,000

Thus, if an antenna is said to have a 20 dB gain over another, it means that the antenna makes the transmitted (or received) signal sound 100 times more powerful than the antenna it is being compared to.

Decibel measurements can be extremely misleading if the reference antenna or power level that is being used for comparison is not clearly stated. Some manufacturers often misstate the gain claims for their antenna by using a non-isotropic (or non-existent???) antenna for comparison. That's why any claims for antenna gain in an advertisement should be taken with large grains of salt unless the reference antenna is clearly stated.

Traveling Waves and Standing Waves

Let's consider what happens when a wave is applied to an antenna. It doesn't matter much whether the antenna current is excited by a radio transmitter or a passing electromagnetic wave; the result is pretty much the same. Take a look at Figure 1-3. In Figure 1-3A, a wave is launched onto the antenna wire. It travels from the source towards the other end. This wave, called the *incident wave* or forward wave, is an example of a traveling wave. That is, the wave travels from one point to another on the antenna wire. When the wave hits the open opposite end of the conductor, it cannot go anywhere so it reverses direction (turning upside down, or "reversing polarity," in the process) and travels back towards the source (Figure 1-3B). This *reflected wave* is also a traveling wave but is traveling in the opposite direction of the incident wave.

The incident and reflected waves interfere with each other, as do all waves that try to occupy the same space. The signal level at any given point on the wire is the algebraic sum (added taking into consideration the polarities of the waves) of the incident and reflected waves. When the waves add constructively, they reinforce each other, producing a *maxima.* Conversely, when they add destructively they produce a *minima* (Figure 1-3C). The location of the minima ("nodes") and maxima ("antinodes" or "loops") tends to be stationary, so the envelope of the combined traveling waves forms a standing wave.

In the other chapters of this book, you will find antennas described as "traveling wave" or

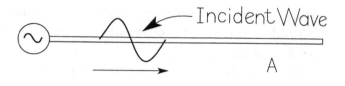

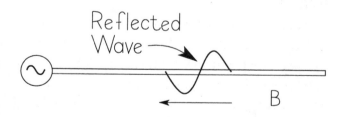

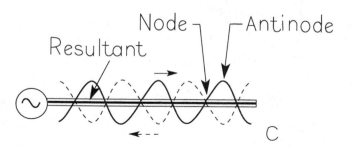

Figure 1-3

"standing wave" designs. A *standing wave antenna* is not terminated at the far ends, away from the receiver, so has incident and reflected components. A *traveling wave antenna* is terminated in a resistance so that the forward wave is absorbed rather than reflected. These concepts will be dealt with further later.

Directivity, Gain, and Aperture

A *directional* antenna is one that prefers signals from a specified direction while excluding or severely attenuating those from other directions. For *omnidirectional* (all direction) transmitting antennas, an analogy is a spherical light bulb (Figure 1-4A) that emits light in all directions; the illumination envelope provided is a large sphere radiating in all directions. Such a source is called omnidirectional because it radiates all directions. But when the spherical lamp is placed at the focal point of a parabolic reflector mirror, its rays are redirected in a single direction (Figure 1-4B). Such a source is directional, in this case unidirectional.

A receiving antenna analogy might be a photocell—an electrical component that responds to light levels—at the focal point of a parabolic mirror. By itself, the photocell responds to light from many directions, and as a result may not have the sensitivity or dynamic range to detect weak light sources in specific directions. But if the photocell is placed at the focal point of a parabolic mirror, then its direction of maximum response will be as shown in Figure 1-4C.

For any given antenna the law of reciprocity tells us that the performance of the antenna on transmit and receive is the same. In our mirror analogy, lamps and photocells placed at the focal point of the parabolic mirror work opposite each other as "transmitter" and "receiver," respectively. A transmit antenna that directs all

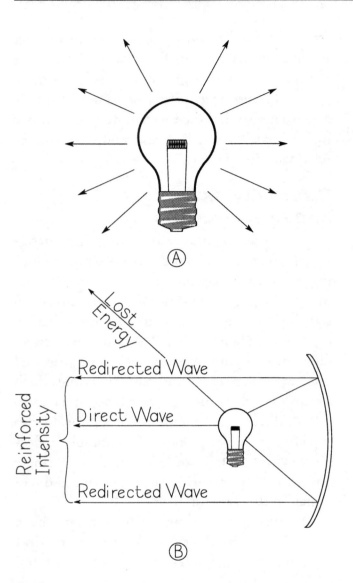

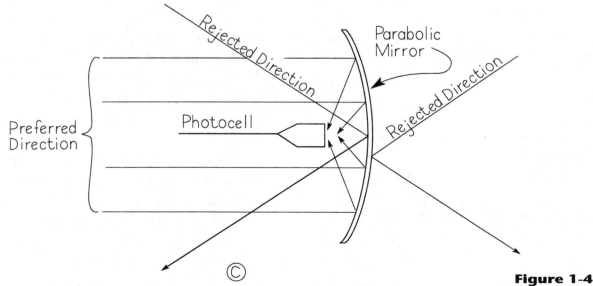

Figure 1-4

of its energy to the south (for example), will only receive stations to the south, and rejects signals arriving from the north, east, and west.

Antennas possess three interrelated properties: directivity, gain, and aperture. We can get a handle on these concepts by considering the basic reference for antenna measurements: the isotropic source. This theoretical construct assumes a spherical point source radiating signal into the air. As the signal travels outwards, the sphere increases in size until it has a diameter R (see Figure 1-5). All of the RF power that was part of that tiny spherical radiator at the center (C) is now distributed over the entire surface of the enlarged sphere. In making comparisons with various antennas, the surface of the sphere is said to have an area of unity (1), and the isotropic radiator is said to have a "gain" of unity. All antenna gains are measured against the unity gain isotropic source. An isotropic radiator is truly omnidirectional because it radiates power in all directions equally.

Directivity means that the RF power radiated by the antenna is not radiated or received in all directions equally, but rather

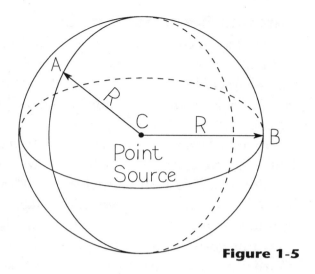

Figure 1-5

area and has a higher power density (watts per unit area). The ratio of the power density (watts per square meter, W/m^2) in the cone to the power density distributed over the entire sphere is the antenna's gain. If a receiver antenna is placed at the distance R from the point source C first on the isotropic source and on the directional antenna, it will receive a louder signal on the directional antenna.

The concepts of gain and directivity are applicable to both receiver and transmitter antennas. Directivity is measured as the angle between -3 dB points. Gain is measured by comparison of the antenna to the isotropic source. A half-wavelength dipole is an antenna that is bidirectional; it radiates a doughnut shaped pattern that looks like a "figure-8" when viewed from above. The gain of the dipole is +1.64 dB compared to the isotropic source.

Receiving antennas also possess a property called aperture, or *capture area*. This concept relates the amount of power that is delivered to a matched receiver to the power density (watts per square meter). The aperture is often larger than the physical area of the antenna, as in the case of the half-wavelength dipole (where the wire fronts

there are preferred directions. Let's assume, for the sake of argument, that the antenna is uni-directional. This antenna, placed at the center of the sphere (C in Figure 1-5) will radiate power towards the surface of the sphere. But because it is directional, it makes a "footprint" on the sphere that is much smaller than the entire spherical surface (Figure 1-6). The radiation pattern is basically a solid with a horizontal angle θ_h and an elevation angle $\theta\chi$. These angles are defined as the points in azimuth and elevation where the power (on a transmit antenna), or sensitivity response (on a receive antenna), falls off by -3 dB from the center of the pattern.

Now we have two situations: the entire sphere with unity surface area, and a conical section from a directional antenna with a surface area less than unity. Directivity is the measure of the extent of the cone of radiation.

If all of the power that had been radiated by the isotropic source is now radiated by the directional antenna, then it is concentrated into a much smaller

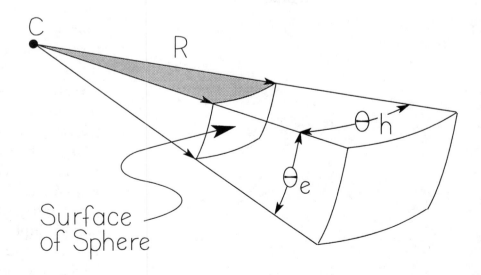

Figure 1-6

a very small physical area), or less as in the case of a parabolic reflector used in microwave reception. Figure 1-7 shows the capture area of a half-wavelength (0.5 λ) dipole. It consists of an ellipse with major axes of 0.51λ and 0.34λ.

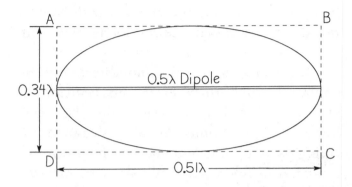

Figure 1-7

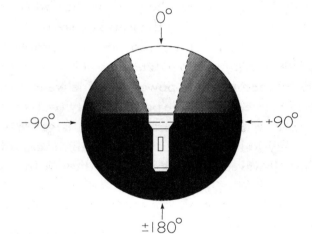

Figure 1-8

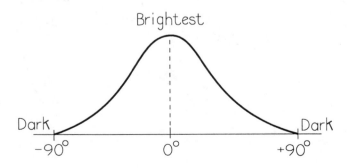

Figure 1-9

Antenna Response Patterns

One way to characterize the performance of an antenna is to plot its response pattern. We can use either of two systems to plot the antenna pattern: polar plot or rectangular plot. Let's consider a flashlight analogy. In Figure 1-8, a unidirectional light beam emerges from the flashlight in a reference direction (which we label zero degrees). The light is brightest at 0°, and falls off in intensity at angles greater than zero until total darkness is reached. This same data, plotted in polar method in Figure 1-8, can be plotted using rectangular coordinates as in Figure 1-9. Light intensity is plotted along the vertical axis, while the angle is plotted along the horizontal axis.

The next few figures show some representative antenna polar plots. These plots represent the horizontal extent—that is, an azimuthal pattern as viewed from above. (Don't forget that each antenna also has a vertical extent, an elevation pattern.) An omnidirectional antenna pattern is shown in Figure 1-10. Such an antenna receives equally well from all directions. Signals arriving with equal strength from any point on the compass will evoke equal responses in the receiver. An advantage of the omnidirectional pattern is that stations from many locations can be accommodated without manually turning the antenna. A disadvantage is that interfering signals cannot be discriminated if they share the same operating frequency. Omnidirectional patterns are commonly associated with single radiator vertical antennas.

A figure-8 antenna polar pattern in shown in Figure 1-11. This pattern is the type of pattern expected from half-wavelength dipoles, certain other horizontal antennas, some loops, and certain multiple radiator vertical antennas. This type of antenna has two preferred directions in which reception is maximized. There are also two rejection or "null" directions in which little signal strength is received. If equal strength stations are located at points "A" and "B" in Figure 1-11, the station at point A will be received with considerably less strength than the station at point B. If the two stations are operating on the same frequency, then the station at "A" is discriminated against, in favor of "B." Thus, a directional antenna provides the ability to solve the co-channel interference problem.

A *cardioid* pattern is shown in Figure 1-12. This pattern is a modified omnidirectional pattern because it allows nearly equal reception in all directions except one despised direction (the null). There are two uses for cardioid antennas. The first is to solve the co-channel interference problem (stations in the null direction are rejected) and the other is to allow unambiguous antenna direction finding. By placing the null on the station of interest, we can tell from which direction it arrived.

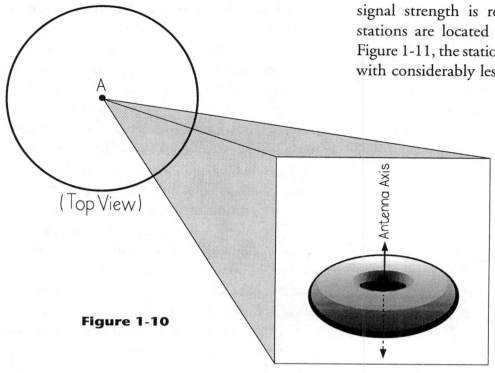

(Top View)

Figure 1-10

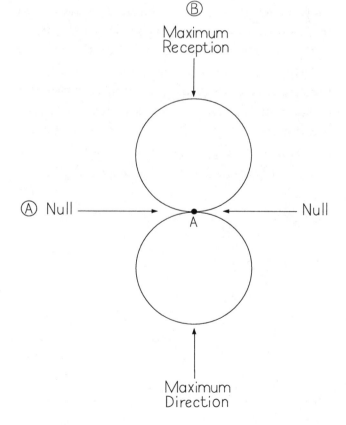

Figure 1-11

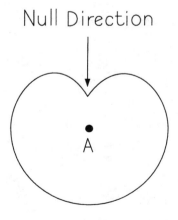

Figure 1-12

A unidirectional beam antenna pattern is shown in Figure 1-13. This pattern is the opposite of the cardioid because it has only one maxima direction and all other directions are nulls. This type of pattern is commonly associated with multi-element Yagi or quad beam antennas, as well as certain multi-radiator vertical antennas.

We can also use the pattern to recognize another facet of antenna design. Note that there is a main lobe in the direction of maximum reception, but there are also other minor lobes (backlobe and sidelobes). These lobes are natural responses of the antenna and represent directions from which attenuated (but non-zero) response is possible. All antennas have these lobes, and the job of the antenna designer is to reduce them as far as theoretically possible.

An elevation antenna pattern is shown in Figure 1-14; this one most nearly matches the beam antenna pattern of Figure 1-13 in that it receives in only one direction. The pattern does not lay parallel to the ground, but rather is elevated by an angle of radiation (α_r). The angle of radiation is often important when designing an antenna for reception from particular areas of the world, although in some cases it might not be practical for receiver owners to accomplish such a goal (it is not impossible, however). The reason for taking care with the elevation pattern is that shortwave signals arrive at the receiver site from the ionosphere at some angle. Ideally, the response pattern of the antenna is oriented to place its highest gain section dead center on the incoming radio signal. For receiver antennas, it might be prudent to call angle of radiation the *angle of maximum response* (AMR).

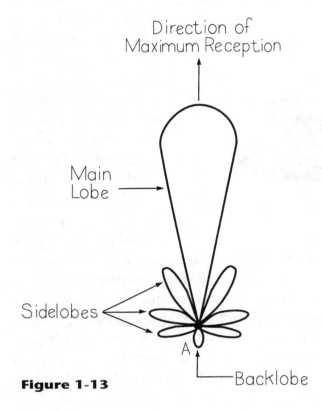

Figure 1-13

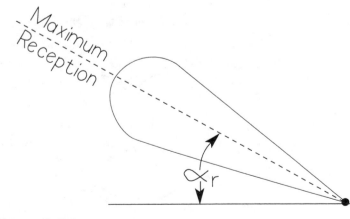

Figure 1-14

Antenna Beamwidth

The antenna beamwidth refers to the relative size of the direction of maximum reception, and is described in units of angle, known as *degrees*. Figure 1-15 shows how the beamwidth is usually determined. The pattern is a bi-directional figure-8, similar to that of the dipole antenna. Line OA defines the direction of maximum reception; A is also the peak signal strength, as represented by the voltage level of the signal. Arc BCD is the line along which the voltage level is 0.707 times the peak voltage. The points where arc BCD intersect the antenna pattern ("B" and "D") are known either as the half-power points or the -3 dB points. These points are relatively easy to measure in practical terms, so are used to define the antenna beamwidth. Thus, the beamwidth is the angle represented by arc BCD and lines OB and OD; for the particular case shown here it is 90 degrees. Note that the response outside the arc region (arc OB and arc OD) is not zero, but is reduced compared to the response inside the region.

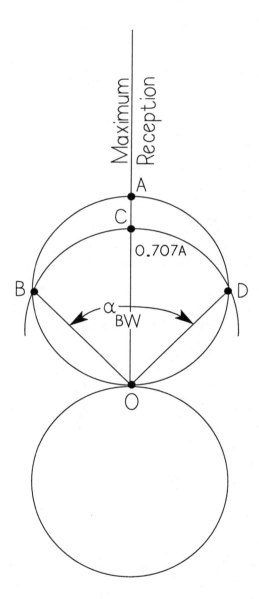

Figure 1-15

Impedance

Impedance is the opposition to the flow of current in an antenna or other circuit. It is the combined effects of ordinary resistance, capacitive reactance, and inductive reactance; like resistance, it is measured in ohms (Ω). The maximum power is transferred between two circuits (like an antenna and a receiver) when their impedances are equal. In a practical antenna system, this means that the antenna, the transmission line between the receiver and antenna, and the receiver antenna input(s) should all have the same impedance so that the radio energy intercepted by the antenna is most effectively transferred to your receiver. The impedances of antennas vary by type and whether or not the antenna is resonant at the frequency the receiver is tuned to. Most contemporary receivers have a 50 Ω antenna input, and several also include a high impedance ("hi-Z") antenna input with an impedance of several hundred ohms. We'll discuss the impedances of different antennas in the pages ahead.

CHAPTER 2

Antenna and Lightning Protection Grounds

A topic of almost perennial discussion among shortwave listeners is the antenna ground connection. A lot of silly things are done in the name of antenna grounding. Some of them work, some of them don't, and some of them are just plain dangerous.

Perhaps the dumbest, most dangerous thing is to not provide a ground.

Several examples of dumb things pop to mind from my own 30+ years of experience. First, I recall a chap—a Novice class ham operator—who lived on the second story of a two-story frame house. He grounded his transmitter and receiver through an 18-foot piece of #22 solid "hook-up" wire. Besides the wire being too small and too long, the "lower end" was ridiculous: it was soldered to a fork stuck into the ground to a depth of about two inches!

Another chap got a top flight electrical ground—but it was ridiculous. In my area, we call this particular ground "Abe's bathtub" because the fellow grounded his ham rig to a massive antique copper bathtub buried six feet underground. Besides wasting a perfectly good (and expensive) antique bathtub, it must've been terribly hard to dig a hole large enough to bury it!!!

Still another guy grounded the receiver to a pipe in the basement of his house—the natural gas pipe! That kind of ground is not only not very good from a radio point of view, but is potentially very dangerous and illegal!

My friend Dave was the chief engineer at a small AM radio station that was erecting a new transmitter site and antenna tower. Noting that there was no sod on the Earth as yet, he laid down a grid of copper wire for hundreds of square meters around the tower. Each row and column of the grid consisted of #10 bare copper wire, and the crossover points between rows and columns were soldered with low resistance silver solder. The entire grid was connected to the antenna tower's ground point. Then the sod company was called in to cover the Earth. When the power company came out, they found that Dave's ground system had a lower AC resistance than the ground they'd installed!

Only a few of us are rich enough to build "Dave's Ground Grid," and few of us own antique copper bathtubs that we are willing to sacrifice. But it's also true that many people do not understand what is a good ground. In this chapter we will look at some aspects of antenna system grounds.

Why Ground an Antenna?

There are two basic reasons to build a ground into the antenna system: lightning and electrical protection and to make the radio system work better. Lightning protection is necessary because antennas sometimes get struck by lightning, and that can set a house on fire or ruin your radio (in a rather spectacular way, incidentally).

Lightning is not "attracted" to the antenna just because it's an antenna, but because it is higher than other objects around (if a nearby tree is higher, then it has a higher probability than the antenna of a strike). A ground does not provide absolute protection against lightning, but it can help tremendously. For some types of antennas, local electrical and building codes require an appropriate ground for lightning protection. Also, your homeowners insurance may require such protection in order to keep the policy in effect, especially if local codes require it. You should use a lightning protection ground even if your local codes and insurance regulations are silent on the matter.

Electrical protection is necessary because radio receivers sometimes short out internally, and that can put 110 volt AC on the chassis. If that happens, then the radio chassis becomes electrically "hot," and very dangerous (perhaps fatally so). A good ground carries the current to Earth, blowing the fuse.

A "good ground" also makes radios work better under the right circumstances, especially with long wire or random length wire antennas (in fact, all so-called "Marconi" style antennas). Antenna and radio performance is improved if the antenna system is provided with a good RF ground.

Lightning grounds, electrical safety grounds, and RF grounds are not necessarily the same thing. For example, a lightning ground that works through a lightning arrestor may be a reasonably good protector for lightning, but is totally ineffective for RF or electrical protection purposes. The idea is to design a ground system that will work for all three functions.

Ground Wires

The ground wire, whether from the receiver or a lightning arrestor, should be made of either aluminum or copper, and be as large as possible. Aluminum clothesline is sometimes used, as is aluminum TV antenna ground wire. Another popular form of ground wire is to use multiple sections of #12 or #14 house wiring connected in parallel at both ends. A lot of people use heavy copper flat braided wire, while others buy a roll of automotive battery ground wire. Still others recycle the outer braided shield of the larger size coaxial cable for the ground wire

(RG-8/U or RG-11/U). The outer insulation, inner insulation, and center conductor are stripped away from the shield. Whatever type of wire is used it should a) be legal under local electrical codes and b) be a large, heavy duty size.

Basic Antenna Ground System

Figure 2-1 shows the basic (and most common) antenna ground system for lightning protection. A lightning arrestor is connected into the antenna download (or transmission line) at some point outside of the building. A heavy ground wire is connected from the "ground" (GND or G) terminal on the lightning arrestor to a ground rod driven into the ground.

The "innards" of a typical lightning arrestor are shown in Figure 2-2A. The antenna lead is represented by a center conductor ("A") that is separated from a pointed ground lug by a small air gap. The air gap is an insulator at low voltages, but when a high voltage lightning strike comes along, the air in the gap ionizes and creates a low resistance path to ground (Figure 2-2B).

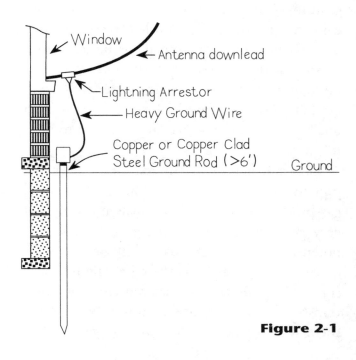

Figure 2-1

Ground rods are available in four-foot, six-foot and eight-foot lengths. Although some are copper, most are copperclad steel. For lightning protection purposes, the four-foot and six-foot lengths are not the best choice. In fact, most local electrical codes require eight-foot lengths. For RF purposes, however, two or three four-foot rods separated by a few inches and shorted together above the surface with heavy wire will suffice. Keep in mind that such an arrangement may not be either legal or smart for lightning protection...if you want multiple ground rods, then drive several eight-footers into the ground.

A somewhat better system is shown in Figure 2-3. On the rear panel of most modern short-wave receivers are two connectors: a coaxial connector for the antenna (ANT), and a ground connection (GND). The latter is usually a machine screw and nut that is attached to the metal chassis of the receiver.

On some receivers, especially older designs, there will be a small phenolic or ceramic strip (see inset to Figure 2-3) with either two or three screw terminal connections. If there are two screws, then one is for the single-wire antenna lead and the other is for the ground connection. On three-wire types, there are two for antennas (A1 and A2) and one for ground (G). If an unbalanced antenna is used with the three-wire type, a shorting wire is connected between A2 and G.

The ground system in Figure 2-3 uses two ground wires. One goes from the ground connection on the back of the receiver to the ground rod, while the other goes from the ground connection on the lightning arrestor to the ground rod. Again, make all wires as heavy as possible.

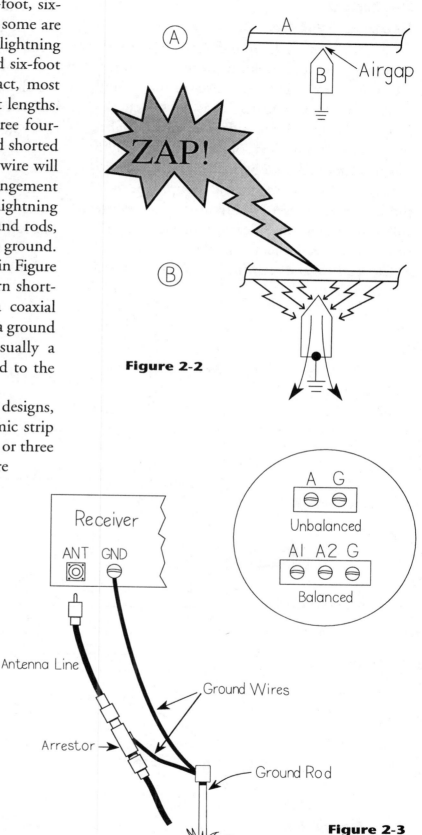

Figure 2-2

Figure 2-3

Switched Ground System

At one time, all ground systems for wire antennas used a large knife switch to connect the antenna to either the receiver or the ground wire, as needed. The idea was to switch the antenna to the ground side whenever a lightning storm approached, or whenever the radio was not attended for a period of time.

Figure 2-4 shows such a set-up. The nice thing is that these old-fashioned switches are still available in some electrical or radio supply stores...I've seen them on sale recently. Mail order electrical and scientific supply sources also carry the switches.

The position shown ("A"), the knife switch connects the antenna downlead to the receiver lead; normal signal reception occurs. But if the switch is flipped to "B," then the antenna downlead is connected to the ground rod through a heavy ground wire.

A lightning arrestor is used in the line. Just because the switch can connect the antenna wire to the ground side does not mean that no arrestor is needed. Besides the fact that the switch can fail, there is always the possibility that a surprise storm or a lapse of memory will occur, and the switch will be in the wrong position.

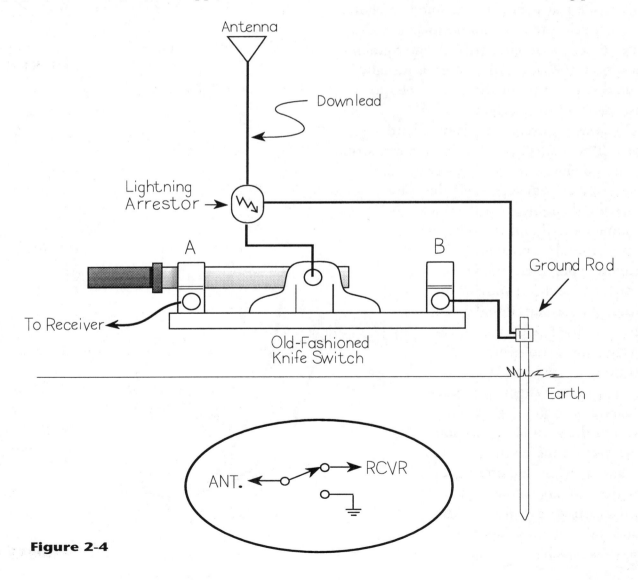

Figure 2-4

Grounds for Vertical Antennas and Towers

The ground systems shown so far are used for horizontal wire antennas. The transmission line or downlead lightning arrestor can be used for any type of antenna, and indeed should always be used. Vertical antennas can be additionally protected, however.

Figure 2-5 shows a method for providing a subsidiary lightning arrestor for vertical antennas. A stiff heavy duty wire, or strip of sheet copper, is placed in close proximity (¼-inch) to the base of the antenna, forming a spark gap for a lightning arrestor. This "arrestor" is connected to the ground rod via heavy wire. This system can be used on either ground mounted or mast mounted vertical antennas. In fact, many commercial vertical antennas have some similar system in place.

Another method is shown in Figure 2-6. This method provides both an RF ground and a lightning protection ground. On vertical antennas, the outer shield of the coaxial cable transmission line forms the ground connection to the receiver. This shield should be grounded via heavy wire to an 8-foot copperclad ground rod that is legal under local codes.

A secondary ground in Figure 2-6 is the quarter-wavelength radial; this is an RF ground. Radials are #14 or #12 (or larger) wire, cut to a quarter-wavelength at a frequency in the center of the band of interest. Of course, for a wide frequency range, such as the high frequency shortwave bands,

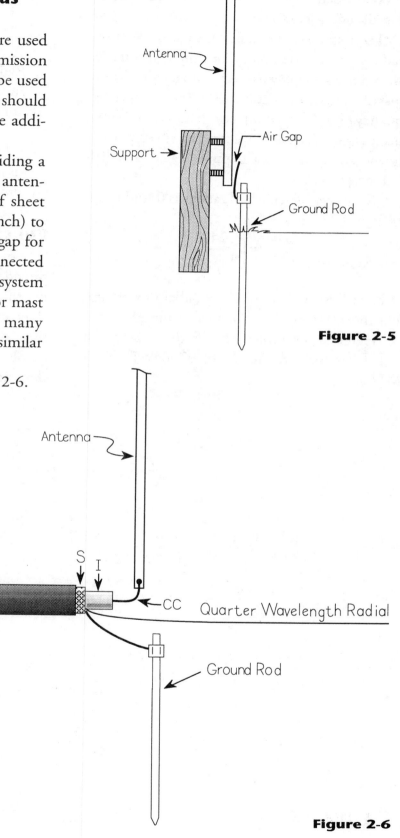

Figure 2-5

Figure 2-6

proper operation requires a multiple radial system for different frequencies a couple megaHertz (MHz) apart. A general rule is to use at least two radials on each frequency, but the real situation is: *the more the merrier.* AM broadcast stations install upwards of 120 radials for a single frequency, but the engineering literature shows decreasing effectiveness above 15 or 16 per frequency. For most SWL purposes, two radials will work well.

The physical length of radials is found from:

$$L_{feet} = \left(\frac{246}{F_{MHz}} \right)$$

Where: L is the length of the radial in feet, and F is the frequency of resonance in megaHertz.

Here's an example: what is the length of a radial cut for a frequency of 9750 kHz (9.75 MHz)?

$$L_{feet} = \left(\frac{246}{9.75} \right) = 25.23 \text{ feet}$$

Radials can be installed either above ground, or buried underground a few inches. For the sake of safety, keep the above ground radials for mast mounted verticals only...bury all others (you don't want anyone tripping over the radial that is installed only a few centimeters above the ground or buried in the grass).

Conclusion

For an antenna to work properly and yet still provide at least reasonable protection against lightning strikes and electrical failures in the receiver, a proper ground system is needed. No form of protection is totally foolproof, or gives absolute protection, but a good ground is better than no protection—by a long shot!

CHAPTER 3

Real World Antennas
Trade-Offs, Construction, and Connections

On the surface, it might appear that constructing and installing a receiver antenna is a relatively simple chore. But when you actually try to do it, the task becomes a bit more daunting! There are a number of factors to consider and things you need to keep in mind when deciding on the best antenna for you, constructing it, and erecting it. If you don't, you might wind up with an antenna that doesn't perform the way you want or that violates local laws. And there's no one "right" antenna for every application or situation. In this chapter, we will take a look at the various factors that go into an antenna decision, including looking at some of the trade-offs (like gain vs. size and cost) that usually must be made. We'll also look at the right way to construct an antenna and make all the necessary connections to get the signal from your antenna to your receiver.

Trade-Offs and Compromises

Antenna selection should take into consideration a number of factors, many of which you can probably think of without me helping you. Often overlooked, however, is the skill of the operator (that's you!). For receiver operators, the ability to know the receiver, how to tune it, how to manipulate the selectivity controls, and how or when to listen, is somewhat more important than any antenna that you can buy or build. While the skilled operator can get more out of a quality antenna than a dud dude, the truth is that she can also trade-off a little antenna capability for other factors if that is appropriate.

One of the most important factors for the SWL/DXer is the angle of arrival typical for signals from the target area at the time and place

of reception. Radio antennas have different elevation angle characteristics, and these must be accounted for in the design if reception of the desired type is to be achieved. In some cases, the height of the antenna off the ground will control the angle of reception. For example, a half-wavelength dipole that is around a quarter-wavelength high will have a main *elevation lobe* (the direction of maximum reception in that plane) nearly straight up, hardly conducive to receiving DX stations that arrive at low angles of 15° elevation.

In general, the DX listener wants to achieve an antenna with a low angle of maximum reception (AMR), while the listener who is after targets in the next state or region needs one with a higher AMR. You have to decide whether you're a DXer or SWL!

Some general guidelines are appropriate if you don't own 43 acres of Texas or any other state. Let's consider a typical suburban or urban single family detached house. Typically seated on a fifth to a third of an acre lot, these homes represent those of a large number of people. A quarter-acre lot has an area of 10,890 square feet, or a square that's about 100+ feet on the side. Depending on where the house and power lines (!!!) are situated, some can accommodate full size horizontal, half-wavelength, antennas down to frequencies of 5 MHz or so. Below that frequency, one needs to consider some form of compensated antenna, such as a coil-loaded dipole. Vertical antennas can be accommodated down to frequencies about 7 MHz in some locations (33 feet high) or higher. Local ordinances and codes may have something to say about how high the vertical can get before mechanical licensing and inspection is required.

People who live in townhouses have a different situation. Besides having lots that are too small for any form of full size antenna in the lower shortwave bands, many of these people have to contend with homeowners' association rules. Generally regarded as a legally binding covenant—thus nearly unbreakable—most such rule books have a provision against any form of outdoor antenna. Unless you can make the antenna nearly invisible to the prying eyes of the homeowners' association toads, then opt for one of the indoor designs even though they are less effective than other designs.

Generally speaking, the possibility of outdoor antennas for apartment dwellers or other rental property residents is limited to nearly, but not exactly, zero. Most of these people will want to opt for an indoor antenna of some sort. However, all is not lost for many people who live in apartments. It is not unusual for apartment owners or managers to grant permission to erect a random length wire to a tree, or a dipole or other antenna on the roof. If you are on good terms with the manager, and can give that person reasonable assurances that they will not assume any unreasonable liability for granting you permission, then they might just grant it. Can't hurt to ask! We'll cover some approaches for apartment and condo dwellers later in this book.

Site Survey

In the sections above we talked a bit about the different choices for an antenna based on the lot size. For the vast majority of readers, the installation site is a primary decision driver, and cannot be overlooked. A friend of mine owned a 43 acre farmette in Texas, and was able to erect just about anything he wanted (including a 1250 foot longwire). My own lot is a 10,000+ square foot suburban mortgage trap, so my choices are considerably more constrained than my friend's.

Others I know (both listeners and ham operators) live in either suburban townhouses or urban row houses, and for both classes their options are tighter than mine. Your own personal situation will have to be assessed before any antenna selection is possible.

If you own your home, then you should have received a copy of the surveyor's platte when you settled, or shortly thereafter. You can make a copy of the actual platte (you don't really want to draw on the original) for purposes of making antenna plans for the site. A ruler and a bit of knowledge will help you plan an antenna installation that makes sense for you.

How Much Antenna Gain?

Gain is a highly desirable attribute of any antenna. Gain makes the signal seem stronger than it really is. And it's not by magic, either, for a higher gain antenna will actually deliver to the receiver antenna input more RF power picked up from the airwaves than a lower gain antenna. But the matter of gain needs some consideration, for gain costs money.

On the positive side: gain means more signal pick-up and less noise (or unwanted signal) pick-up, so a better signal-to-noise ratio is achieved. Dollar for dollar, up to some unspecified but flexible limit, a dollar spent on the antenna system provides better results than a dollar spent on preselectors and fancy receiver features. For ham operators, a $3000 antenna does a lot more overall good than a $3000 linear amplifier. Thus, it might seem that antenna gain is everything.

But consider gain in another light. A gain of +3 dB means doubling the received power level. Sounds like a lot of increase, huh? Nah, not really—remember our discussion of decibels back in Chapter 1? On some receivers 3 dB is a single S-unit on the S-meter, while on other receivers 6 dB (quadrupling the power level) is required to register a 1 S-unit increase. It's also true that human operators have difficulty distinguishing two reasonably strong signals that are a single S-unit apart. For example, the difference in perception of two signals, one S-6 and the other S-7, is in the decimal dust category. The 3 dB, *a la* 1 S-unit, difference only makes a real difference when you are searching for the really weak ones, where a signal that is 1 S-unit (3 dB) above the noise floor is hearable and a weaker one is not. For listeners chasing weak DX, the difference may be worth it, but for others it is a marginal benefit in the trade-off equation. It is generally held (that is, people I agree with say) that a 20 dB difference (about 6 S-units) is required for comfortable listening if two signals are present at the same time.

Noise Considerations

One of the factors that can make you wonder why you paid so much money for such a poorly performing radio is local noise pick-up. One of the most important controlling factors in radio reception is *signal-to-noise ratio* (SNR), the relative strength of the signal versus the "noise floor." Some noise is inherent in the receiver, while other noise is inherent in the atmosphere. The on-board noise created by the receiver cannot be helped, while atmospheric noise is attenuated at least somewhat by using a directional antenna with gain. The noise problem can be quite complex, and is beyond the scope of this book (especially since many noise problems are not helped by antenna design). But what is a matter of concern, and what you can do something about, is man-made interference. That type of noise can be helped by proper design and installation of the antenna.

Man-made noise comes in a lot of different forms. Sparking electrical contacts, which are found in switches and motors, will produce a static-like noise or an abrupt "pop!" (if a single operation type of device, like a switch). Some motors produce a "whirring" sound when they run. A "frying eggs" hash-like noise is produced by those infernal light dimmer controls used to replace switches in houses. Some of those dimmers are so noisy that replacing them with regular switches is the best solution. A scratchy arcing noise is sometimes produced by the local power lines if they are not in good repair.

Perhaps the worst offenders in the neighborhood are television receivers and video cassette recorders. There are three basic problems seen. First, if you have cable, then there is a wideband coaxial cable entering your home carrying scores of signals that raise intermodulation possibilities to new heights of glory (or ignominy). The cable must become "leaky" to RF before the problem can occur in any large degree. You might want to get the cable company to repair the cable as a solution. Second, the 15734 Hz mis-shapened squarish wave used in the TV horizontal deflection system produces "birdies" that appear every 15.734 kHz up through the spectrum...even into the low-band VHF region. Finally, there is the 3.58 MHz color oscillator used on color televisions.

Listen at that frequency on a good TV night and you may hear severe birdies at 3.58 MHz and they splash a few dozen kiloHertz either side of 3.58 MHz...which wouldn't be so bad were it not for the fact that they appear on harmonics of 3.58 MHz as well. In my neighborhood, I can tell from the 15.734 kHz and 3.58 MHz noise in my receiver when a popular TV show is on...and if lots of people are taping a movie then some frequencies in the lower shortwave bands become almost useless to me.

Antenna design and installation can make a difference in suppressing these noise sources, especially if the antenna is directional. The null in the directional antenna pattern can be aimed at the offending noise source, reducing its overall amplitude at the input of the receiver. While that position may also attenuate desired signals from that direction, it may be a reasonable trade-off for a specific SNR problem.

Where you locate your antenna is a factor in noise pick-up. For example, power line noise tends to fall off dramatically with distance, so placing an antenna as far away as possible will help tremendously. Keep in mind that a "safe" distance from a hazards point of view might be too close for the SNR point of view. Avoid locating any antenna near either power lines or cable television wires even when hazards are not the primary concern.

Permits and Legal Stuff

One necessary reminder is that your local government might have some interesting ideas—legal requirements, actually—concerning your antenna installation. Their electrical, mechanical, and zoning codes must be observed. There is a great deal of similarity between local codes because most of them are adaptations from certain national standards. But there are enough differences that one needs to consult local authorities. Indeed, you may need a license or building permit to install the antenna in the first place, and it may be illegal for you to install any antenna! Before you decide on a final design or purchase the materials for it, make sure that you are permitted to install it.

About thirty years ago, a friend of mine in a radio club found out that his county had an ordinance that said an outdoor antenna must be double its own height plus 50 feet from the nearest property line. He received a summons after a complaint from a neighbor. In a county full of quarter-acre home lots, however, that was a ridiculous law. Very few outdoor TV antennas met that strict requirement! So Hal went to the court house and asked for 50,000 complaint forms. Using a local county directory, he proceeded to fill out the same complaint as he'd

received against every homeowner in the area. The county board repealed the law during the next meeting.

Fortunately, you won't have to worry about building permits or other legalities for most wire antennas unless you are erecting masts or towers to support them. However, you should check on any local regulations pertaining to antennas just in case. If your property is covered by any restrictive covenants dealing with antennas, these can usually be found in the prospectus, sales contract, or deed for the property.

Save all paperwork regarding any building permit or other written authorization you might need, including inspection decals or papers, and the original drawings (with the local building inspector's stamps). If a casualty occurs, then your insurance company may elect to not pay off if you have violated an electrical, mechanical, building, or zoning code. That clause may be overlooked by an enthusiastic antenna builder, but it could prove to be a costly oversight if something happens.

Installing Antenna Masts

In the absence of the side of a building, or a natural antenna support such as a tree, it becomes necessary to provide a support. There are three ways this can be done: grow a tree; erect a tower; or erect a mast. The first alternative isn't terribly practical because one would have to wait for a decade or two before the tree was tall enough to do you any good. The second alternative is so costly that only a few can afford it. The third alternative is what this section is all about.

Masts are typically shorter than towers. Although 50-foot telescoping masts are available, they are also a bit rare. For purposes of this discussion, we will assume a maximum height of less than 30 feet. Such masts can be bought or built from a number of different materials.

One source of metal masts is stores that sell

television receiver antenna parts, such as home supply dealers and many local electronic parts distributors. Although getting rarer in this age of nearly universal cable TV wiring, TV antenna parts are still sold in electronics catalogs. Masts and hardware are also sold by ham radio equipment dealers.

There are two basic forms of TV antenna mast. The most elegant (and costly) are the telescoping slip-up masts. These masts consist of two, three, or four sections, each smaller diameter than the next, so that they fit inside one another. When the assembly is collapsed, they will be no more than six to eight feet long, depending on the design and the final erected height. To install, each mast section is raised to a certain height, where some alignment holes line up, and a steel pin is placed through both diameters to help stabilize the assembly. If the mast is more than 15 to 18 feet high, then it is common practice to use guy wires, which means a guy ring is needed to hold the wires.

A less expensive TV mast consists of several five or ten foot sections that can be joined end to end. These mast sections are built with one end tapered and the other flared so that sections can be joined together. If a guy ring and wires are used, these masts are successful to about 30 feet high, although I am not happy with them over 20 feet because they tend to get unstable above that height. When selecting

mast sections for this type of mast, avoid the cheap thin wall steel or aluminum varieties, and opt instead for the thick walled steel versions. Even thin wall steel will collapse when loaded too much.

Wooden masts can be built, and in the following sections one such design will be discussed. These masts can be made to 25 or 30 feet with good stability, especially if a good grade of pressure treated lumber is used.

Figure 3-1 shows one method for installing shorter masts, say up to about 15 feet high. The mast is fastened to a chain link fence post by U-bolts buffered with short pieces of "2x4" lumber. The bottom end of the mast is anchored in a concrete filled cinder block (large size preferred). You can buy repair or patching cement in small bags at Harry and Harriet Homeowner hardware stores, in case you don't want to buy an entire seven cubic yard truckful.

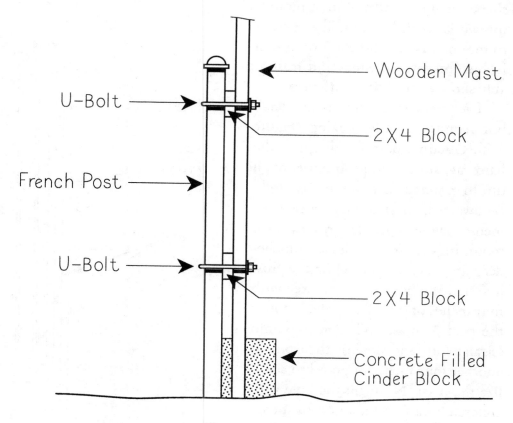

Figure 3-1

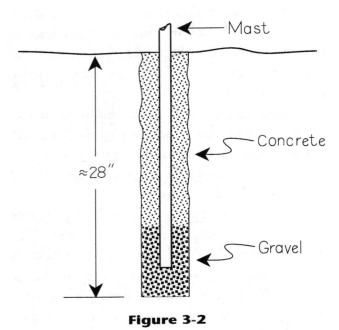

Figure 3-2

If the fence post is firmly anchored in a concrete plug, and is in good shape, then this form of mast mounting works well. You would not want to mount a beam and rotor on top of it, but for wire antennas and reasonably short verticals it is sufficient.

Lacking a fence post is not fatal, but requires a little digging (Figure 3-2). Obtain a posthole digger at the hardware store, and grub out enough dirt to mount a post, or the mast itself. Be aware of local ordinance requirements for the depth. In my area, such mountings are to be at least 28 inches deep in order to get below the frost line. Fill the bottom of the hole with four inches of gravel, and then mount the post or mast. When it is plumb (straight up and down), then put in another four inches of gravel to stabilize the mast. Next, fill the hole with concrete to a point about four inches below the surface.

Homebrew Wooden Mast

Figure 3-3 shows a beefy 25-foot mast that will work for a lot of sites that lack a natural means for mounting an antenna. The lumber to use for this antenna is pressure treated 2x4s, the kind normally recommended for outdoor use on decks and other structures. This type of lumber typically comes in 8-foot, 10-foot, 12-foot, and 16-foot lengths, with some stores offering 20-footers. The idea is to stack the lengths three deep (except at the top) to provide strength.

In the scheme shown in Figure 3-3, the bottom section consists of two 12-foot 2x4s, with two 8-footers, stacked on top of each other, sandwiched between them. Additional 8-footers on top of the bottom section, properly sandwiched together, form the upper section.

The lumber elements are fastened together with either ⅜-inch or 5/16-inch bolts, fitted with flat washers, lock washers, and hex nuts as

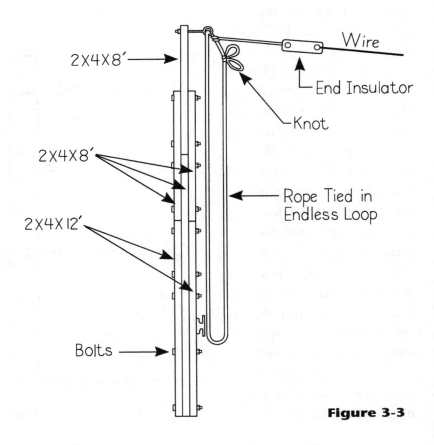

Figure 3-3

needed. Some people like to use two hex nuts on top of each other such that the outer provides additional holding for the inner. Figure 3-4 shows the details on how to do this.

Masts tend to be fixed, and not easily lowered. But you will want to install, change, or repair the antenna from time to time, so you will want some means for getting to the antenna wire. The traditional way is to install a pulley at the top of the mast so that an endless loop rope can be used to raise and lower the wire like a flag on a flag pole. I don't like that system. Pulleys can rust and jam or break. I used a pulley on a mast in the late 1950s, but one time the rope slipped out of the pulley's wheel race, and jammed in between the wheel and the housing. After that, my mentor and tormentor, Mac Parker (W4II), showed me a neat little trick to get around that problem: screw-eye bolts. The mast of Figure 3-3 has a screw-eye bolt mounted at the top (see detail in Figure 3-5). The rope is passed through the eye of the screw-eye, and tied off to form the endless loop. A boater's "deck cleat" at the base of the mast, about waist level, is used to secure the rope at the bottom end. This system has worked great for me over the years, and I never had a repeat of the pulley disaster.

Another form of ground mounted mast is shown in Figure 3-6. The actual mast can be a telescoping mast, a 2x4 mast, a wooden handrail (if sturdy enough). This mount is designed for installation against the side of a house or other building. The base of the mast is anchored in a cement footer such as those used for supporting porches and outdoor decks. The bottom of the 2x4 is fastened to the footer using a U-channel, of the sort used for anchoring stud-

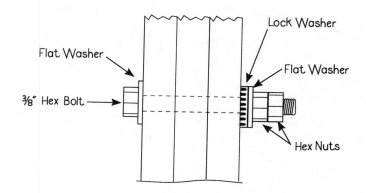

Figure 3-4

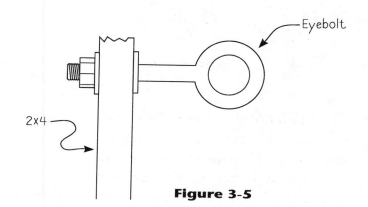

Figure 3-5

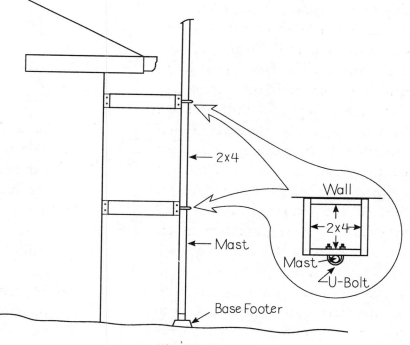

Figure 3-6

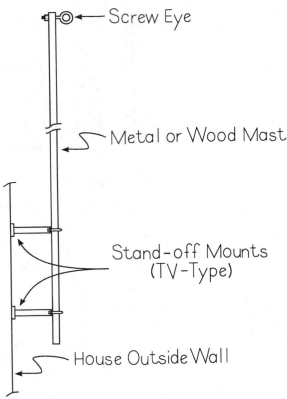

Figure 3-7

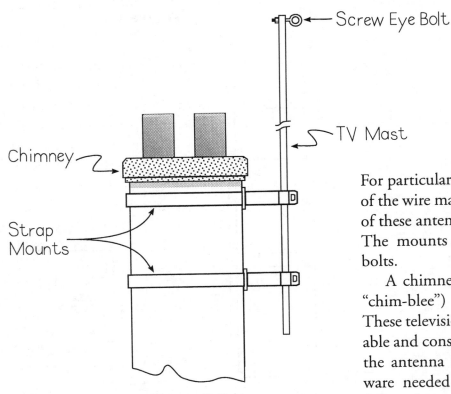

Figure 3-8

ding in houses, or the supports in car ports. The mast is supported at two points from braces attached to the house outer wall. These braces should be long enough to clear the roof overhang and gutter by an inch or two, but not much longer. Detail in the inset of Figure 3-6 shows typical construction for the braces. Actual dimensions will depend on the offset needed. A U-bolt holds the mast to the brace. At least two heavy duty wing bolts, or other through wall fasteners, are used to hold the brace against the wall. Figure 3-7 shows a wall mount that uses television antenna hardware to hold an antenna mast. This type of installation can be made close to the roof line of the house. The actual mast can be wooden handrail stock (if sturdy and robust), or metal television antenna masts. The standard TV masts come in ten foot lengths, and the best are made of steel. Place a screw-eye bolt at the upper end in the same manner as other masts.

The mast is held to the wall with stand-off mounts. These come in 4-inch, 6-inch, 8-inch, 12-inch, and 24-inch sizes. For a ten foot mast, use the smallest size that will clear any obstacles. For larger, heavier, or longer masts, use a heavier grade. For particularly long antennas, the wind weight of the wire may be substantial. If you design one of these antennas, use a heavier grade of mount. The mounts are held to the wall with wing bolts.

A chimney (or, in my part of the country, "chim-blee") mount is shown in Figure 3-8. These television antenna mounts are easily available and consist of a pair of stainless steel straps, the antenna mast clamps, and the bolts/hardware needed to secure the straps. To install, follow the manufacturer's directions. They will

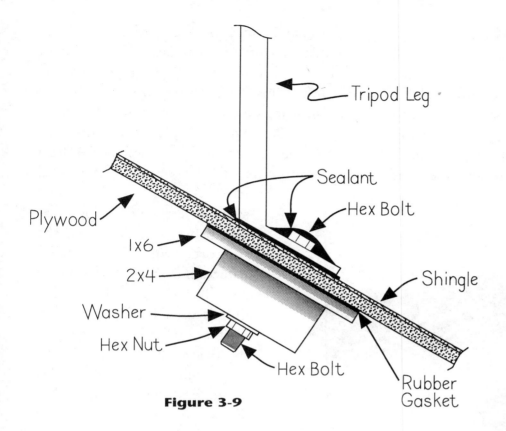

Plywood

1x6

2x4

Washer

Hex Nut

Hex Bolt

Tripod Leg

Sealant

Hex Bolt

Shingle

Rubber Gasket

Figure 3-9

the peak is the most common location. Follow the manufacturer's directions in installing a tripod. Typical detail of how the legs are installed on the roof is shown in Figure 3-9. A typical tract house (and many custom house) roofs consist of a layer of plywood, ⅝- to ¾-inch thick, covered with tar paper and shingles. The bolts that hold the legs must pass through the roof, and that opens two issues: strength and waterproofing.

The strength issue is addressed by backing the roof, inside the attic or loft, with a 12-inch length of 1x6 lumber and a similar length of 2x4. Some people also use a 6-inch 1x6 lumber on the outside under the tripod leg's mounting tab.

The waterproofing issue is extremely important. If rain water or snow infiltrates around the bolt, then it will rot the roof, causing a tremendous repair bill. A sealant is placed between the mounting tab and the shingle (or outside 1x6, if used). Use proper roofing sealants. Traditionally that meant roofer's tar, but today hardware stores sell several different forms (select a good one), although all share a specific characteristic: they're gooey and messy. After all is correctly mounted, dab lots of sealant all over the assembly, completely covering it. Some installers use a rubber gasket inside the attic/loft that prevents any water that gets in from migrating further. Periodically (like annually) inspect the mount both inside the roof and outside on the roof, for evidence of water infiltration…or pick another mounting method.

call for you to wrap the straps around the chimney, and then cinch them tight. It is best practice to make sure the straps are horizontal to the ground, or it will look like the dickens and may lose some strength. Don't kink the straps while spritzing with them, or they will never go on right. As with other TV mast antennas, a screweye bolt at the top will make it easy to use a rope to raise and lower the antenna wire for installation and servicing.

A safety note is in order here. Those straps are easily installed, but it should be a two person job. The reason is that the act of putting them into place will get a single installer into some silly looking and very awkward (hence dangerous) positions. I've done it, but consider it dumb to attempt without assistance.

Another approach is to use a tripod roof mount such as those used to support TV antennas. These tripods can be mounted at any point on the roof, even on the slope, although straddling

End and Center Insulators

When constructing a wire antenna, you will need end insulators to electrically isolate the copper wire antenna radiator element from the support rope. Most wire antennas also require a center insulator. Insulators also provide a certain amount of mechanical strength in the connection between the radiator wire and the rope supports.

Figure 3-10

Figure 3-11

Insulators may be made of glass, glazed ceramic, or synthetic materials such as nylon or Teflon.™ Most of those sold in stores today are of synthetic material, although used ceramic and glass insulators are frequently seen at hamfests. Figure 3-10 shows two typical insulators. The larger type can be used for high power ham radio transmitter antennas as well as general receiver antenna use. It provides a much larger degree of isolation between the wire and the supports (which presumedly reduces end effects) and is mechanically stronger. The smaller unit is used for smaller transmitter antennas and general shortwave receiver antennas.

A popular type of center insulator is shown in Figure 3-11. This type uses an SO-239 "UHF" coaxial connector, so it will mate directly with the PL-259 coaxial connectors used on many antennas. The wire radiator elements are connected to heavy duty solid copper wire "pigtails" protruding out each end of the center insulator. A different form of center insulator consists of a hollow body of PVC-like plastic material with connections for the antenna wire made to, and supported by, a pair of screw-eye terminals on either side.

Some center insulators similar to Figure 3-11 contain *balun* transformers. "Balun" stands for "balanced to unbalanced," and is used to match a "balanced" antenna (such as a dipole) to an unbalanced feedline (such as coaxial cable). Some baluns also do impedance transformations. For example, ordinary dipoles use 1:1 balun transformers since the center impedance of ordinary dipoles is approximately 75 Ω. However, folded dipoles use 4:1 baluns since their center impedance is closer to 300 Ω.

Connecting to End and Center Insulators

There are two goals to keep in mind when making the connections to either end insulators or center insulators. First, you want a strong, reliable mechanical connection that won't come loose under the buffeting the antenna will receive. Winds and weather can take a terrible toll on wire antennas, so a good, reliable mechanical connection is mandatory. The second goal is to make a good electrical connection. After all is said and done, the antenna is still an electrical device connected into an electrical circuit.

Let's deal with end insulators first. This method works no matter what type of end insulator you use. The radiator wire is #14 stranded antenna wire, which means it is either hard drawn copper wire, or copper-clad steel wire, such as that sold under the trade name of Copperweld. When working with antenna wire, be aware that it kinks up very easily. In fact, experienced antenna erectors claim that gremlins or RF demons exist whose main function in the universe is to put permanent kinks in your wire. When the wire kinks, it is nearly impossible to get the kink out of the wire so that it looks good again. The antenna will perform as well, but the spot where the kink occurred always exists to tell the world: *you're kinky.*

Figure 3-12

The first step in connecting the antenna wire to the insulator is to pass the wire through one of the holes in the insulator (Figure 3-12). Leave six to eight inches of "free" wire. Next, double the free end of the wire back on itself, and then wrap the end around the main body of the wire; leave about 0.75- to 1-inch of loop to permit the insulator to move freely. Wrap the free end around the main body of the wire with six to eight wraps.

If a downlead is installed, as it will be on one end of Marconi style antennas, then strip away about two inches of its insulation, and then wrap the bare downlead wire around the main antenna wire four to eight times, as shown in Figure 3-13.

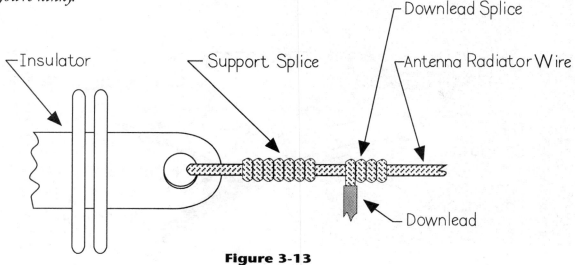

Figure 3-13

The final step is to solder the connections. The purpose of the solder is not to add mechanical strength, but to ensure the electrical connection in the face of potential corrosion and oxidation. Use either 50/50 or 60/40 lead/tin resin core solder.

Connecting to the center insulator depends on the type of center insulator that is used. Figure 3-14 shows the use of an ordinary end insulator as a center insulator for a dipole or other balanced antenna. The two wire radiators are spliced onto the insulator in the normal manner for end insulators. The coaxial cable is stripped such that its center insulator and conductor are routed to one of the antenna radiators, while the braid (outer conductor) is routed to the other. Both are spliced to their respective radiator elements. One popular method is to use the pigtails left over from making the two support splices as electrical connections for the coaxial cable.

In some cases, the body of the coaxial cable is wrapped around the center insulator and tied off with string, cord, or fishing line in order to provide mechanical support for the connections. If you use the "split coax" method, then strain relief is essential.

The method of connection shown in Figure 3-14 is not recommended because it is mechanically weak and open to the weather. It is common to find water infiltration into the coaxial cable, which deteriorates its performance. It is better to use a regular center insulator or balun transformer.

Figures 3-15 and 3-16 show both forms of center insulators; Figure 3-16 also represents typical balun transformer connections. In both forms, the antenna transmission line to the receiver is made through the SO-239 on the center insulator, and its mating PL-259 coaxial connector on the coax cable.

The type of center insulator shown in Figure 3-15 uses a heavy, solid copper wire pigtails protruding from inside the insulator. Before beginning the splice, "tin" the pigtail. That is, heat it with the soldering iron and spread a thin coating of 50/50 or 60/40 lead/tin resin core solder all over each pigtail. It should look "silver plated" after it is tinned without lumps of solder on the wire.

The antenna wire is laid alongside the copper pigtail, in contact with it, and is then passed through the hole in the insulator, doubled back on itself, and finally wrapped around both the pigtail and its own main body six to eight times. It thus resembles an ordinary end insulator sup-

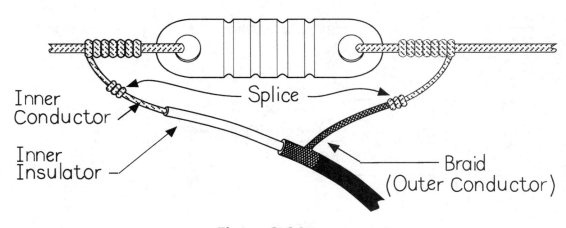

Figure 3-14

Figure 3-15

Figure 3-16

from the body of the insulator (use long-nose pliers) in order to facilitate the use of tools and to prevent melting the plastic when heat is applied to solder the connection. Pass the end of the wire all the way into the terminal, pass both sets of flanges, and then crimp the flanges over the wire with longnose pliers in order to form a good mechanical joint. Next, solder the terminal and wire together.

Connecting to the Receiver

There are a number of different methods for connecting the antenna download or transmission line to the radio receiver or transmitter. Figure 3-17 shows a collection of connectors that are sometimes used for radio receiver and transmitter connections to the antenna. The leftmost is the PL-259 "UHF" coaxial connector. This type of connector is used extensively on transmitters, transceivers and, increasingly, modern radio receivers. Next to it is the smaller BNC coaxial connector. This connector has replaced the PL-259 on radio test equipment, but is not used very often on receivers or their antennas except for portables. I've seen only one receiver that is not a hand-held portable that uses BNC connectors. The single pin connector to the right of the BNC is an ordinary banana plug. It is used with single wire banana jacks or "five-way binding posts" on the receiver. It is used today only on receivers, and has not been used for transmitters since the World War II era. Finally, there is an old-fashioned alligator clip. It is not used at all on transmitter antenna leads, but is sometimes used temporarily, for test purposes only, on receivers. Figure 3-18 shows how the alligator clip is connected to a coaxial connector.

port splice, except for the pigtail in the core. Using the soldering iron or gun, solder the splice thoroughly in the same manner as for support splices.

The method for connecting the other type of center insulator, as well as balun transformers, is shown in Figure 3-16. Pass the antenna wire through the eyelet, and "support splice" it in the manner similar to the end insulator; leave about eight to ten inches of wire free when you pass it through the eyelet (the goal is to have about five inches after the support splice is made).

The end left over from making the support splice is connected to the terminal lugs fastened to the eyelet. It is prudent to pull the lug away

Figure 3-17

In the foreground in Figure 3-17 are two adapters. The device on the left side is a right-angle PL259-to-SO239 adapter. It is used to reroute the coaxial cable 90 degrees. The second adapter is one that allows an SO-239 UHF connector to mate with a piece of coaxial cable that uses a BNC connector on the end.

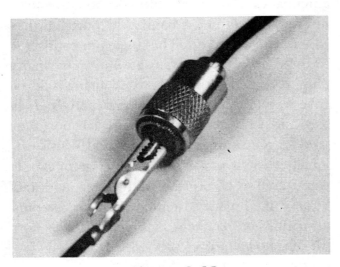

Figure 3-18

There are two basic methods for connecting single wire antennas to non-coaxial antennas. Some receivers are equipped with two terminal antenna blocks (Figure 3-19A), in which one is for the antenna ("ANT" or "A") and the other is for the ground connection ("GND", "GRND" or "G"). Other receivers are equipped with three terminal antenna blocks, labeled "A1", "A2" and "G" (Figure 3-19B). These receivers can use a balanced transmission line, such as twin-lead, parallel line, or twisted pair line), but are most often connected to a single wire line. When single line is used, it can be converted into the unbalanced form similar to Figure 3-19A by connecting a wire jumper between terminal "A2" and "G"; that is, by strapping one side of the antenna connector to ground.

The method of choice for connecting the wires is through the use of cable ends, or "spade lugs," as shown in Figure 3-19A. However, if you must use just the exposed wire, then do it like Figure 3-19C. Strip the end of the insulated download wire about ⅜-inch and then form it into a loop that has a diameter slightly larger than the body of the screw terminal. If the wire is stranded, then tin the stripped end to prevent it from fraying and shorting to the adjacent terminal. Place the loop under the screw in the direction of tightening for the screw ("clockwise"). The idea is to cause the loop to close on itself under the screw when the screw is tightened. If you place the loop under the screw in the counterclockwise manner, then it will open when the screw is tightened…and come loose.

A means for connecting the single wire antenna to a portable shortwave radio is shown in Figure 3-20. Of course, the direct way is to use an alligator clip on the end of the download and connect it directly to the telescoping whip

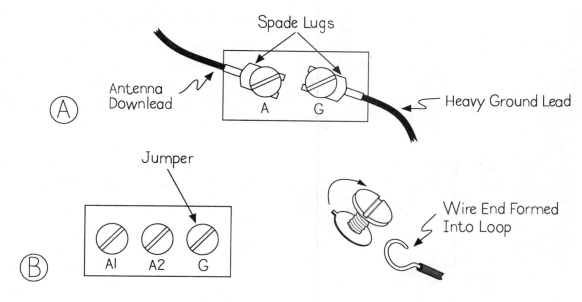

Figure 3-19

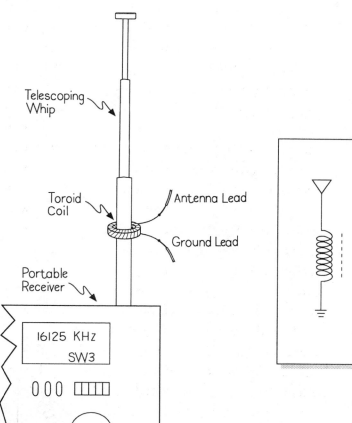

Figure 3-20

antenna of the radio. But that may cause damage to the radio if static electricity charges build up on the antenna. The method of Figure 3-20 is indirect because it relies on inductive coupling through a toroidal inductor coil.

The coil is wound on a toroidal core that has an inside diameter that will just fit loosely over then bottom portion of the whip antenna when the wire windings are in place on the core. That usually means a T37 or T50 core. For low bands (< 7 MHz), use about 20 turns of #26 enameled wire over the core; for higher bands (> 7 MHz) use eight to ten turns of #26 enameled wire. Connect one end of the coil to the download, and the other to the ground lead. An equivalent circuit is shown in the inset to Figure 3-20.

Be a bit careful when adding an external antenna to a portable short-wave radio. Some of them are quite sensitive, and already provide compensation for the small telescoping whip antennas. If an external antenna is used, then signal levels may prove excessive and the radio will overload badly.

CHAPTER 4

Transmission Lines

The subject of transmission lines can be easy or hard, depending on how we want to make it. The reason is that a transmission line can be a very complex circuit. Indeed, it is a lot more than a simple electrical conductor to connect a load (antenna) to a source (receiver or transmitter). In this chapter, we will take a practical descriptive approach. If you want a slightly more technical (read "mathematical") approach, see my other antenna book, *Practical Antenna Handbook* published by TAB Books/McGraw-Hill. In this book, you will find the various types of transmission line described, along with some information on connecting them to receivers.

Single-Wire "Downleads"

Certain types of antennas (Marconi, random wire, Tee, Windom, etc.) require a single conductor "download" from the antenna feedpoint to the receiver. These antennas are the simplest, and on some the "download" is not a true transmission line. Even so, the installation advice given here also applies to those simple downloads.

Transmission Lines

Perhaps the simplest true transmission line that we'll consider is the parallel line. Several of the types of transmission line that are discussed below are basically parallel conductor lines. Figure 4-1 shows the basic transmission line circuit based on a parallel conductor line. This type of transmission line consists of two identical conductors, parallel to each other, separated by a "dielectric" ("insulator" to us commoners) between the signal source and the load. In a transmitter, the "source" is the transmitter, while the "load" is the antenna.

There are three impedances in the circuit of Figure 4-1. First, there is always an internal impedance on any device, and this is represented by resistance R_s in Figure 4-1. Second, there is the load impedance, represented by R_L, which is the impedance of the antenna. Finally, there is a *characteristic impedance* (Z_o), also sometimes called surge impedance, that is an attribute of the transmission line itself. For practical purposes, we need only know a few things about characteristic impedance. First of all, we

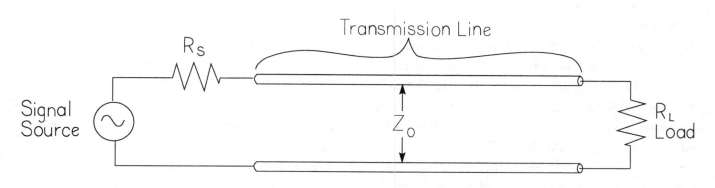

Figure 4-1

can rely on the so-called "naive" (because it's non-mathematical) definition. This definition is based on the fact that in all electrical circuits, antennas and transmission lines included, the maximum power transfer between a source and a load occurs when the impedances are matched. That is, Z_o is that impedance that, when the transmission line is terminated in it, will allow the maximum power transfer between the line and the load. A proper transmission line is one that has a characteristic impedance, Z_o, that is equal to both the source and load impedances. Remember: characteristic impedance, which is used to order or make transmission line, is merely an attribute of the line. Nothing at all mystical about it!

In the discussion above, I alluded to a situation where not all of the power is transferred to the load. Where does it go? After all, the Law of Conservation of Energy is inviolable in any frame of reference not created by a sick mind. Figure 4-2 shows what happens by a little *gedankenexperiment* (mind experiment). Figure 4-2A shows the same sort of circuit as in Figure 4-1, although for simplicity's sake only the load end is shown in detail.

Suppose that the signal generator at the left end of Figure 4-2A blurts out a single pulse of electrical signal energy (Figure 4-2B). It will be launched onto the transmission line and travel from the source end to the load end. When it comes to load, different things happen under different circumstances. If the load impedance, R_L, happens to equal the characteristic impedance Z_o of the line, then all of the signal is absorbed by the load (Figure 4-2C). In the case where the load is an antenna, some of it is radiated into space as a radio signal, while some of it is used to make heat. But if there is an impedance mismatch, such that $Z_L \neq Z_o$, then only some of the signal is absorbed by the load; the rest of it is reflected back towards the source

(see Figures 4-2D and 4-2E).

The reflected signal is a loss to the system. In receiver systems, the signal "source" is the antenna, which is excited by a passing electromagnetic wave. The signal set up in the antenna acts as if it were a signal generator with an internal impedance equal to the antenna's feedpoint impedance. The load is the receiver input impedance seen across the antenna terminals. If the antenna impedance, transmission line impedance, and receiver input impedance are mismatched, then there will be a loss situation where less signal than is possible reaches the receiver.

The situation actually found in radio receiver and transmitter antennas is shown by the rope analogy in Figure 4-3. Real signals, except in esoteric applications like radar, are continuous sine waves, which can be simulated by connecting a rope to a hard, immovable wall, and then moving the free end up and down in an oscillatory manner. The sinusoidal incident (or *forward*) wave thus imparted to the rope propagates towards the wall, where it reflects and propagates in the opposite direction (*reflected* wave). If the oscillation continues, when the forward and reflected waves combine they form a system of standing waves, with nodes (minima) and antinodes (maxima). (You remember these terms, don't you?) The nodes are spaced a half-wavelength apart, as are the antinodes; the distance between a node and either adjacent antinode is a quarter-wavelength.

But antenna systems are not ropes on walls, so we have to transform the analogy to the real world. In the case of the antenna system, the "rope" is the transmission line, while the oscillation is in the form of a sine wave electrical signal. Figure 4-4 shows the voltage situation as a function of line length (expressed in wavelengths) for several situations. The current waveform could just as easily been measured, and the results would be the same. In this scheme, the

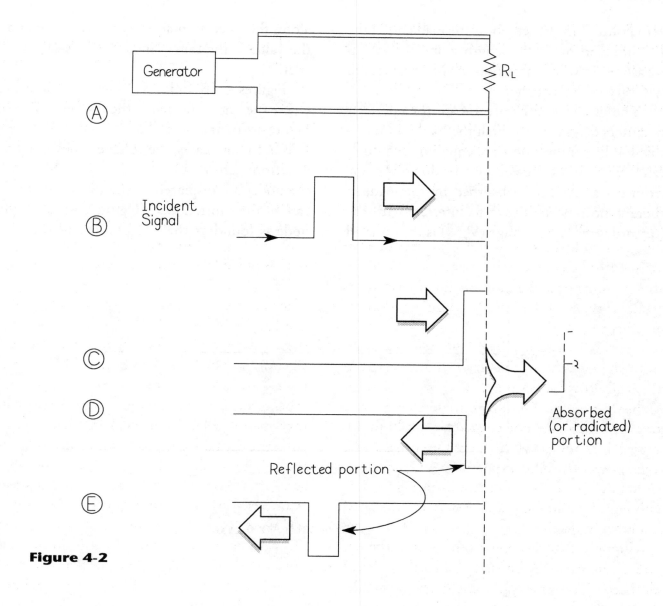

Figure 4-2

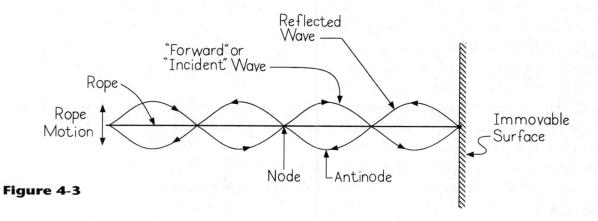

Figure 4-3

zero point of measurement is the load end of the transmission line. The length along the line is measured in wavelengths, so the physical length will vary with frequency.

The situation in Figure 4-4A is for a perfectly matched system in which the load and transmission line impedances are equal to each other ($Z_L = Z_o$). All of the energy sent down the line from the generator is absorbed by the load, so there is no reflected wave to interfere with the forward wave. The voltage (V_{max}) is the same all

along the line; no matter where you measure it the value is the same. Such a line is said to be "flat."

Figures 4-4B and 4-4C show the situations where the line is shorted at the load end ($Z_L = 0$, Figure 4-4B) and open-circuited ($Z_L = \infty$, Figure 4-4C). In both cases, the voltage varies along the line from zero to a maximum value, V_{max}, but the nodes are displaced in the two cases. In the case of the shorted load (Figure 4-4B), the first node is found at the $\lambda/2$ point, and others at

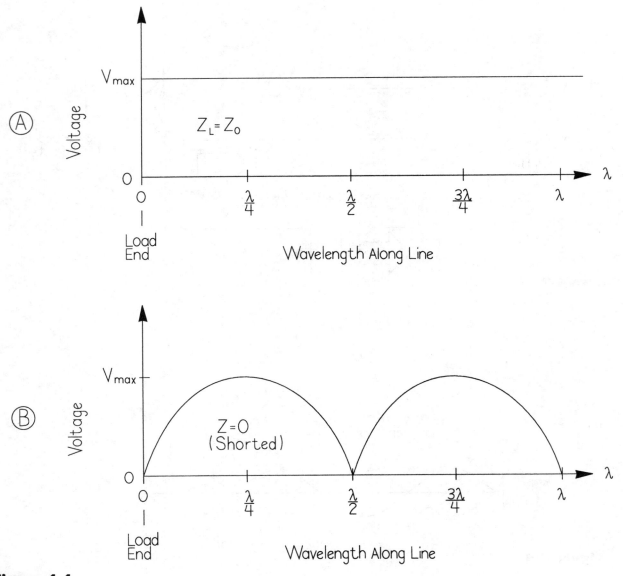

Figure 4-4

integer multiples of λ/2 (Nλ/2) thereafter. In the case where the line is open-circuited (Figure 4-4C), the first node occurs at the λ/4 point, and others are spaced half-wavelength apart down the line from there. The location of the nodes is often used in troubleshooting faulty antenna transmission lines to determine whether they are open or shorted.

In most healthy antennas, if the line isn't flat it will resemble Figure 4-4D. In this case, the voltage along the line will vary from an antinode maxima (V_{max}) to a node minima (V_{min}) at half-wavelength intervals along the line. The first minima occurs at the load end, while the subsequent minima (nodes) are spaced half-wavelength apart from there. The first thing to note is that the minima voltages are not zero, but have some non-zero value. This situation indicates a line that is mismatched, but is neither open nor shorted.

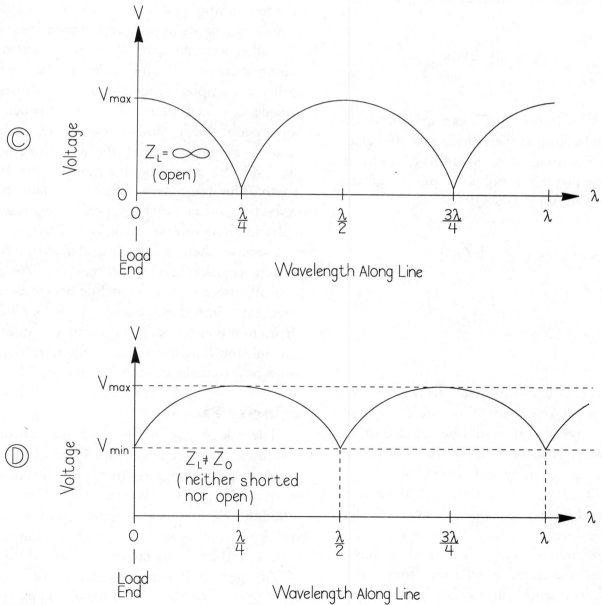

Figure 4-4

Standing Wave Ratio (SWR)

The ratio of the maxima and minima voltages is called the voltage standing wave ratio (VSWR), or simply *standing wave ratio* (SWR). Both terms are equally valid, and yield the same number, so take them as synonyms. The "VSWR" term merely refers to the fact that the measurement was made using voltage, rather than current ("ISWR"). The VSWR is the ratio of minimum and maximum voltages, or:

$$VSWR = \left(\frac{V_{max}}{V_{min}} \right)$$

The VSWR (or SWR) can also be determined by looking at the ratio of load and characteristic impedances, arranging them to produce a positive number of one or greater (1.2:1 is valid, 0.8:1 is not):

$$VSWR = \left(\frac{Z_o}{Z_L} \right)$$

or,

$$VSWR = \left(\frac{Z_L}{Z_o} \right)$$

whichever produces a number of 1:1 or greater.

The SWR represents a loss in the system. Wherever possible, it should be reduced to 1:1 or as close as possible to 1:1 if the ideal cannot be achieved. In practical terms, however, a VSWR of 2:1 is not a terribly bad antenna system, and on receivers up to 3:1 can be tolerated if absolutely necessary. Transmitters, on the other hand, have to absorb their own large power level when the signal is reflected from a mismatched load and will malfunction at lower SWR figures than a receiver. Most ham trans-

mitters with solid-state final power amplifiers tend to start shutting down the power level as VSWR gets larger than 1.4:1 or so, and are essentially shut off at 3:1. On receivers, a high SWR just means crummy performance.

There are only two legitimate ways to get VSWR to 1:1. First, the antenna can be adjusted to resonance (antenna element length or the value of inductance or capacitance in series with the antenna element). If the impedance is not equal to the feedline impedance, then either an antenna tuning unit or broadband matching transformer needs to be used between the two. The other legitimate way is to use an antenna tuning unit, or matching network, that transforms a complex impedance to a resistive impedance equal to the feedline impedance. Some people—who don't know any better but should—erroneously think that you can adjust the SWR by adjusting the transmission line length. This error derives from two false premises: first, the fact that it appears so because of faults in the simplest forms of VSWR meter and, second, there is some impedance transformation occurring in transmission lines. (We can, after all, use a transmission line as a quarter-wavelength impedance transformer.) Don't fall victim to this error—adjust the antenna, not the transmission line, unless (and only unless) you know how to make a matching section.

Velocity Factor

The velocity factor (V or VF) of transmission line is the percentage of the speed of light at which a signal propagates in the line, expressed as a decimal. If c is the speed of light (300,000,000 meters per second), and v is the velocity of the signal in the transmission line, then v/c is the velocity factor (V). Typical values of V range from 0.66 for certain types of coaxial cable to very nearly 1.0 for parallel open conductor line.

Types of Transmission Line

Now let's take a look at some of the most popular forms of transmission line used with radio receivers. We won't discuss every type; some are too esoteric or specialized (like for microwave applications) to have much relevance to SWL needs. The three basic types of transmission line that we will discuss are: parallel conductor line, twin-lead (of which there are two subtypes), and coaxial cable.

✦ *Parallel Conductor Transmission Line*

Parallel conductor transmission lines consist of two wires, run parallel to each other, and separated by air (which serves as the dielectric) as in Figure 4-5. As a result of having an air dielectric, the velocity factor of the parallel line is typically close enough to 1.0 that it is rated at 0.999 or 1.0. Wire sizes typically used are #12 down to #22, and much of the time the wire is uninsulated (however, enamel or formvar insulation is probably a good idea). In practice, the wires are held apart a constant distance S by plastic, ceramic or other insulators; these insulators are often called *spacers* in honor of the fact that their main function is to maintain a constant separation between the two wires.

The characteristic impedance of the parallel wire transmission line is set by the center-to-center spacing between the conductors (*S*), and the diameter of the wire used for the conductors. Typical values of impedance for parallel line run from about 250 Ω to 1200 Ω, with 400, 450, 500, 600, and 800 Ω being the most commonly encountered (you can match these values with antenna feed requirements). I am going to give you the equation for figuring out the impedance because it's a factor

under your control should you elect to make your own parallel line (which is often the case). The equations for coaxial cable and twin-lead are not given because these factors are not under your control...you typically buy the stuff already made (I've met only one guy in 35 years of playing with radios who built his own coaxial cable, and it was a nitrogen gas-filled experimental type—the guy fancied himself an inventor). The formula is:

$$Z_o = 276 \log \left(\frac{2S}{d} \right)$$

Where:

Z_o is the characteristic impedance in ohms
S is the center-to-center spacing between conductors
d is the diameter of the conductors (assuming both conductors are identical)
[Both S and d are in the same units.]

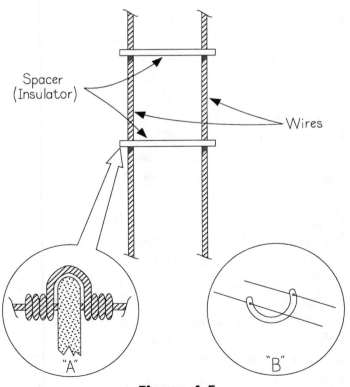

Figure 4-5

The diameters of common AWG wire sizes, needed for "d" in the equation above, are as follows:

Wire Size	d
10	0.1019
12	0.0808
14	0.06408
16	0.05082
18	0.04030
20	0.03196
22	0.02535

Parallel line is typically made using solid wire conductors, although some is seen using stranded wires. Care must always be taken in handling parallel line to avoid kinking it, for the kinks become permanent immediately on occurrence. The problem is that these discontinuities mess up the impedance and create a glitch in the SWR exhibited by the line.

In some cases, you may build your own parallel line from a spool of wire and a collection of spacer insulators. While the store-bought variety has spacers molded onto the wire, the homebrew variety typically uses spacers that are a slip fit at best. In order to secure the spacer along the line, a jumper arrangement as shown in inset "A" to Figure 4-5 is used. The two main conductors are passed through the holes in the spacer, and a short piece of wire is spliced such that it mechanically bridges the spacer. The purpose is not electrical connection, but rather mechanical strength.

The spacers used in parallel line will be either straight, as in the main illustration of Figure 4-5, or will be U-shaped as shown in insert "B" to Figure 4-5. The purpose of this type of spacer is to maintain the center-to-center spacing while increasing the electrical pathway taken by leakage currents that flow on the surface of the spacer. Both contaminants and rain water can seriously reduce the normally very high electrical resistance, and this effect is lessened by using the U-shaped spacer design.

✦ *Twin-Lead Transmission Line*

Twin-lead transmission line (Figure 4-6) is a special variety of parallel line that uses a plastic material as the dielectric separating the conductors rather than air. Because the plastic is dielectrically different from air, the velocity factor of twin-lead is lower than for parallel line. Typically, twin-lead has a velocity factor around 0.82.

Twin-lead comes in two main varieties. The 300 Ω twin-lead (Figure 4-6A) is designed for television antenna installations. Early TV antennas used folded dipole driven elements and required an impedance close to 300 Ω for proper matching. As a result, the low cost transmission

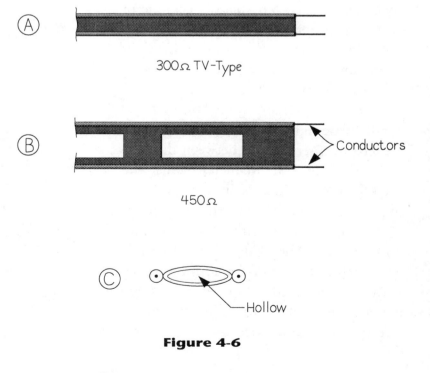

Figure 4-6

line designed for TV use had that impedance. It is also used for several different forms of short-wave antenna, FM broadcast band folded dipoles, and VHF/UHF monitor antennas. The other type of twin-lead is the 450 Ω type (Figure 4-6B), which is about twice the width of the TV type line. This twin-lead is intended for transmitting antennas, although certain receive antennas also can use it. Most commercial 450 Ω line has rectangular holes cut into the insulation, which improves the loss of the line and increases the velocity factor a small amount.

Like parallel line, twin-lead should never be kinked or tied in a knot. In addition, neither type of line (parallel or twin-lead) should be twisted on itself when installed or subjected to any sharp angle turns.

A special type of 300 Ω twin-lead with a hollow air core (Figure 4-6C) is sometimes seen. It consists of a fatter dielectric element that is hollow in the center. This special lead is intended for UHF television installations.

✦ Coaxial Cable Transmission Line ("Coax")

Perhaps the most common form of transmission line for shortwave receivers is coaxial cable (Figure 4-7). "Coax" consists of two conductors arranged concentric to each other, and is called "coaxial" because the two conductors share the same center axis. The inner conductor will be a solid or stranded wire, while the other conductor forms a shield. For the coax types used on receivers the shield will be a braided conductor, although some multi-stranded types are also sometimes seen. Coaxial cable intended for television antenna systems has a 75 Ω characteristic impedance, and uses metal foil for the outer conductor. That type of outer conductor results in a low-loss cable over a wide frequency range, but does not work too well for most applications outside of the TV world. The prob-

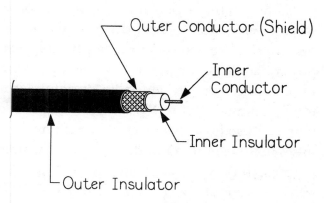

Figure 4-7

lem is that the foil is aluminum, which doesn't take solder. The coaxial connectors used for those antennas are generally Type-F "crimp-on" connectors, and have too high a casualty rate for other uses.

The inner insulator separating the two conductors is the dielectric, of which there are several types: polyethylene, polyfoam, and Teflon are common (although the latter is used primarily at high UHF and microwave frequencies). The velocity factor (V) of the coax is a function of which dielectric is used, and is:

Dielectric Type	Velocity Factor
Polyethylene	0.66
Polyfoam	0.80
Teflon	0.70

Coaxial cable is available in a number of characteristic impedances from about 35 Ω to 125 Ω, but the vast majority of types are either 52 Ω or 75 Ω impedances. Several types that are popular with receiving antenna constructors include:

RG-8/U or RG-8/AU	52 Ω	Large diameter
RG-58/U or RG-58/AU	52 Ω	Small diameter
RG-174/U or RG-174/AU	52 Ω	Tiny diameter
RG-11/U or RG-11/AU	75 Ω	Large diameter
RG-59/U or RG-59/AU	75 Ω	Small diameter

Although the large diameter types are somewhat lower loss cables than the small diameters, the principal advantage of the larger cable is in power handling capability. While this is an important factor for ham radio operators, it is totally unimportant to SWLs. Unless there is a long run (well over 100 feet) where cumulative losses become important, then it is usually more practical on receiver antennas to opt for the small diameter (RG-58/U and RG-59/U) cables—they are a lot easier to handle. The tiny diameter RG-174 is sometimes used on receiver antennas, but its principal use seems to be connection between devices (such as the receiver and either a preselector or antenna tuning unit), in balun and coaxial phase shifters, and in instrumentation applications.

Installing Coaxial Connectors

One of the mysteries faced by newcomers to the radio hobbies is the little matter of installing coaxial connectors. These connectors are used to electrically and mechanically fasten the coaxial cable transmission line from the antenna to the receiver. There are two basic forms of coaxial connector, both of which are shown in Figure 4-8 (along with a United States cent for size comparison). The larger (all silver colored) connector is called the *PL-259* UHF connector, and is probably the most common form used on radios (don't take the "UHF" too seriously). The PL-259 is a male connector, and it mates with the *SO-239* female coaxial connector.

The smaller connector in Figure 4-8 (partially black) is called a *BNC* connector. It is used mostly on electronic instrumentation, although some receiver antenna uses are seen (especially in hand-held radios).

The BNC connector is a bit difficult, and very tedious, to correctly install, so I recommend that you do as I do: buy transmission line with them already mounted. But the PL-259

connector is another matter—it is relatively easy to install besides not being readily available already mounted.

Figure 4-9 shows the PL-259 coaxial connector disassembled. Also shown in Figure 4-9 is the *diameter reducing adapter* that makes the connector suitable for use with smaller cables. Without the adapter, the PL-259 connector is used for RG-8/U and RG-11/U coaxial cable. With the correct adapter, it will be used with smaller RG-58/U or RG-59/U cables (different adapters are needed for each type).

The first step is to slip the adapter and threaded outer shell of the PL-259 over the end

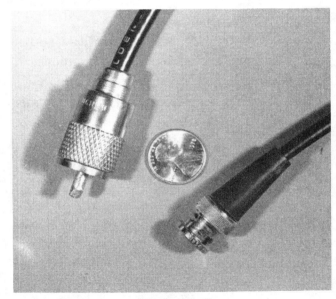

Figure 4-8

Figure 4-9

of the cable. (You will be surprised at how many times the connector is installed, only to find that one of these components is still sitting on the workbench…requiring the whole job to be redone.) If the cable is short enough that these components are likely to fall off the other end, or if the cable is dangling particularly long distance, then it might be wise to trap the adapter and outer shell in a knotted loop of wire (note: the knot should not be so tight as to kink the cable).

The second step is to prepare the coaxial cable. There are a number of tools for stripping coaxial cable, but they are expensive and not terribly cost effective for anyone who doesn't do this stuff for a living. You can do just as effective a job with a scalpel or hobby knife (like the kind sold under the "X-acto" name), either of which can be bought at hobby stores and some electronics parts stores. Follow these steps in preparing the cable:

1. Make a circumscribed cut around the body of the cable ¾-inch from the end, and then make a longitudinal cut from the first cut to the end (Figure 4-10A).

2. Now strip the outer insulation from the coax, exposing the shielded outer conductor, as shown in Figure 4-10B.

3. Using a small pointed tool, carefully unbraid the shield. Be sure to separate the strands making up the shield. Lay it back over the outer insulation, out of the way.

4. Finally, using a wire stripper, side cutters, or the scalpel, strip ⅝-inch of the inner insulation away, exposing the inner conductor (Figure 4-10C). You should now have ⅝-inch of inner conductor and ⅜-inch of inner insulation exposed, and the outer shield "de-stranded" and laid back over the outer insulation.

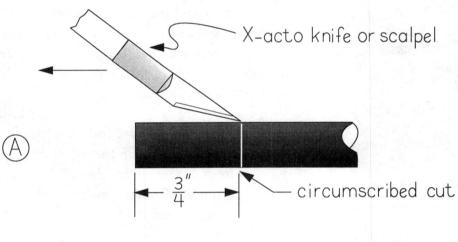

X-acto knife or scalpel

Ⓐ

$\frac{3}{4}''$ circumscribed cut

Ⓑ

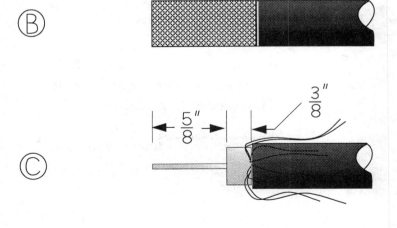

Ⓒ $\frac{5}{8}''$ $\frac{3}{8}''$

Figure 4-10

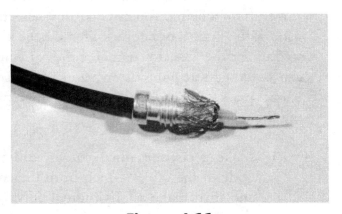

Figure 4-11

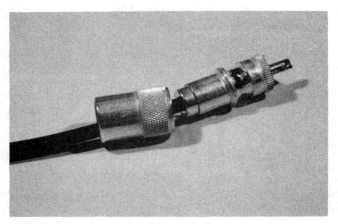

Figure 4-12

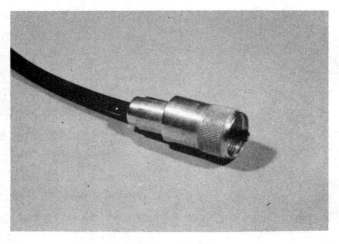

Figure 4-13

Next, slide the adapter up to the edge of the outer insulator. Lay the unbraided outer conductor over the adapter (Figure 4-11). Make sure that the shield strands are neatly arranged, and then—using side cutters—neatly trimmed to avoid interfering with the threads. Once the shield is laid onto the adapter, slip the connector over the adapter and tighten the threads (Figure 4-12). Some of the threads should be visible in the solder holes that are found in the groove ahead of the threads. It might be a good idea to use an ohmmeter or continuity connector to make sure that there is no electrical connection between the shield and inner conductor (which would indicate a short circuit).

Soldering involves using a hot soldering iron. The connector will become dangerously hot to the touch. Handle the connector with a tool or cloth covering.

◆ Solder the inner conductor to the center pin of the PL-259. Use a 100-watt or greater soldering gun, not a low-heat soldering pencil.

◆ Solder the shield to the connector through the holes in the groove.

◆ Thread the outer shell of the connector over the body of the connector (Figure 4-13).

After you make a final test to make sure there is no short circuit, the connector is ready for use.

Handling and Installing Transmission Lines

Transmission lines are relatively simple to use, but do require some care in handling. Some general rules or guidelines are:

1. For all types of transmission line, you want to avoid extremely sharp bends and kinks. Those kinks will inevitably cause a VSWR discontinuity, and reduce the performance of the antenna.

2. If it is necessary to route transmission line around a corner, then make the turn over a gentle arc with about one foot radius or more.

3. Avoid, wherever possible, running transmission lines close to metallic objects such as gutter downspouts. Of course, *don't even THINK of running them close to power lines!*

4. Run the transmission line along a wall, floor, or roof using stand-off insulators (Figure 4-14). These insulators consist of a screw-eye end with a plastic center insulator plug. There are several types, all originally made for the TV antenna and cable TV industries, and they differ in the manner of fastening: machine screw, wood screw, and case hardened masonry nail types are all readily available. Most people will use the wood screw or masonry nail types for outside walls or roofs. Care should be taken on roof installations to not penetrate inside the roof; otherwise, a water wicking situation will exist and it could rot

the roof (use overhanging portions). Getting the transmission line inside the house is a bit of a trick. If you have brick or masonry walls, then a hole can be drilled in the wall at an appropriate place. A hammer and star bit can be used (for those who like hard manual labor). Most people would prefer to use a tungsten carbide masonry bit on a slow-speed electric drill to make the hole. Be sure to wear goggles when doing this job, for dust and chips fly about and are dangerous to your eyes.

On brick walls, make the entrance hole in the mortar line between bricks, for it's a lot easier than drilling through brick. Note that old brick and mortar which has been weathered for many years becomes extremely hard—so hard, in fact, that you might want to consider an alternate route into the building. I've worn out several carbide masonry bits on a single installation where

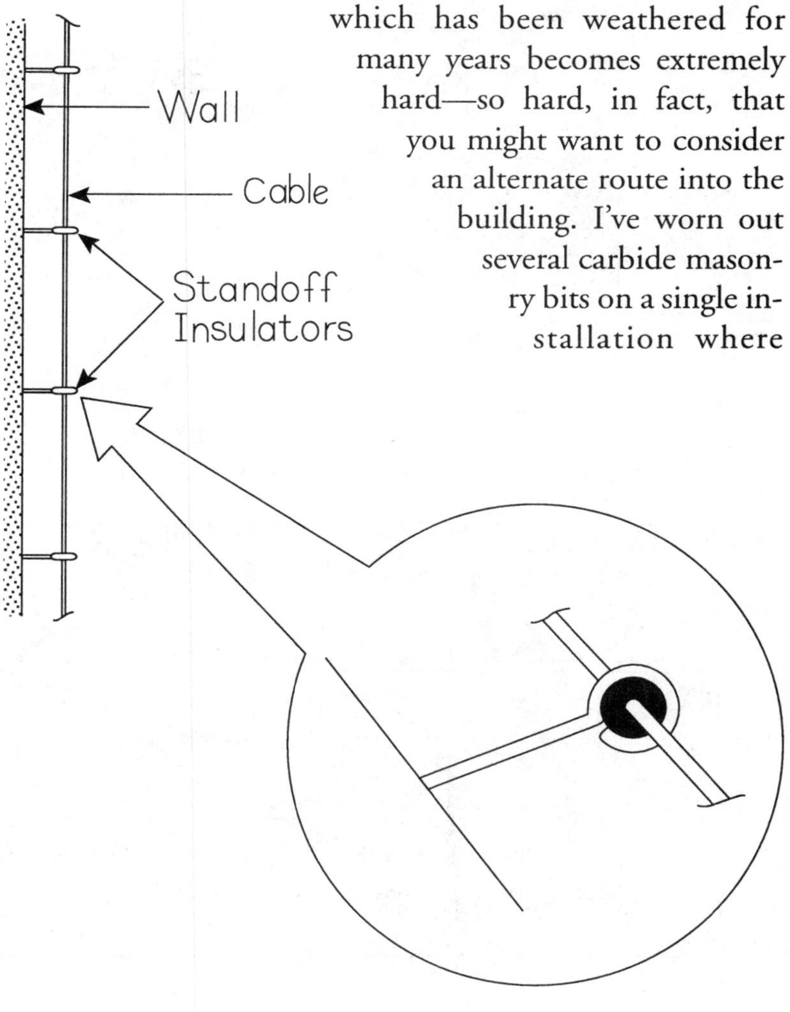

Figure 4-14

100-year old reused brick was used to build the house, and the mortar line was too thin to cut into effectively.

Cinder block walls are used on a lot of houses, and even brick houses frequently have cinder blocks in the basement and for a few feet above the surface. Cinder block is usually built with two hollow chambers (see Figure 4-15), one on either side of the center line. The best place to drill the hole is in these chambers. To find an appropriate spot, first find the center line of the

block. Once the center line is marked, split the distance to either edge and drill at that point (it should be right in the center of the block, if the block was built normally). Keep in mind that an extra long bit is needed for drilling through most cinder blocks (eight to 14 inches thick, depending on the block).

There is a right way and a wrong way to install cable at the wall entrance site. Figure 4-15 shows both ways. The wrong way is to bring the cable in from above, and then pass it through the wall. The problem is that water runs down the cable and into the hole. Even if the hole was waterproofed with caulk or RTV silicone seal, the material will eventually deteriorate and allow water to wick into the house. There are two steps to avoiding water damage. First, use a drip loop of 12 to 24 inches of cable looped gently below the point of entrance, and then brought in from below. Second, fill the excess diameter of the hole with a generous glob of caulk or silicone seal. Inspect the seal every so often (six to 12 months) to guard against deterioration or trauma damage.

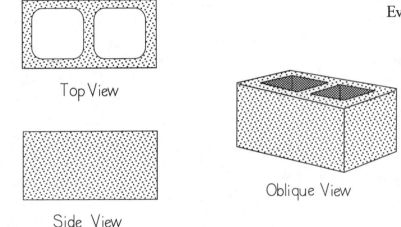

Top View

Side View

Oblique View

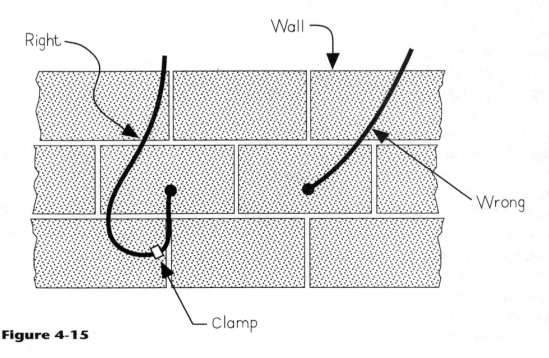

Right

Wall

Wrong

Clamp

Figure 4-15

Wood frame and siding houses (like mine) are even easier to install a transmission line in. My house is like millions of other houses built in the post-war period (that's World War II, for you kids who don't remember it). It has a cinder block basement that extends about two feet above grade. A 2x4 heel plate supports the system of 2x4 studs that frames the house. The inside of the frame is covered with dry wall, while the outside is covered with plywood sheathing and aluminum siding (some houses use vinyl siding). This method of construction is shown in cross section in Figure 4-16.

In some houses, like mine, there is a ten inch space between the top of the cinder block, which is two feet above grade, and the heel plate, and this space is occupied by the floor joists for the first floor above the basement. I am able to drill holes in this space to the outside, and that is where my antenna transmission lines pass into the house. Alternatively, as shown in Figure 4-16, a fist sized (or smaller) square hole can be cut in the dry wall in an unobtrusive spot to accommodate locating the cable. In either case, you can either pass the cable directly into the house, or use a double ended female co-axial "barrel" connector, as shown. These connectors are threaded over their entire cylindrical body so that a pair of hex nuts can be used to secure the connector to the wall. I've found it wise to caulk or silicone seal the hex nut against water wicking. Of course, a drip loop is essential.

"But," laments the dear reader ("dear reader" is a fancy way of saying "you"),

"I rent my house, and the landlady is a real *{expletive deleted}* and won't let me drill a ¾-inch hole in the side of her *{expletive deleted}* house." There is a way out, other than just doing and paying the consequences. Figure 4-17 shows a method that I used on several occasions. You can fashion a flat piece of wood planking (1x6 works nicely, as do narrower widths) to fit under the moving part of the window. At least one friend of mine used a 4-inch high metal panel intended for a rack mount for this purpose. Coaxial barrel connectors, stand-off feedthrough insulators and other connectors can be mounted on the wood panel to pass antenna wires into the house. The connectors and the top, bottom and side edges of the panel should be caulked against the weather. In addition, some means must be found to secure the window to prevent DSBGs (dirty, smelly, bad guys) from burglarizing the place via an open window (besides stealing the family silver, your pistol, hunting rifle and your kilobuck radio, they will likely also damage the antenna wire).

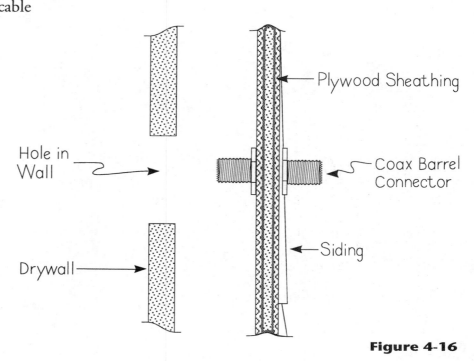

Hole in Wall

Drywall

Plywood Sheathing

Coax Barrel Connector

Siding

Figure 4-16

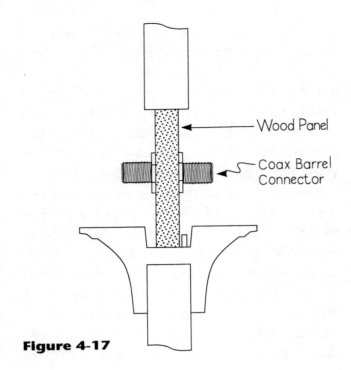

Wood Panel

Coax Barrel Connector

Figure 4-17

An alternative that can be used on both casement and sash windows is to break out a pane of glass, and replace it with either metal, wood or plastic of about the same thickness. A little glass putty, and the panel is secured in place.

Whichever method you select, don't forget the darn drip loop! It'll save you a lot of potential water damage. Besides, every radio or TV pro who sees your installation will know one thing for sure: no drip loop indicates an enthusiastic amateur who doesn't know *{expletive deleted}* from Shinola did the job. They will shake their heads in pity, amazement, and despair at your embarrassed expense...which might just be worse than water damage if that pro is your mother-in-law.

CHAPTER 5

Simple "Quick and Dirty" Antennas

The antennas discussed in this chapter represent what are probably the most commonly used "antlers" in the shortwave radio listening community. They are not necessarily optimum from a technical point of view; indeed; they are probably NOT optimum, but are often the best choice for nontechnical SWLs because of practical considerations. Despite not being technically the best antennas, they will return as much performance as many listeners can use, so they may well be your best choice.

Random Length Antenna

Perhaps the most common shortwave antenna in the entire world is the random length wire antenna shown in Figure 5-1. It is the antenna most likely to be found in the owner's manual of even some of the most sophisticated shortwave radio receivers. The random length antenna is untuned, and consists of a healthy length of wire strung up between two supports.

The antenna wire should be #14 hard drawn stranded copper wire, or (preferably) #14 stranded steel wire that is copperclad to lower the resistance to radio frequency signals. The ends of the wire are supported by end insulators (EI in Figure 5-1) and a rope to the support structure. The rope ought to be a good grade of synthetic material, rather than cotton clothesline or other cheap type, in order to withstand the rigors of outdoor living.

The supports for the random length antenna can be the house, a nearby tree, or a wooden or metal mast erected especially for the purpose. DO NOT USE power poles, telephone poles, cable TV poles, or other utility poles for an antenna support. It might be convenient, but it could also be dangerous...and is illegal in nearly

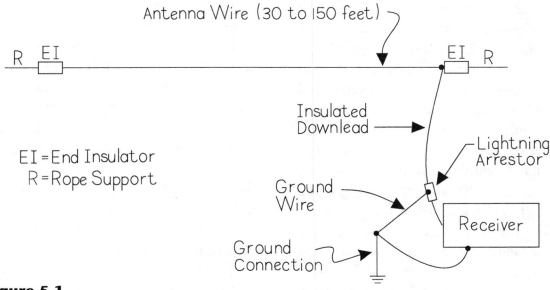

Antenna Wire (30 to 150 feet)

EI = End Insulator
R = Rope Support

Insulated Downlead
Lightning Arrestor
Ground Wire
Receiver
Ground Connection

Figure 5-1

all localities. The antenna wire should be well clear of the support structure, so use at least five feet of rope and more if needed. For well filled-out trees, the antenna wire should be entirely clear of the leafy crown of the tree so that no physical interference (and therefore potential damage) or signal loss occurs.

The signal is carried to the radio receiver by a downlead. The downlead consists of a length of insulated wire of #14 to #22 size. It must be insulated, even though the antenna wire need not be insulated, for both safety reasons and to prevent signal loss by accidental grounding. Make sure that the downlead doesn't touch anything metallic or the ground even if it is insulated.

The random length antenna can be erected at almost any angle, from sloping downward to straight up in the air (in which case it is a vertical). The best performance will be seen if the antenna wire is horizontal to the ground and is as high as practical. 20 to 30 feet seems to be a practical height for many SWLs, and it works just fine...100 feet is better, but isn't terribly practical. After all, if you can afford a 100-foot tower, you can afford a better antenna!

The random length antenna works best if the wire is run in a single direction so there are no bends in the wire as it runs from one support to another. If you must bend the wire, however, this can be done with minimum violence to its performance. Don't overdo it, however. Keep at least 50% of the length in one direction and have no more than two bends.

Many people simply run the downlead into the house, directly to the radio receiver, without going through a lightning arrestor. That may be quick 'n' dirty, but it's also dumb. Lightning strikes are not very likely, but if they come the arrestor will divert a large portion of it to ground. The lightning arrestor may save the receiver (no guarantees, however), and is likely to prevent the house from catching fire (again,

Nature does what it must so no guarantees). Even if the house does catch fire, your insurance is more likely to pay off if an approved lightning arrestor is used in the circuit. Another factor is that local electrical codes might require a lightning arrestor, so use it!

The ground connection is necessary for the antenna to reach its best performance. Some shortwave receiver manuals recommend a cold water pipe as the ground. I don't think they make very good grounds today now that cold water pipes are typically made of polyvinylchloride (PVC) or some other plastic material. Even if you have metal pipes, it is usually preferable to use an eight-foot copperclad steel ground rod driven into the Earth so that only a few inches show. The ground wire from the receiver and the lightning arrestor should be as heavy as possible (but for different reasons).

The random length antenna is a good basic antenna, but doesn't perform as well as some of the other antennas found in this book. Use it if you please, but realize that other alternatives exist.

The "Tee" or "Top Hat" Antenna

The Tee antenna shown in Figure 5-2 is a reasonably popular version that is related to the random length antenna of Figure 5-1. Like the random length antenna, it is untuned and non-resonant. It differs from the random length antenna in that a portion of the downlead is used as a vertical antenna section. The vertical section should be ten to 30 feet long, and runs at a right angle down from the antenna wire. The rest of the downlead can be routed as convenient for your particular case.

One popular way to make a Tee antenna is to place the downlead connection directly over the point on the house where the receiver is located (or where the wire goes into the house).

The supports are at either end of the structure, or at some angle. The idea, however, is to bring the downlead off at as close to a right angle as possible.

In my own experiments, the Tee antenna doesn't seem to have any advantage over the random length antenna of Figure 5-1, but doesn't seem any worse either. It will make a convenient antenna for those readers who have supports (like trees) that would take the antenna wire directly over the building. As in the case of the random length antenna, use a lightning arrestor and ground connection with the Tee antenna.

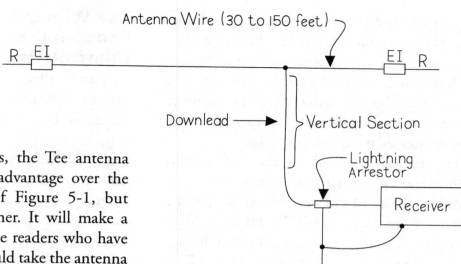

Figure 5-2

Tunable Random Length or Long Wire Antenna (Marconi Antenna)

The random length antenna of Figure 5-1 is not usually resonant at a wide range of frequencies (it is resonant at a few frequencies). That means that the impedance of the antenna varies with frequency and can show wide excursions

over a large range of possible values. The non-resonant random length and Tee antennas are poor impedance matches at most frequencies, but that situation can be rectified by using an antenna tuning unit (ATU) at the feed end of the antenna, as shown in Figure 5-3.

If an inductor (L1) is inserted into the circuit in series, i.e., by connecting terminals B-to-E and A-to-F, then the antenna will act as if it were longer than the actual length (for any given frequency). Alternatively, if a capacitor (C1) is inserted in series with the wire, as by connecting D-to-E and C-to-F, then the antenna will act as if it were shorter than the actual length on any given frequency. Conversely, we can build a simple L-section antenna coupler by connecting A-to-F, B-to-D-to-E, and C-to-ground.

There are actually three cases in which

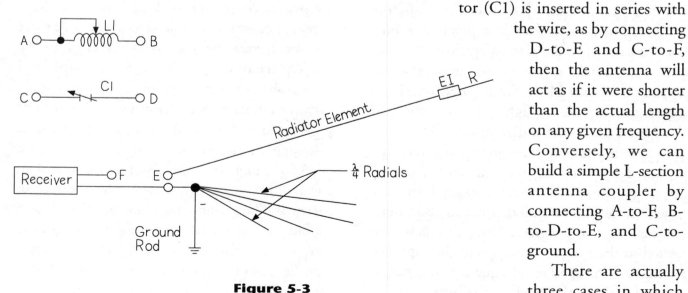

Figure 5-3

this tuned random length antenna might be used. If the antenna wire is less than a quarter-wavelength long at the operating frequency, then the inductor is inserted into the line with the antenna wire. For use with the L-section coupler shown in the inset, the antenna element needs to be greater than a quarter-wavelength.

For the upper end of the HF region (> 14 MHz) use a variable or tapped inductor of 18 µH (or so) and a capacitor of 140 pF. For the entire range of the 3 to 30 MHz HF band, then use a 365 pF capacitor and a 28 µH inductor. For less than 3 MHz, try up to 1100 pF of capacitance, which can be built using a two or three section "broadcast variable" capacitor. There are several antenna tuning units which are commercially available and suitable for tuning random wire or Tee antennas. These are discussed in Chapter 13.

Any wire antenna is enhanced by using a series of quarter-wavelength radials connected to the ground point. The ground rod is also used (for lightning protection), but the radials improve the performance on the bands for which the radials are cut. The length of each radial (in feet) is $246/F_{MHz}$ or (in meters) $75/F_{MHz}$. Use at least two radials for each band of interest (although, up to 120, the "more the better"…but two to four is a practical limit). For the sake of pedestrian safety in your yard, bury the radials a few inches underground. A spade or shovel blade can be used to "slit" a trench that is wide enough to press a wire into it, without the need for digging holes.

The random length antenna can sometimes be tuned by watching the S-meter on the receiver, but the effect is sometimes small (so tune slowly and watch carefully). You can also tune it "by ear" on many signals. Once the dials connected to the rotary inductor and the capacitor are marked for band and frequency, they can be retuned without the need for the instrument.

The Window-Coupled Random Length or Longwire (Marconi Antenna)

Random length and longwire antennas (the two are sometimes confused with each other) are easily built Marconi-style antennas. They consist of a radiator element consisting of a length of wire (Figure 5-1), supported by end insulators (EI) and ropes (R). An insulated wire downlead is routed through a window or wall to the receiver. If the antenna has an unknown length, then it is a random length and may or may not offer directivity (depending on frequency). The long wire has a length that is at least two wavelengths long (2λ), and offers directivity on the lowest operating frequency (2λ), and higher frequencies.

But what if you can't pass the lead through the window; for example, when it's too cold to have the window open 1/16-inch for the window sill strap used by SWLs for this purpose? There is a solution: use a *window capacitor*. That's right, a window capacitor. The glass of the window pane is a reasonably good dielectric for a capacitor, and has sufficient area to make a parallel plate capacitor. Cement copper foil on both sides of the window pane (Figure 5-4), so that the two pieces register with each other without overlap. Solder the downlead to the outside piece of copper, and the lead to the receiver to the inside piece of copper. Because the copper and glass forms a capacitor, the antenna is electrically shorter than its physical length would otherwise suggest, so add about 15% of the length that you might ordinarily use for any given frequency.

A lightning arrestor is absolutely essential on any antenna, so don't overlook it on this type of antenna! The ground terminal on the arrestor should be connected to an eight-foot ground rod that is driven into the Earth, through a short length of heavy wire (consult local electrical codes).

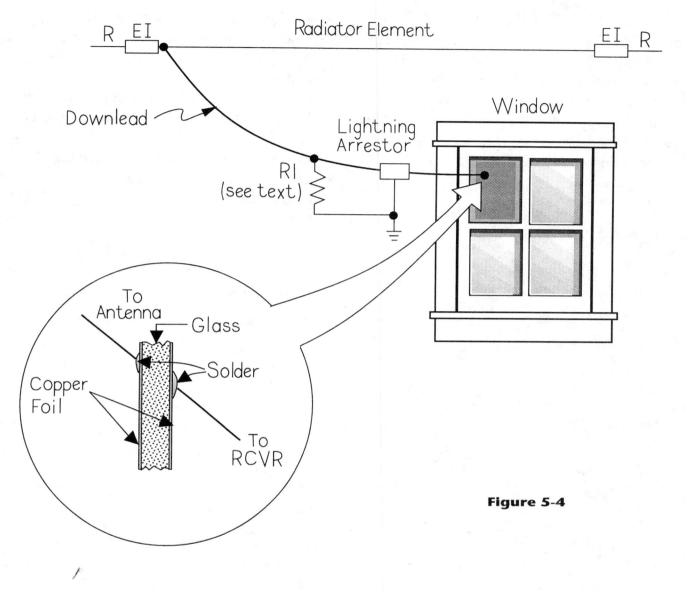

Figure 5-4

A problem sometimes seen on longwire antennas is static electricity build-up. The electricity comes from local fields, including distant lightning, and other physical phenomenon. It can reach scores of dozens of kilovolts, and can seriously damage the input circuitry of the receiver (even though not generally harmful to humans, unless you're startled by the shock and fall off your ladder). The solution to this problem is to place a resistor (R1 in Figure 5-4) between the ground and the downlead. Many people place the re-

sistor across the lightning arrestor because the arrestor makes a decent mounting support for the resistor. Use a value of resistance between 200 kilohms and 2 megohms. However, in constructing the resistor use at least ten 2-watt resistors in series; i.e., for a 1 megohm resistor use ten 100 kilohm, 2-watt resistors connected in series. The reason for this is to prevent the static electricity from arcing over the resistor...we want to drain it off, not zap it to ground (Yes, Virginia, resistors have voltage ratings).

A more conventional means of passing a single wire downlead through the window is shown in Figure 5-5. The conductor through the window is an insulated flat strap (available where antenna supplies are sold) that fits beneath the movable part of the window and the window sill. It will mold into the channel that receives the moving part. The window is then dropped down onto the flat strap.

The window doesn't quite close all the way when the flat strap is used (despite what the installation instructions say). If you live in a cold region of the country, then you might want to either use a different approach or be sure to seal the window. I found that the adhesive-backed foam weather stripping sold at Harry and Harriet Homeowner do-it-yourself stores works well. One type is round, and will mold directly to the window sill and sash (see inset in Figure 5-5).

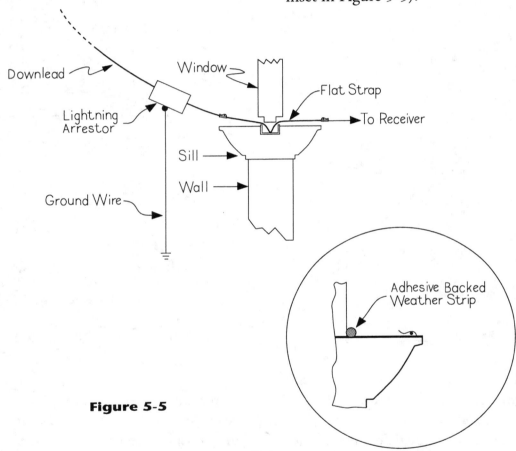

Figure 5-5

CHAPTER 6

The Dipole and Its Relatives

Dipoles have long been favorite antennas with receiver owners, and there are several reasons for this popularity. One of them is that the dipole has a bit less than 2 dB gain over an isotropic radiator because it is bidirectional instead of omnidirectional (Figure 6-1). For a transmitter, antenna gain provides increased effective radiated power in the transmission direction. There is no real increase in actual power, but because the total power is directed into limited directivity it acts as if there were more power being generated. For receiving, antenna gain means that any given station in that direction can be heard louder even if only the smallest amount—2 dB isn't even one S-unit on the receiver S-meter.

The dipole also provides two deep nulls of its ends, which is possibly the dipole's best advantage for SWLs. You can reduce loud interference by strategically placing an antenna null in that direction.

The final reason dipoles are popular receiving antennas is their utter simplicity. Just take a bit of wire, some insulators, a 1:1 balun coil (if you want to do it right), and you're in business!

Regular Dipole

Figure 6-2 shows the simple dipole. The radiator elements (A) are each quarter-wavelength long, and are made of copper wire. Use #12 or #14 wire size; smaller sizes tend to break too easily.

The overall length of the wire element ("L" in Figure 6-2) is one half-wavelength, and is found from the equation

$$L_{feet} = \frac{468}{F_{MHz}}$$

where: L_{feet} is the length in feet, and F_{MHz} is the operating frequency in megaHertz. Because the dipole usually must work over a wide range, it is normally cut for a frequency close to the center of the desired band of operation. This equation is used close to the Earth's surface, and contains a 5% reduction in length because of "end

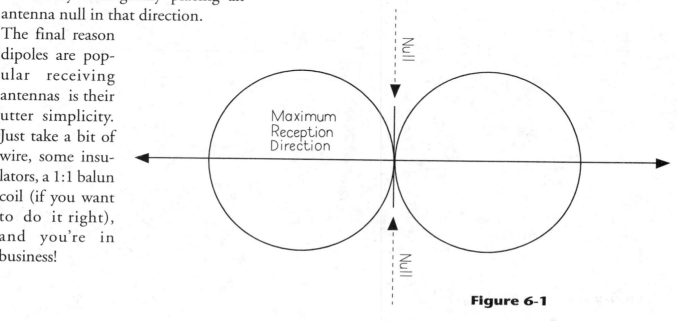

Figure 6-1

effects." In free space (that is, many wavelengths above the Earth's surface) the factor "468" becomes 492.

Let's look at a real-world example. Suppose we want a dipole cut to a frequency of 11750 kHz with an overall length of L and the length of each element A. The solution is found by:

$$L_{feet} = \frac{468}{11.750} = 39.83 \text{ feet}$$

Length "A" is one-half of L_{feet} or
$$\frac{39.83}{2} = 19.92 \text{ feet}$$

The factor ".92" feet can be converted to inches by multiplying it by 12, that is: 0.92 inch x 12 = 11.04 inches ≈ 11 inches. Thus, the antenna is made of two wire elements, each being 19 feet and 11 inches long.

The radiator element is broken into two portions, each of which are half the length found by the equation above, or a quarter-wavelength long. The ends of the wires are tied off to a rope mechanical support via ceramic, glass, or plastic end insulators (EI in Figure 6-2). The feedpoint, where the line to the receiver is connected, is the center of the antenna where the two quarter-wavelength radiator elements are supported by a center insulator or 1:1 balun transformer.

Dipole Radiation Patterns

Figure 6-1 shows the conventional "figure-8" pattern normally associated with dipole antennas. This pattern is azimuthal—that is, as viewed from above. It consists of two main lobes along the same maxima axis, with low-reception nulls along an axis at right angles to the main lobes. The main lobes represent the directions of maximum reception signal strength (when pointed at a transmitting station), while the nulls represent

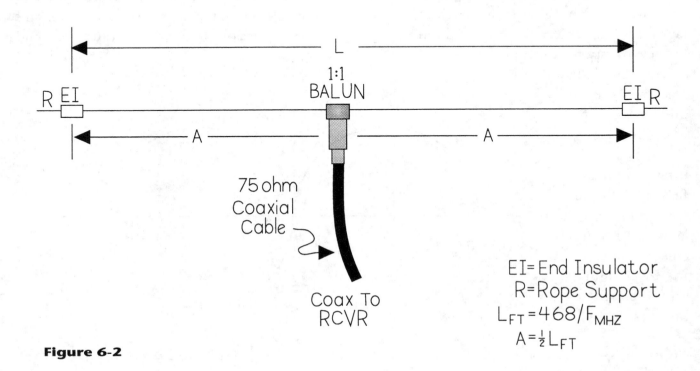

Figure 6-2

points of minimum signal strength.

The pattern of Figure 6-1 is actually only a partial view. It represents only the horizontal cut. Real antennas have a three dimensional radiation pattern with both vertical and horizontal extents. Figure 6-3 shows the three dimensional pattern (Figure 6-3A) relative to the antenna axis. The horizontal figure-8 pattern is shown at Figure 6-3B, while the vertical extent for a perfect dipole in free space is shown in Figure 6-3C.

The vertical extent radiation pattern is a function of the distance of the antenna above ground. The version shown in Figure 6-3C is for a perfect, free space dipole. If the antenna is less than a quarter-wavelength above ground, the pattern will be highly distorted. The variation of

the pattern from the ideal of Figure 6-3C is due to reflections from the Earth's surface immediately below the antenna combining with the radiated signal.

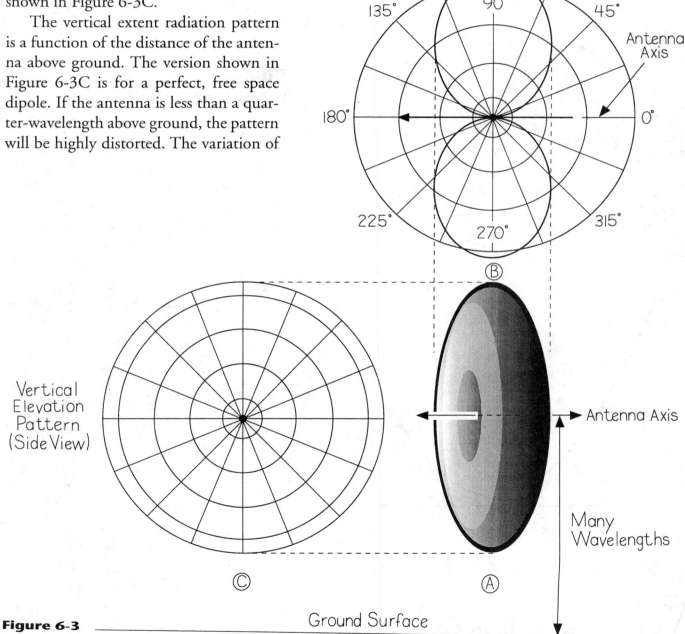

Figure 6-3

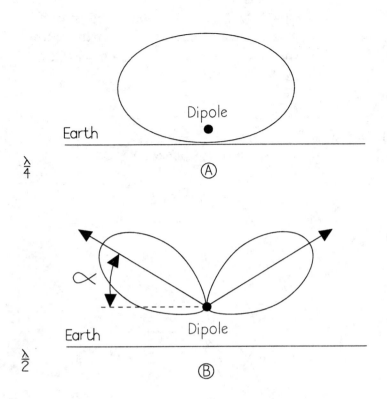

Figure 6-4

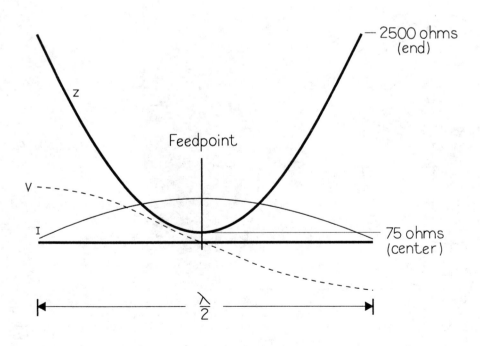

Figure 6-5

By the Law of Reciprocity, the same problem occurs in receiving antennas. Figure 6-4A shows the approximate pattern from a dipole located a quarter-wavelength above the Earth's surface, while Figure 6-4B shows the pattern existing when the dipole is a half-wavelength above ground.

The angle α in Figure 6-4B is the radiation angle. This angle is critical when determining where signals will be received from at any given time and frequency.

Dipole Feedpoint Impedance

When a dipole is electrically excited, either by a transmitter at the feedpoint or by an intercepted radio wave, an electrical current flows in the radiator. This current oscillates back and forth at the transmitted frequency. Neither the current (I) nor the voltage (V) are constant over the entire length of the radiator element. Figure 6-5 shows the distribution of voltage (dotted line) and current (thin solid line) along the length of the half-wavelength radiator. These two elements (V and I) are related to the impedance by the ratio V/I. Note that the voltage crosses a minimum and current rises to a maximum at the feedpoint. Because the feedpoint is located in the middle of the half-wavelength dipole, we can conclude that the dipole is a current fed, rather than voltage fed, antenna.

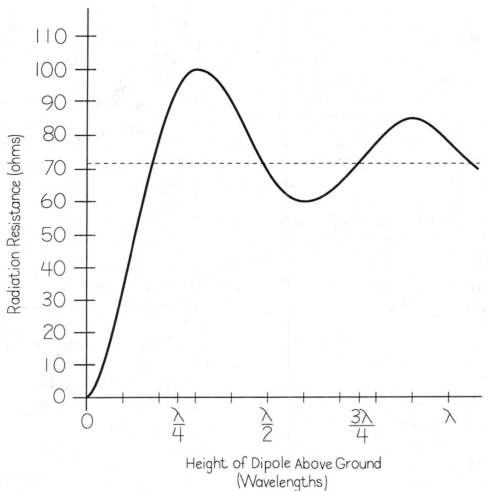

Figure 6-6

We can also note that the impedance drops to a minimum at the feedpoint, and rises to about 2500 Ω at the ends. In an ideal dipole in free space—or so far above the ground and away from other objects as to simulate free space—the feedpoint impedance is close to 73 Ω. As a result, such a dipole makes a good match to 75 Ω coaxial cable. Unfortunately, the situation is not so simple in real life. Figure 6-6 shows that the actual impedance is a function of the distance of the antenna above the Earth's surface. The impedance is close to the ideal 73 Ω only at intervals of a quarter-wavelength until the antenna is so far above ground that the impedance variations converge to the ideal point. While these facts are of more importance to transmitter operators, they are also important for you if you want to maximize the effectiveness of your antenna system.

Coaxial cable is used as the transmission line between the dipole and the receiver; one end of the antenna is connected to the center conductor of the coax, while the other end of the antenna is connected to the outer shield of the coax. The coaxial cable makes a good impedance match for most practical dipoles. In general, RG-59/U, RG-11/U, or some other 75 Ω coaxial cable is used for the transmission line. For receiver antennas, the smaller sized RG-59/U cable is suitable (hams sometimes have to use the larger size cable because of the high power level of their transmitters).

Dipole Erection Pointers

Dipoles are relatively easy to erect. You need to identify or build two support points: a roof peak, wall, tree, mast, and so forth. The path between the two support points is ideally oriented in the direction to be rejected—at right angles to the direction of desired signals. These points should be at least 10% further apart than the length of the antenna. UNDER NO CIRCUMSTANCES SHOULD A PATH BE CHOSEN THAT REQUIRES THE ANTENNA TO BE NEAR OR OVER A POWER LINE!!!

The Folded Dipole

The folded dipole is a half-wavelength antenna consisting of parallel radiator elements (like twin-lead) shorted together at the ends (Figure 6-7). These antennas are typically "broader band" than conventional dipoles, so they remain useful across a wider frequency range away from the resonance point. The length of the radiator element is approximately the same as a regular dipole for the same frequency, namely 468 divided by the desired receiving frequency expressed in MHz.

These lengths are, by the way, approximate. The actual length will probably be slightly shorter, although there is a small possibility of it being a bit longer. The actual length depends on the electromagnetic environment at your location because house structures, trees, and height above the ground can affect

the resonance and feedpoint impedance. Also, when twin-lead is used, the velocity factor of the specific brand that you buy may affect length. The actual length is found by trimming or lengthening the antenna from the formula length, until minimum VSWR is reached on the frequency of operation that you desire.

The feedpoint connection is established by cutting one of the radiator elements, and attaching the transmission line. Because the free space impedance of the dipole is around 280 Ω, it is a good match to 300 Ω television type twin-lead cable. The twin-lead is stripped at the ends, the exposed wires are twisted together, and then soldered (see Inset A of Figure 6-7). Similarly, one of the wires in the twin-lead is snipped at the center and about one-half inch stripped back in either direction. A transmission line is prepared from a piece of twin-lead, and it is soldered to the radiator element ends (see Inset B in Figure 6-7).

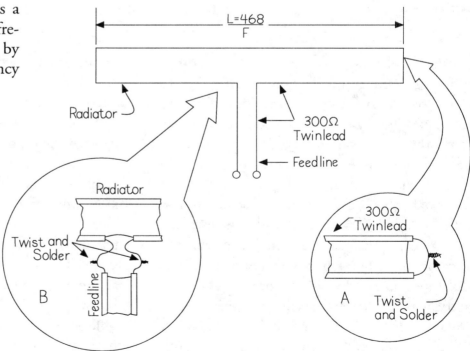

Figure 6-7

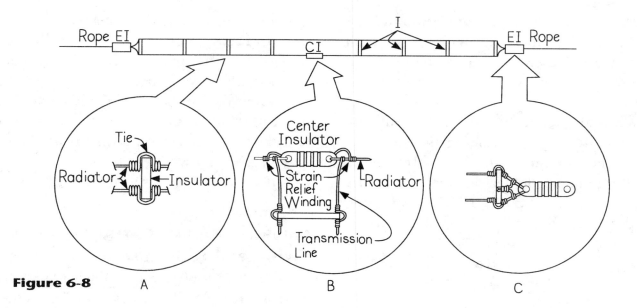

Figure 6-8   A   B   C

The 300 Ω feedline to the receiver is not a good match to the 50 Ω output impedance used by most equipment sold today. In addition, this transmission line is balanced, while the standard receiver antenna input is unbalanced (designed for coaxial cable). The folded dipole made with either twin-lead or parallel transmission line should be connected to the receiver through an antenna tuner (usually a good idea for any antenna) that is equipped with a balanced output in addition to the normal unbalanced or coaxial cable output. These tuners have an internal 4:1 impedance ratio balun ("*bal*anced *un*balanced") transformer.

The folded dipole shown in Figure 6-8 uses a more traditional method of construction ("pre-twin-lead"). Many experienced people prefer this method to the twin-lead method. The radiator element is made from #12 or #14 stranded copper wire. The wires are spread four to six inches by using spreader insulators ("I" in Figure 6-8) every five feet or so. The best insulators are the ceramic types that are made for the purpose, but these are hard to come by these days except at hamfests. Alternatives include segments of PVC plumbing pipe, plastic, plexiglass, or even old toothbrushes (don't laugh, it worked!). Each insulator is secured in place by a tie wire made of the same wire stock as the antenna radiator (Inset A in Figure 6-8). The tie wires are twisted and then soldered.

The feedpoint of the wire folded dipole (Inset B in Figure 6-8) is insulated with a standard antenna center insulator (which are easily available everywhere). The feedline is 300 Ω parallel transmission line, and it is connected to the radiator between the center insulator and the strain relief winding. The latter winding is made by looping a "tail" through the insulator, and around the radiator wire (back on itself), wrapping it around the radiator four or five times. Both the electrical connection from the transmission line and strain relief wrapping are soldered.

The end insulator is similarly handled (Inset C in Figure 6-8). A spreader insulator at each end is wired in the normal way (Figure 6-8, Inset A), but the ends of the radiator are twisted together in a normal insulator for support by a rope. If you use regular parallel wire antenna insulators, then it is possible to buy a type with a hole in the center. If these are used, then the support insulator can be eliminated, and the rope attached to the center hole. As with all antenna connections, the end connections and tie wires should be twisted tightly together and then soldered.

When the antenna radiator elements are identical sizes, and the spacing is four to six inches, then the impedance transformation is 4:1, as for antenna folded dipole. Other values (from 0.1:1 to 16:1) can be achieved by varying the spacing and respective conductor diameters. (See *The ARRL Antenna Book* for design graphs and equations if you're interested. If you use the 15th edition, look on page 2-33.)

Alternate Feed Using a Balun

An alternate method of feeding a folded dipole is shown in Figure 6-9. In this system, a 4:1 balun transformer is connected directly to the feedpoint, transforming the impedance to a value four times lower than the natural impedance ($\approx 300\ \Omega/75\ \Omega$). As a result of transforming the

feedpoint impedance, this antenna can be fed from 75 Ω coaxial cable.

Using a balun transformer at the feedpoint also helps the antenna pattern by balancing the currents in the two halves of the radiator. That nice pattern in Figure 6-1 is idealized for a perfect antenna. In practical antennas, it can get quite ragged, but with a balun at the feedpoint it comes much closer to the ideal.

Solving THE BIG PROBLEM on Twin-Lead Folded Dipoles

As early as 1960, I learned the hard way that there is a major problem with twin-lead folded dipoles. Because twin-lead uses #16 or #18 wire, and it is typically soft-drawn copper rather than copper clad steel, these antennas break a lot. A little wind, or a bit of ice, and *plooop!* The antenna breaks and falls to the ground. Sometimes old fashioned metal fatigue causes these antennas to simply drop to the ground. Regardless of the mechanism, however, the result is the same: you're out of business until repairs are made.

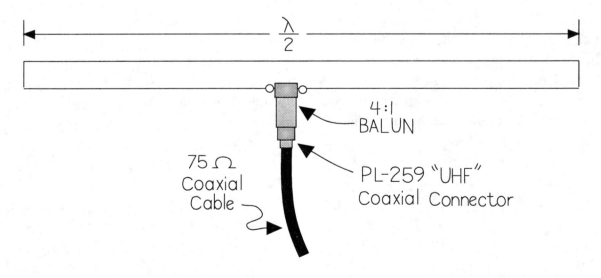

Figure 6-9

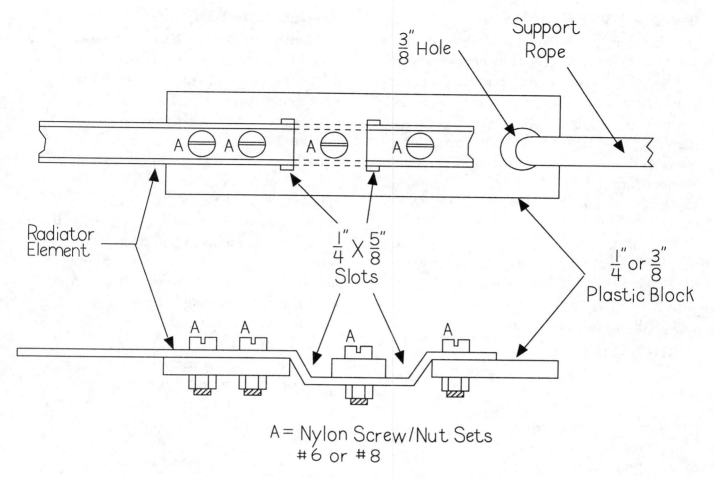

A = Nylon Screw/Nut Sets
#6 or #8

Figure 6-10

As a sad-faced teenager I told my mentor, the late "Mac" Parker (W4II), of the problem. He chuckled, and then drew out a little drawing...which was somewhat like Figure 6-10. The end insulators (shown here) and the center insulator are made from ¼-inch plexiglass, Lucite, or other form of strong, nonconductive plastic material. A pair of ¼-inch slots, about two inches apart, are cut into the center. It is easy to make these slots by starting with a ¼-inch drill, making a hole at either end of the slot-to-be, and then removing the material between them with a rat tail file. A series of five screw holes are made at the points indicated. If #6 screws are anticipated, then drill 5/32-inch holes (¼-inch for #8). A ⅜-inch hole is drilled at one end for the support rope (both ends for a feedpoint insulator). In order to prevent cracking, the ⅜-inch hole should be at least its own diameter away from any edge.

The twin-lead is prepared by using a drill, leather punch, or ordinary paper hole punch to cut holes into the twin-lead. Pass the end of the twin-lead across the front side of the insulator, through the first slot, across the back side of the insulator to the other slot, and through this slot back to the front side. The twin-lead is fastened to the insulator block using nylon (NOT metal) machine screws and hex nuts. It might be useful to use a second nut on each screw, tighten it, and then superglue it in place.

Inverted-Vee Dipoles

The inverted-Vee antenna (Figure 6-11) is the answer for many receiver owners who do not have two supports from which to hang a regular dipole, or who have insufficient space to stretch out the regular dipole. The inverted-Vee is supported at its center by a mast, pole, corner of the roof, or other supporting structure. The radiator elements are sloped downward at a composite angle (Φ) of 90° or more (closer to 120° is usual).

The inverted-Vee is a half-wavelength long, but the physical length is about 6% greater than for an equivalent half-wavelength dipole on the same frequency. An approximation of the physical length can be found from:

$$L_{feet} = \frac{498}{F_{MHz}}$$

This length is then trimmed by experimentation using ordinary antenna tuning methods.

Loaded Short Dipoles

Many people do not have the physical space to build a regular dipole antenna, especially at today's real estate prices. Fortunately, there are some things that can be done for the situation. Perhaps the most popular way to shorten a dipole is to insert an inductor in each element (L1 and L2 in Figure 6-12). This antenna is called the *inductively loaded shortened dipole*. The overall length of the antenna ("A" in Figure 6-12) is shorter than a half-wavelength. The inductor coil is located at a distance ("B" in Figure 6-12) from the feedpoint, which can be anything from zero to about 75% of the overall length ("A"). Since this is a receiving antenna only, you can place the coils at the ends of the radiator elements if you wish.

Figure 6-13 gives us a means for determining the inductive reactance required of L1 and L2 by knowing the relative length of the antenna. Only three curves are given here: A = 0.1L, A = 0.5L, and A = 0.9L. The

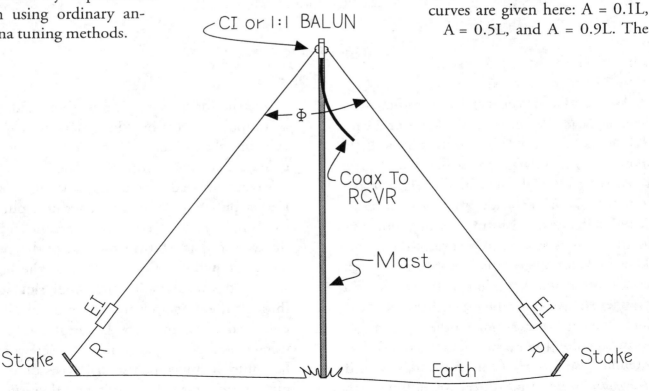

Figure 6-11

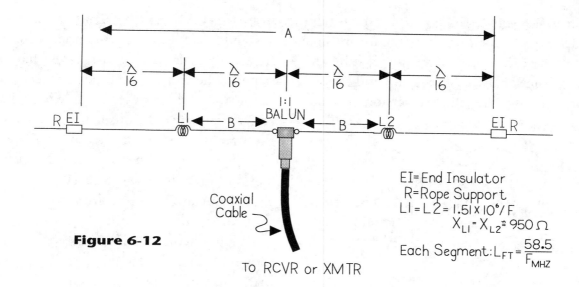

Figure 6-12

EI = End Insulator
R = Rope Support
$L1 = L2 = 1.51 \times 10^6 / F$
$X_{L1} = X_{L2} = 950\ \Omega$

Each Segment: $L_{FT} = \dfrac{58.5}{F_{MHZ}}$

horizontal axis shows the location of the inductors as a percentage of the overall length $[(A/B) \times 100\%]$. For example, suppose that we want to build a 7.2 MHz antenna that is 50% of the normal size. The length A is $[(468/7.2) \times 0.5] = 32.5$ feet; each element is therefore $32.5/2 = 16.25$ feet long. The coil is placed at the 50% point in each 16.25 foot (16'3") element. The 50% coil location line (read off "B" axis) intersects the 50% antenna size curve at about 850 Ω. The inductor should be designed to have an inductance of 850 Ω at 7.2 MHz, or $X_L/2\pi F = [(850\ \Omega)/((2)(3.14)(7.2\ \text{MHz}))] = 18.8\ \mu H$.

As is true with all antennas, these design guidelines, whether the equation for a half-wavelength antenna or the chart of Figure 6-13, are always approximate. They will get you into the ballpark, but you will need to use a tuning method to bring the resonant frequency to the exact point desired. You can do this by adjusting either the inductance or the overall length of the antenna. Use a noise bridge, impedance bridge, or some other means for finding the resonant point.

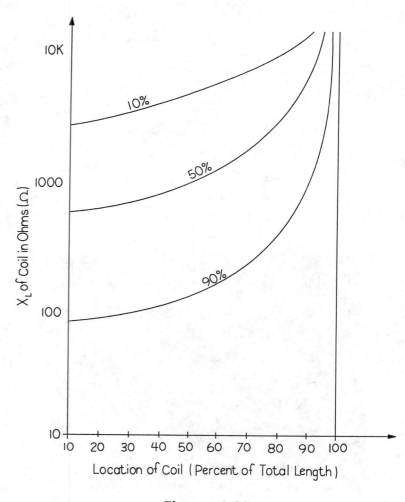

Figure 6-13

Figure 6-14 shows three possible methods for connecting the loading inductor to the antenna. In each case, the coil is supported by an insulator of the sort used for the end and center insulators. Usually, the shorter versions of the insulators work best. In Figure 6-14A the coil is a standard cylindrical "solenoid wound" coil (meaning it has a length greater than its diameter). The coil is sometimes connected exactly as shown, while in other cases (where the coil is larger diameter) the insulator passes coaxially through the center of the coil. Figure 6-14B shows the same type of mounting for a coil wound on a toroidal core; Figure 6-14C is similar but uses a larger size toroid that can be slipped over the insulator.

A pair of commercial dipole loading coils are shown in Figure 6-15. These coils appear to be made from PVC pipe stock with a PVC cap on either end. The coil is made from insulated wire wound in the space between the end caps. These are available from a variety of ham radio and electronics parts sources.

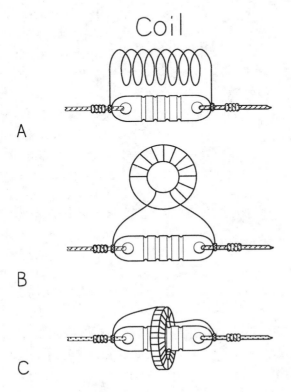

Figure 6-14

The Tilted, Center-Fed Terminated, Folded Dipole (Loop Antenna)

Figure 6-16 shows the *tilted, center-fed terminated, folded dipole* (TCFTFD) antenna, which is a special case of a loop antenna and a folded dipole antenna. The inventor, Navy captain G.L. Countryman (W3HH), once called it a "squashed rhombic" antenna. The antenna is a widely spread folded dipole, and is shorter than a conventional folded dipole. It must be mounted as a sloper, with an angle from its upper vertical support of 20 to 40°.

The feeding of the antenna is conventional, with a feedpoint impedance close to 300 Ω. A 75 Ω coaxial cable is connected to the bottom half of the antenna through a balun transformer that has a 4:1 impedance ratio. At the top side of the antenna, the "feedpoint" is occupied with a termination resistor of 370 to 430 Ω (390 Ω, 1 or 2 watts, makes a good compromise for receiving antennas).

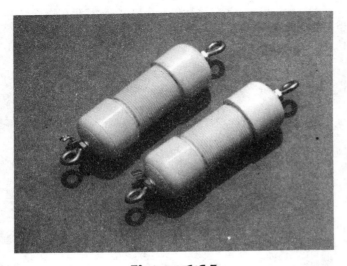

Figure 6-15

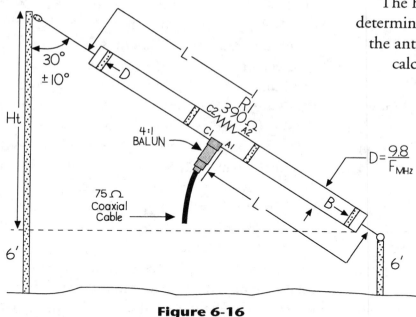

Figure 6-16

The spread (D) of the antenna wire elements is found from:

$$D_{feet} = \frac{9.8}{F_{MHz}}$$

The spreaders are preferably ceramic, strong plastic, or thick-walled PVC pipe. The spreaders can be made of wood (1x2 stock or 1-inch dowels) for receive antennas if the wood is properly varnished against the weather.

The overall length of the antenna is calculated a little differently from most antennas. We need to calculate the lengths *from the feedpoint to the middle of the spreaders*, which is also the length from the middle of the spreaders and the terminating resistor. These lengths (A1-B, A2-B, C1-D and C2-D) are found from:

$$L_{feet} = \frac{164,000}{F_{kHz}}$$

Four sections of wire, each with a length defined by the equation above, are needed to make this antenna.

The height of the upper antenna support is determined by trigonometry from the length of the antenna from end-to-end (not the length calculated for D, but approximately twice that length), and the angle. For example, at 7 MHz the lengths are 23.4 feet, and the spreaders are one foot. Thus, the overall physical length, counting the two element lengths and half of both spreader lengths, is [2 x 23.4 feet - (2 x 0.5)] foot, or 45.8 feet. If the angle of mounting is 30°, then the antenna forms the hypotenuse of a 60/30 right triangle. If we allow six feet for the lower support, then the upper support is:

$$\text{Height} = 6 + L \cos \Theta$$
$$= 6 + (45.8 \cos 30) = 45.7 \text{ feet}$$

This antenna has a low angle of radiation, and at a tilt angle of 30° (considered ideal) it is nearly omnidirectional.

The termination resistor can be mounted on a small piece of plastic, or alternatively as shown in Figure 6-17, it can be stretched across the end insulator in the manner of the inductors in the previous section. Use a 390 Ω, 2-watt resistor for this application.

Resistor

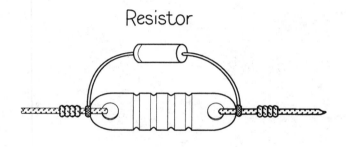

Figure 6-17

Wideband and Multiband Dipole Antennas

The dipole is reasonably wideband for receiving applications, but "wideband" normally means scores of kiloHertz above and below the resonant frequency. At frequencies removed from this range, however, the antenna is less effective and acts much like a random wire antenna. Let's look at two methods of "widebanding" a dipole.

First, the method of Figure 6-18 is basically two dipoles connected to the same feedline, but tuned to slightly different frequencies. At the higher end of the HF spectrum, only a few inches difference in physical length are needed to wideband the antenna several hundred kilo-

Hertz. For example, if the one dipole (A1/A2) is cut for 25 MHz, and the other for 26 MHz, the length difference is only about 8.6 inches.

Keep in mind that all dipoles are already "multiband" antennas, provided that the other bands are odd harmonics of the half-wavelength natural frequency. Thus, an antenna cut for a half-wavelength on 4500 kHz, is also a ¾-wavelength resonant antenna for 3 x 4500 kHz, or 13500 kHz. The two-lobe "figure-8" pattern of the half-wavelength dipole splits into four distinct lobes, so the antenna is not as directional on the higher frequency.

The simplest, most straightforward method of multibanding a dipole is to connect several dipoles to the same feedline, as shown in Figure 6-19.

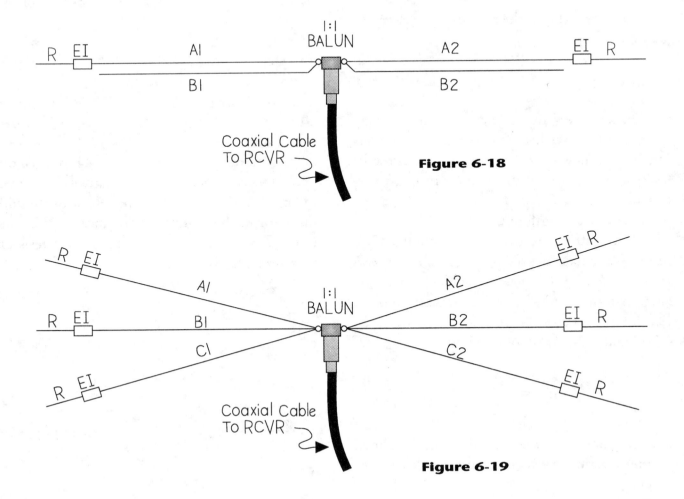

Coaxial Cable To RCVR

Figure 6-18

Coaxial Cable To RCVR

Figure 6-19

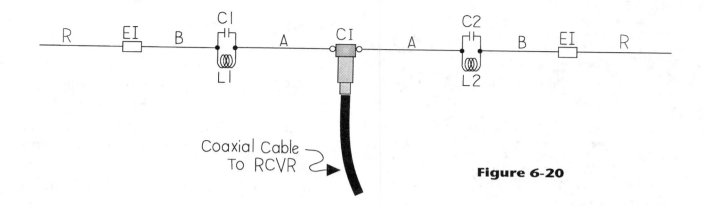

Coaxial Cable
To RCVR

Figure 6-20

Each dipole has a low impedance near its half-wavelength resonant frequency, and a high impedance at other frequencies. The antennas can be harmonically related to each other only if the even harmonics are used (third harmonics are already resonant—see above).

Use the usual formula for a standard dipole to determine the physical length of each antenna. Like any dipole, the formulas are only approximate, and some means for tuning the antenna are necessary for maximum efficiency. Each antenna is independent, so make the calculation for each band of interest.

Some people use a single multiconductor cable to form the dipole sections. For example, electric cord (two conductors), antenna rotor wire (four or five conductors), and computer flat cable (up to 100 conductors!) have all been used for multiband dipoles. These wires are, however, weaker than regular antenna wire and antennas built with them will most likely have a greater failure rate than regular antennas.

Trap Dipoles

One approach to building a multiband dipole antenna is to use resonant traps in a single wire dipole, as shown in Figure 6-20. Each trap is a parallel resonant inductor (L)–capacitor (C) tuned circuit. One of the properties of the parallel LC tuned circuit is that it offers a high impedance at its resonant frequency but a very low impedance to all other frequencies. Such a trap might offer an impedance of 20,000 Ω or so to the resonant frequency and a low impedance (< 100 Ω) at all other frequencies. Thus, for a high frequency, the sections marked "A" in Figure 6-20 are used; the trap isolates the rest of the antenna length for those frequencies. Each "A" section represents a quarter-wavelength element of a half-wavelength antenna.

At a lower frequency, the trap is not a factor so the resonant frequency is determined by the lengths consisting of A+B for each quarter-wavelength section. The resonant frequency is also affected by the inductor of the trap, and follows rules approximating those of the loaded trap dipole in the previous section. Typically, for any given resonant frequency, the antenna will be 68 to 75% of the non-trap physical length given earlier by the standard dipole equation.

A little "cut and try" experimentation will result in a resonant antenna. In general, the best advice is to adjust the length of the highest frequency sections ("A") first, and then work out in sequence.

Figure 6-21 shows a commercially available trap for shortwave antennas. Although it is relatively easy to design and build antenna traps for receiving antennas, they are also relatively low in

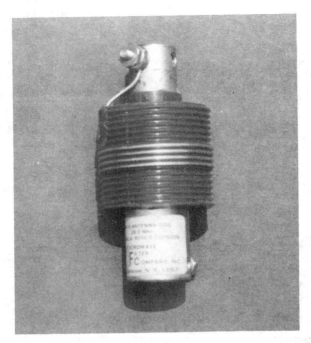

Figure 6-21

Balun Transformers

As we noted earlier, the word *balun* is actually an acronym made from the first syllables of *bal*anced and *un*balanced. A true balun transformer will convert a balanced load into an unbalanced load, such as from a balanced dipole to an unbalanced coaxial cable transmission line. The balun may, or may not, provide impedance transformation depending on the design. Two common impedance ratios are 1:1 and 4:1. The 1:1 balun transformer is typically used with conventional single-wire dipoles fed with 75 Ω coaxial cable, while the 4:1 are used with folded dipoles or elsewhere if a 4:1 or 1:4 impedance transformation is needed (they are bidirectional and can be used "backwards").

The typical balun today is wound on a ferrite toroidal core, although air core and ferrite rod solenoid wound (cylindrical) are also possible. Figure 6-23A shows the basic toroidal balun, Figure 6-23B shows the solenoid version, and Figure 6-23C the "bazooka" style. For receiving antennas, the FT-37 and FT-50 sizes are adequate. Typically, for the 3 to 30 MHz high frequency (a.k.a. HF) range, use

cost and readily available from suppliers of radio antenna goods.

Figure 6-22 shows a long multiband trap antenna that is usable for a large number of bands. Each trap (T1, T2, T3) is resonant on successively lower frequencies. Otherwise, the antenna is very similar to the trap dipole of Figure 6-20.

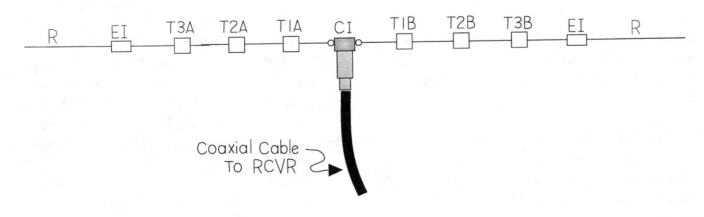

Figure 6-22

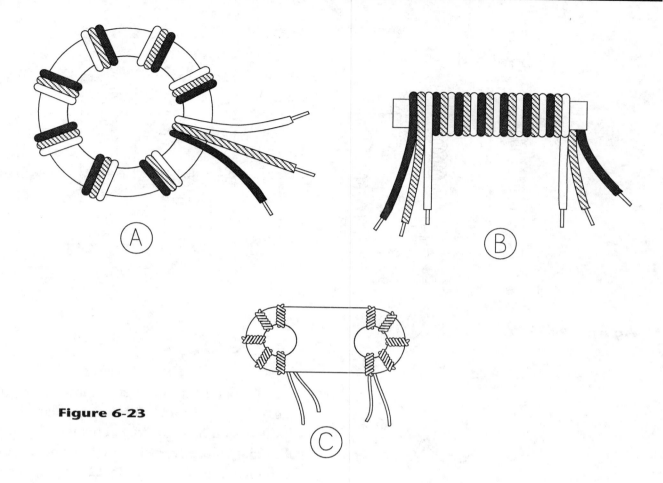

Figure 6-23

six turns on the CF-123 or ten turns on the FT 200-61 (they have different permeability values), of #12 or #14 enameled or formvar coated solid wire.

Each transformer is either bifilar or trifilar wound. That is, each turn consists of two or three wires wound close together, depending on the design. Some builders twist the wires together in a drill mandrel, but I don't recommend this practice because it is both dangerous and does not work as well as the flat winding schemes.

The pattern of windings is shown in Figure 6-24 for three different cases: 1/1, 4/1, and 50 Ω/75 Ω. The balun coil shown in Figure 6-24A provides balanced to unbalanced transformation, but the impedance transformation is 1:1. Note that it uses three windings,

trifilar wound, on a single core. This type of transformer is used on ordinary dipoles which provide a 75 Ω load, and are fed with 75 Ω coaxial cable (such as RG-59/U or RG-11/U).

Why would anyone want a 1:1 balun transformer? The reason is simple, especially when one looks at the antenna patterns produced by conventional dipoles with and without a balun transformer at the feedpoint. The idealized figure-8 pattern that is normal for a dipole is distorted by radiation caused by currents flowing on the outside conductor of the coaxial cable. Ideally, this current is geometrically balanced by currents flowing in the opposite direction in the inner conductor, but that ideal is rarely achieved. The problem is alleviated by the 1:1 balun transformer, and the pattern restored to very near the ideal.

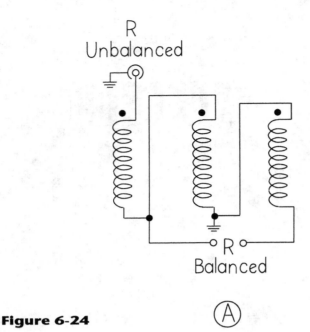

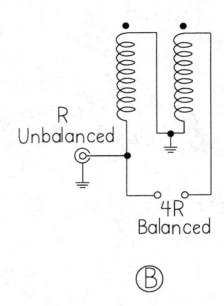

Figure 6-24

A 4:1 balun transformer is shown in Figure 6-24B. This transformer uses two bifilar wound windings over a single core. This is the type of balun that will convert the 300 Ω impedance of the folded dipole to the 75 Ω impedance of coaxial cable.

Both of the balun transformers shown in Figure 6-24A and Figure 6-24B are broadband RF transformers, and will cover a wide range of impedances. For example, the 1:1 transformer can also work with 52 Ω coax, while the 4:1 transformer will convert the 200 Ω impedance of certain loop antennas to 50 Ω for coax input.

The balun transformer of Figure 6-24C is a little different. It will match 75 Ω loads to 50 Ω transmission line. It uses two silvered mica capacitors for frequency compensation. Note that the number of turns for coil L1 is one-half the number of turns for L2 and L3 (3 turns and 6 turns for CF-123 forms, and 5 turns/10 turns for FT-200-61 forms). This winding protocol differs from the other baluns where all windings have the same number of turns.

CHAPTER 7

Longwire Antennas
Single Wires, Vee Beams, Rhombics, and Beverages

Longwire antennas have an almost legendary appeal to receiver owners because they are simple in concept, easy to construct, relatively low in cost, and provide both gain and directivity at reasonable cost. Although longwires can be very long (> 2λ is the minimum length), especially at low frequencies, they are manageable for many people. These antennas become more manageable at higher shortwave frequencies, such as the 19, 13, and 10 meter bands, where one wavelength is relatively short physically.

Just how long is "long" for a longwire antenna? For the lower HF and medium wave bands, 500 to 800 feet just begins to be considered "long," while at 25 MHz a mere 150 feet is considered "long." Vic Clark (W4KFC), former American Radio Relay League (ARRL) president, once told me of seeing a long, heavy copper wire mounted on telephone poles along a railroad track in Peru. He at first thought it was an old-fashioned telegraph line, but later found out that it was a low VLF band Vee-beam longwire antenna that was 24 miles long per leg! Vic officially visited that radio station later during the same trip in his capacity as the director of a U.S. Coast Guard engineering laboratory.

My first experience with longwires was a little unusual, especially since it occurred in the two-meter amateur radio band (144 to 148 MHz) where longwire antennas are not exactly common. A ham radio club station was located in a local Red Cross chapter house. Among the several antennas used at the station were a nine element two-meter Yagi directional beam antenna and a 120 foot long HF trap dipole (3.5 to 30 MHz). One winter evening, the late Johnnie Harper Thorne (K4NFU), who eventually became a well known antenna expert, and myself went to the station to work a few two-meter stations (those were pre-repeater days). Our first contact was a chap we had worked many times before; he was located about 90 miles to the east. That evening, he was louder than normal (good conditions?), and the receiver S-meter registered about two S-units higher than normal. At first, we thought he had installed either a new antenna or a power amplifier, and made some comment to that effect. "No" he averred, "nothing's new." It turned out that I had accidentally connected the HF trap dipole to the two-meter transceiver. Its 120 foot length was more than 12 wavelengths long at 146 MHz—far more than the minimum requirement for a longwire antenna. Furthermore, the main lobes of such a long longwire antenna would be off the ends of the antenna and was thus pointed at the other station. Of course, the frequency selective traps were ineffective at two-meter band frequencies.

Perhaps my companion that evening remembered the longwire many years later. When he moved to Texas and bought a 43+ acre farmette, he erected a 1250 foot longwire antenna about 30 feet off the ground. When I used it in July 1984, it performed a whole lot better than I anticipated. I owe Johnnie Thorne a debt of gratitude for his instruction not only on longwire antennas, but also on loop antennas (on which he was particularly expert).

The horizontally polarized longwire's

popularity with receiver owners is due to several different factors. One factor is that it provides gain and directivity at certain harmonically related frequencies (and in one version on non-harmonic frequencies). With the possible exception of odd multiples of a quarter-wavelength, at other frequencies the antenna acts like a very long random length wire antenna. Another receiver advantage is that its very long length provides a very large aperture, so the amount of signal energy captured is also large.

There is also the matter of the angle of radiation and reception (ARR or α). DX antennas need low, horizon-kissing angles. A longwire that is installed $\geq \lambda/2$ from the ground will exhibit values of α of 10 to 15°.

Finally, there is a *diversity effect* sometimes seen on longwires. When the ionosphere is unsettled, an incoming signal's arrival angle may change (see Figure 7-1) over the course of a few seconds, resulting in the fading phenomenon. Because of its length, the fading signal can change, yet remain within the antenna's aperture, thus reducing fading under the right circumstances.

There are several "flavors" on the longwire antenna menu: resonant single wire longwires, nonresonant single wire longwires, Vee beam longwires, and rhombic beam longwires. In addition, there is a related class of antennas called Beverage or wave antennas. We will discuss all of these antennas in this chapter.

Resonant Single Wire Longwire Antennas

Let's first take a look at the simple unterminated resonant (a.k.a. "periodic") longwire antenna made from a single wire radiator. Interestingly enough, although the longwire antenna looks terribly Marconian—like an antenna that is tuned against ground—it is actually Hertzian when the physical length is more than two wavelengths ($\geq 2\lambda$).

A fundamental form of longwire antenna is shown in Figure 7-2. It consists of a wire radiator element that is at least two wavelengths ($\geq 2\lambda$) long. One can visualize the longwire antenna as a set of series-connected half-wavelength dipoles strung end to end. Unlike certain other long wire (but not "longwire") antennas, the "dipoles" are out of phase with each other, as indicated in Figure 7-2 by the "+" and "-" signs along the antenna length. It is the interaction of the waves on the various sections that forms the pattern for reception.

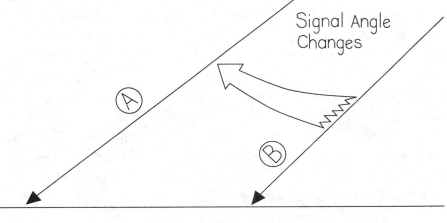

Figure 7-1

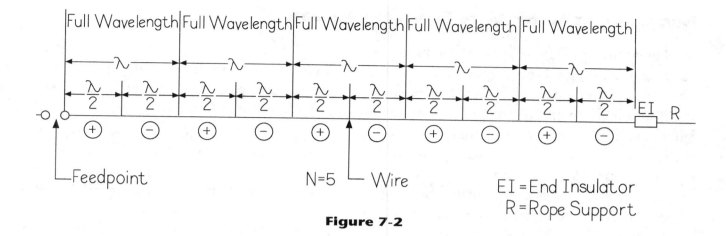

Figure 7-2

Longwire Length

Resonant longwire antennas are designed to lengths that are multiples of a half-wavelength, provided that they are at least 2λ long. Unlike certain other resonant antennas, the performance of the longwire does not change a great deal with moderate changes in frequency. The exception to the rule is that the angle of radiation and reception changes rapidly with changes in length for antennas that are less than about 3λ long. The actual cut physical length is actually slightly shorter than $N\lambda$, as seen by the equation:

$$\text{Length}_{\text{feet}} = \frac{984(N - 0.025)}{F_{\text{MHz}}}$$

Where:

Length is in feet (ft)

F_{MHz} is the lowest operating frequency in megahertz (MHz)

N is the integer number of wavelengths desired for the length

Let's look at an example and find the length of a 2λ single wire resonant longwire for the 60-meter tropical broadcast band (4.75 to 4.995 MHz). Because the lowest frequency in the band is 4.75 MHz, the antenna is designed for that

frequency. This is contrary to the practice on other forms of antenna where a frequency in the middle of the band is selected (e.g. 4873 kHz).

$$\text{Length} = \frac{984(2 - 0.025)}{4.75\,\text{MHz}}$$

$$\text{Length} = \frac{(984)(1.975)}{4.75\,\text{MHz}}$$

$$\text{Length} = \frac{1943.4}{4.75} = 409\,\text{feet}$$

That 409 foot antenna also worked well on its harmonics. For example, the second harmonic is the 31-meter band, the third harmonic overlaps the 20-meter ham band and a fixed point commercial radio band, the fourth harmonic is the 19 MHz fixed point band that also includes the Russian Salyut and Mir space station beacons, the fifth harmonic is a fixed point band plus the 12-meter ham band, and so forth.

A constraint on the use of other frequencies is that the antenna becomes very heavily capacitive reactive ($-X_c$) at frequencies where the antenna is an odd multiple of quarter wavelength. An equivalent inductive reactance ($+X_L$) can be used to cancel the capacitive reactance (i.e., a coil is placed in the circuit).

Nonresonant Single Wire Longwire Antennas

The resonant longwire antenna mentioned above is a standing wave antenna because it is unterminated at the far end. A signal propagating from the feedpoint, or any point along the length as happens in receive antennas, towards the open end will be reflected back towards the source. The interference between the forward and reflected waves sets up stationary standing waves of current and voltage along the wire.

A *nonresonant longwire* is terminated at the far end in a resistance equal to its characteristic impedance. Thus, the incident waves are absorbed by the resistor rather than being reflected. Figure 7-3 shows a terminated longwire antenna. The receiver end is like the feed system for other longwire antennas, but the far end is grounded through a terminating resistor, R1, that has a resistance (R) equal to the characteristic impedance (Z_o) of the antenna (R = Z_o). When the wire is 20 to 30 feet above the ground, Z_o is about 500 to 600 Ω.

The radiation pattern for the terminated longwire is a unidirectional version of the multi-lobed pattern found on the unterminated longwires (Figure 7-4). The angles of the lobes vary with frequency, even though the pattern remains unidirectional. The directivity of the antenna is partially specified by the angles of the main lobes. Figure 7-5A shows how angles of the main lobes change with respect to antenna length in wavelengths. For the sake of comparison, the gain over a dipole is shown in Figure 7-5B. It is interesting to note that gain rises almost linearly with Nλ, while the directivity function changes rapidly at shorter lengths (above three or four wavelengths the rate of change diminishes considerably). Thus, when an antenna is cut for a certain low frequency, it will work at higher frequencies, but the directivity characteristic will be somewhat different at each end of the spectrum of interest.

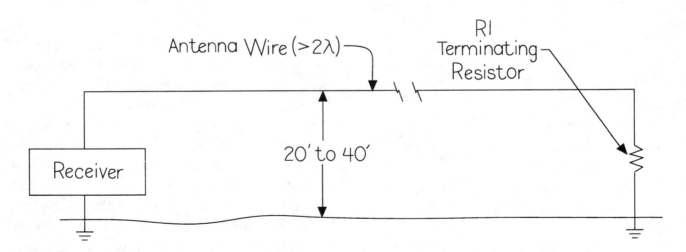

Figure 7-3

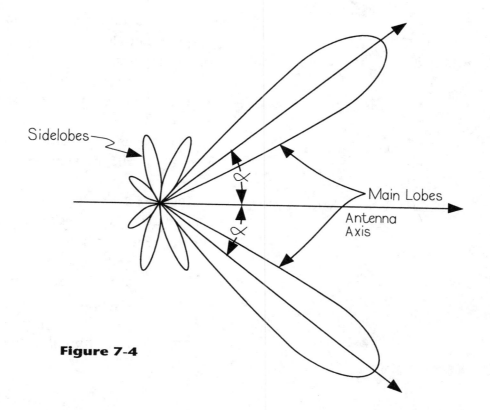

Figure 7-4

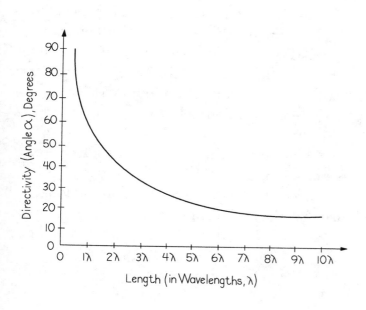

Figure 7-5A

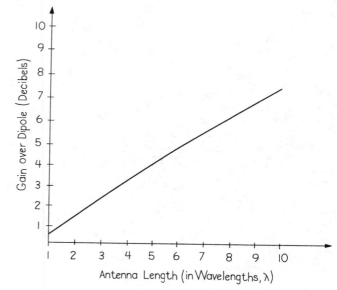

Figure 7-5B

Longwire Antenna Radiation/Reception Characteristics

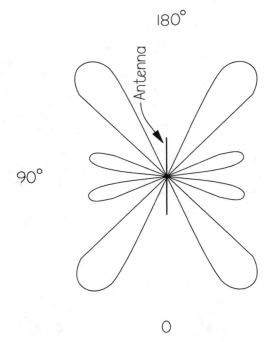

36° main   2λ
75° -5dB

Figure 7-6A

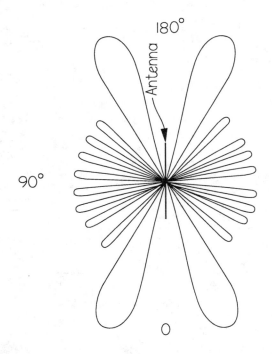

5λ main 22
47, 62, 72, 83

Figure 7-6B

The radiation pattern of longwire antennas is quite complex, even though the antenna is physically simple. This complexity is due in part to the fact that the half-wavelength segments radiate or receive out of phase with each other. If all segments were in-phase, then the patterns would be somewhat simpler. As it is, the complexity of the patterns is very "wavelength dependent."

Figure 7-6 shows two situations. A two-wavelength (2λ) pattern is shown in Figure 7-6A. There are four major lobes positioned at angles of ±36° from the longwire. There are also four minor lobes—the strongest of which is -5 dB down from the major lobes—at angles of ±75° from the longwire. Between all of the lobes are sharp nulls in which little reception is possible.

As the wire length is made longer, the angle of the main lobes pulls in "tighter"—that is, towards the wire. As the lobes pull in closer to the wire, the number of minor lobes increases. At 5λ (Figure 7-6B), there are still four main lobes, but they are at angles of ±22° from the wire. Also, the number of minor lobes increases to sixteen. The minor lobes are located at ±47, ±62, ±72, and ±83° with respect to the wire. The minor lobes tend to be -5 to -10 dB below the major lobes.

When the longwire gets very much longer than 5λ, the four main lobes begin to converge along the length of the wire and the antenna becomes bidirectional. This effect occurs at physical lengths greater than about 20λ.

In general, the following rules apply to longwire antennas:

- On each side of the antenna, there is at least one lobe, minor or major, for each half-wavelength of the wire element. For the overall element, there is one lobe for every quarter-wavelength.

- If there is an even number of lobes on either side of the antenna wire, then half of the total number of lobes are tilted backwards and half are tilted forwards; symmetry is maintained.

- If there is an odd number of lobes on either side of the wire, then one lobe on either side will be perpendicular to the wire, with the other lobes distributed either side of the perpendicular lobe.

Longwire Feed Systems

A longwire antenna can be fed either at the end, or at any current maxima ("loop") along its length. The current loops occur in the middle of half-wavelength segments. If a longwire is to be for single frequency operation, then an appropriate low impedance current loop can be selected. Unfortunately, these very simple antennas grow terribly complex (in theory of operation, if not construction) once the frequency for which any given feed point in a current loop changes. Sliding to another received frequency changes the location of the maximum current spots because the physical definition of "half-wavelength" also changes. For multi-frequency operation the best solution is to end-feed the antenna.

The "ideal" feed system is shown in Figure 7-7. It uses an antenna tuning unit right at the antenna feedpoint. The impedance to be matched is typically 500 Ω. An argument for this system is that any practical untuned parallel transmission line will re-radiate some signal, contributing an unwanted vertically polarized element to the antenna pattern. By placing the ATU at the feedpoint, the problem is greatly reduced—coax, properly terminated, is less likely to re-radiate than open feeders. (Or at least that's the popular myth about coax…which may or may not be true—makes a good story, anyway.) Although some people have successfully used this system by motorizing the tuning elements in an ATU, remote mast mounted ATUs are still a bit rare.

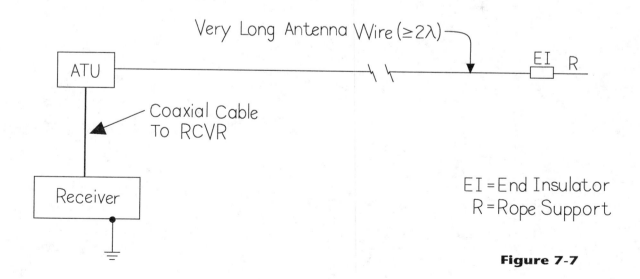

Figure 7-7

A popular alternative is shown in Figure 7-8. This feed system is the old fashioned "Zepp" method. The antenna tuning unit is co-located with the receiver, and is connected to the longwire antenna line thorough 500 Ω parallel conductor transmission line. Although the correct line is 500 Ω "open" parallel line, a good substitute is 450 Ω insulated twin-lead. It will substitute nicely for the open parallel line, causing only a small VSWR increase. It is quite suitable for nearly all SWL applications and is less of a hassle than open line.

A disadvantage of the simple Zepp feed method is that the integrity of the antenna pattern depends on currents in both parallel conductors being equal. This situation occurs naturally only when the physical length of the antenna is an integer multiple of a half-wavelength for the frequency being received. At other frequencies, the currents are unequal and that increases the pattern distortion. Also, installation problems, like one conductor being closer (too close) to a gutter or alumi-

num siding than the other, can distort the current flow and thus the antenna receive pattern.

The use of a quarter-wavelength matching section to feed the longwire is shown in Figures 7-9A and 7-9B. Both versions use 600 Ω parallel transmission line. You can either purchase such line ready-made or make it yourself. The 600 Ω characteristic impedance can be realized by spacing #16 solid wire at four inches, or #14 wire at five inches. The physical length of the quarter-wavelength stub is $246/F_{MHz}$ (the velocity factor being negligible here). The method of Figure 7-9A uses a matching nonresonant (untuned) parallel transmission line to the receiver that is tapped at a point that will make the required impedance transformation. This matching system only works on a single band. The other method, shown in Figure 7-9B, connects untuned parallel 600 Ω line to the open-circuited bottom of the stub. This feed system will work on only one band as nontuned feeders, but if an antenna tuning unit

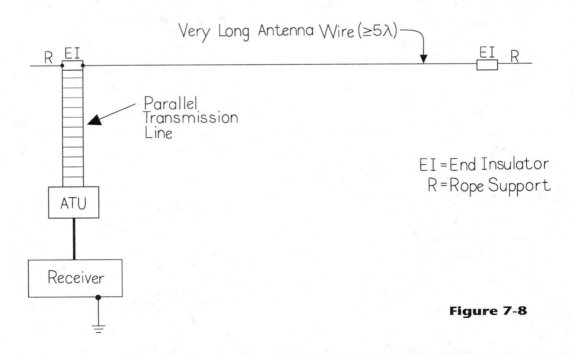

Figure 7-8

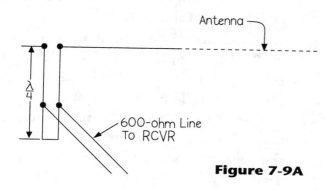

Figure 7-9A

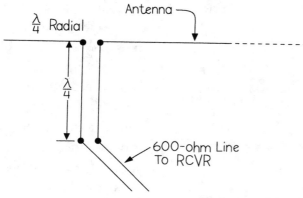

Figure 7-9B

is provided it will also resonate the feeders at higher frequencies. Some people provide a balun transformer to connect to the stub. A 9:1 transformer will reduce the 600 Ω impedance to about 67 Ω, which is not a bad match to either 52 Ω or 75 Ω coaxial cable.

A way to improve the situation is to use a quarter-wavelength radial connected to the "cold" side of the parallel transmission line (see Figure 7-10). The purpose of the radial is to provide a counterpoise ground (as opposed to a real Earth ground) connection for the longwire antenna. The radial is a wire that is cut to a quarter-wavelength in the center of the band of interest. The length is:

$$L_{feet} = \frac{246}{F_{MHz}}$$

or, in meters:

$$L_{meters} = \frac{75}{F_{MHz}}$$

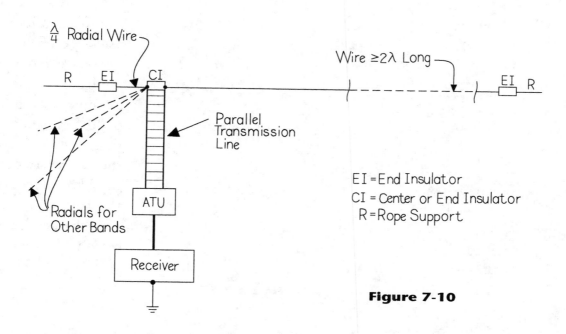

EI = End Insulator
CI = Center or End Insulator
R = Rope Support

Figure 7-10

The antenna shown in Figure 7-10 is fed with 500 Ω parallel transmission line, as were the others, even though it has a counterpoise radial ground. Although considered "best" for ideal installations, practical installation problems usually militate against parallel line. A method for using coaxial cable transmission line is shown in Figure 7-11. In this version, a 4:1 balun transformer (T1) is inserted at the feedpoint. The balun converts the feedpoint impedance to a value that is one-fourth as large, or 125 Ω. Although further impedance transfor-

mation can be done, in order to better match a standard coaxial cable impedance, the resultant 125 Ω impedance results in only a 1.67:1 VSWR when connected to 75 Ω coax like RG-59/U or RG-11/U. While that VSWR might concern ham operators (because of VSWR shut-down circuits in transmitters), it doesn't seriously affect receiver owners.

Radials are a key component to resonant longwires—indeed, for nonresonant longwires too. Unfortunately, the radial is also relatively long and may consume a bit of valuable lawn space needed for the longwire. For example, a two-wavelength longwire designed to receive 6000 kHz and up has a length of 324 feet, and the radial for 6000 kHz is 41 feet long, for an overall length end-to-end of 324 + 41, or 365 feet. It is possible to shorten the radial length by inserting an inductor in series with the radial (Figure 7-12). A general rule is to use a coil that has an inductive reactance of 900 Ω at a frequency in the center of the band of interest. For example, in the 5950 to 6200 kHz international shortwave broadcast band, the center frequency is 6075 kHz. The coil makes the antenna tuning a little sharper, but this is a reasonable trade-off for most users lacking proper space.

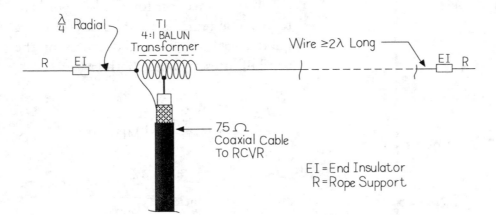

Figure 7-11

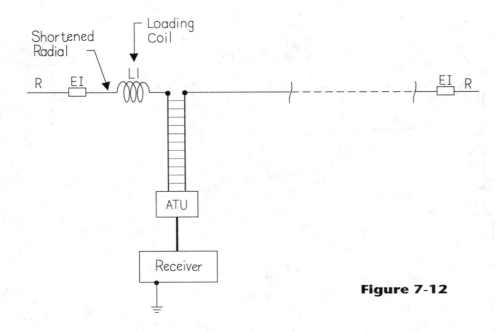

Figure 7-12

Longwire Termination Resistors

The *aperiodic*, or nonresonant, longwire antenna requires a termination resistor at the end opposite the receiver connection. This resistor should have a resistance value equal to the characteristic impedance of the antenna wire. The resistor should be either a carbon composition or metal film type (because those are noninductive). Don't use a wirewound resistor, even those purporting to be "noninductive." Those resistors are noninductive only at low audio frequencies...which means they actually have enough inductance to upset circuits in the RF frequency range. Termination resistors should have a power rating of either 1-watt or 2-watt, with the latter being preferred for receiving antennas.

While the concept of a termination resistor is easy to draw in book illustrations, it's a little harder to implement in practice. One of the problems is that the grounded end of the resistor must be well grounded, and a length of wire between the resistor and the ground rod—no matter how thick—is NOT a good ground connection at RF frequencies. However, there are two easily implemented solutions to the problem.

One solution is to use an *airborne* counterpoise ground, a quarter-wavelength radial, as shown in Figure 7-13. An end insulator separates the radial wire from the antenna wire, and a 1-watt or 2-watt termination resistor bridges the insulator. If possible, the resistor should be shrouded inside of a waterproof plastic box.

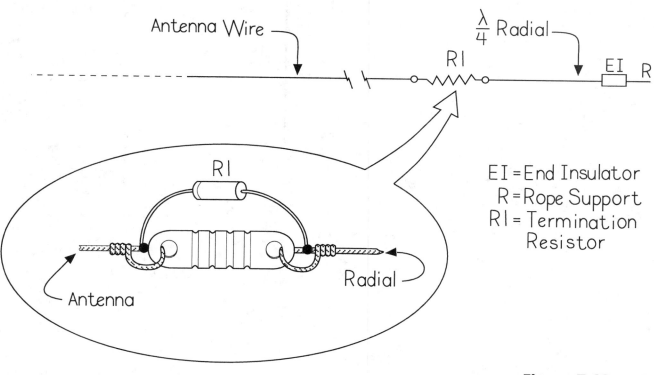

Figure 7-13

The other solution is to use a system such as shown in Figure 7-14. This method places the resistor at the top of a six to eight foot copperclad steel ground rod (driven into the ground so that only a few inches show). A long, heavy duty machine screw or bolt connects the box to the ground rod; U-bolt clamps make both the electrical connection and the mechanical fastening.

Note that a series of radials are also connected to the ground rod. These radials are ideally a quarter-wavelength long (length in feet equals $492/F_{MHz}$), but

when buried (and made with bare wires) considerably shorter wires will do. There should be at least four radials per band, although one or two are better than none. As always, the radials should be buried for safety reasons—pedestrians can trip over radials on the surface, and receive serious injury for which you might be liable.

A stand-off insulator connects the other end of the resistor to the antenna wire. The wire can be either a vertical downlead, at the cost of some distortion to the receive pattern, or sloped over a relatively long distance to the resistor housing.

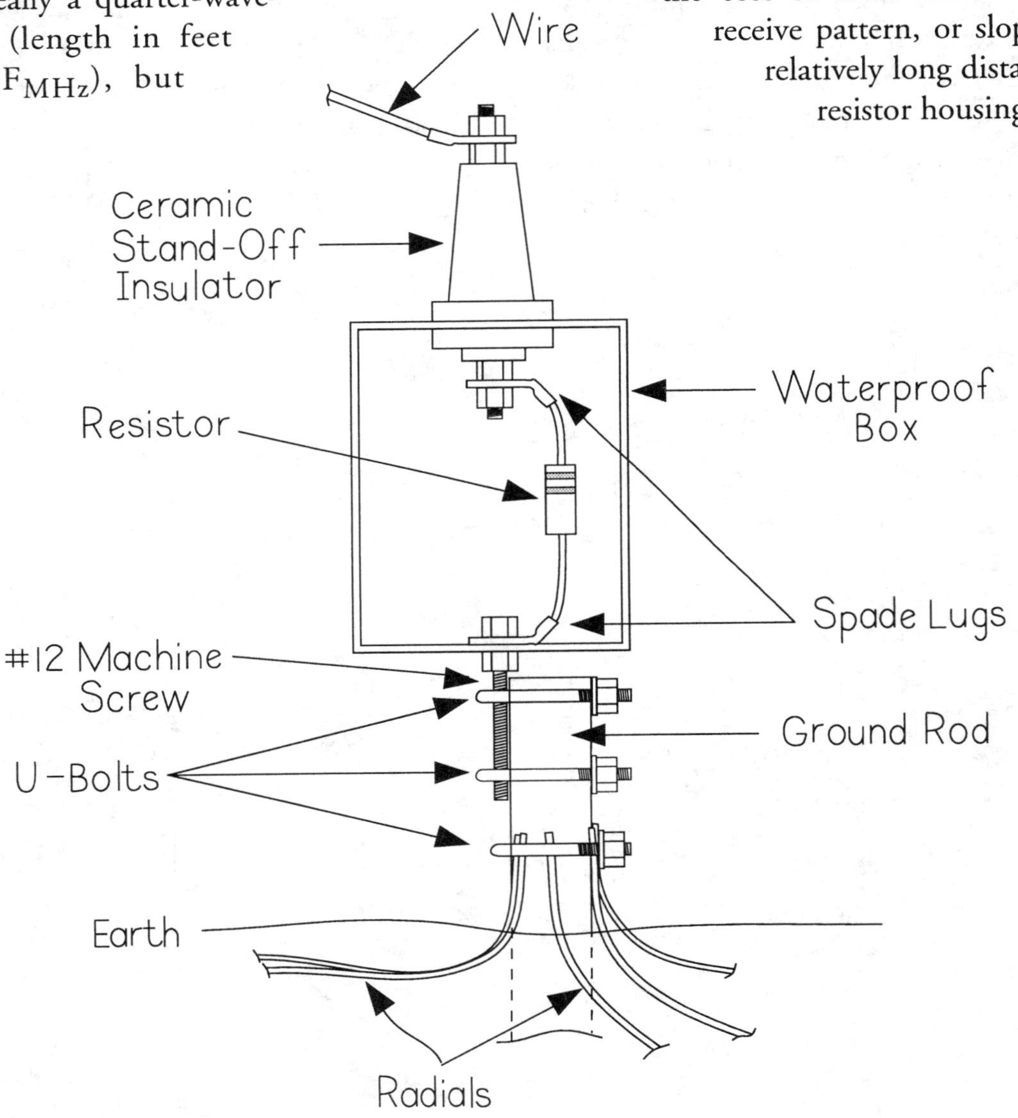

Figure 7-14

Vee Beams and Rhombic Beams

Longwire antennas can be combined in several ways to increase gain and sharpen directivity. Two of the most popular of these are the Vee beam and the rhombic antennas. Both forms can be made in either resonant (unterminated) or nonresonant (terminated) versions.

✦ Vee Beams

The Vee beam (Figure 7-15) consists of two equal length longwire elements (Wire-1 and Wire-2), fed 180° out of phase with each other, and spaced to produce an acute angle between them. The 180° phase difference is inherent in connecting the two wires of the Vee to opposite conductors of the same parallel conductor feedline.

The unterminated Vee beam of Figure 7-15 has a bidirectional pattern that is created by summing together the patterns of the two individual wires. Proper alignment of the main lobes of the two wires requires an included angle between the wires of twice the radiation angle of each wire. If the radiation angle of the wire is β, then the appropriate included angle is 2β. The list below shows the optimum included angles for various wavelength Vee beam antennas. For antennas with included angles given below, the radiation pattern elevation angle is close to 0° (i.e. horizontal). To raise the pattern a few degrees, the 2β angle should be slightly less than these values.

Nβ	2β
1	90
2	73
3	58
4	50
5	44
6	40
7	36
8	35

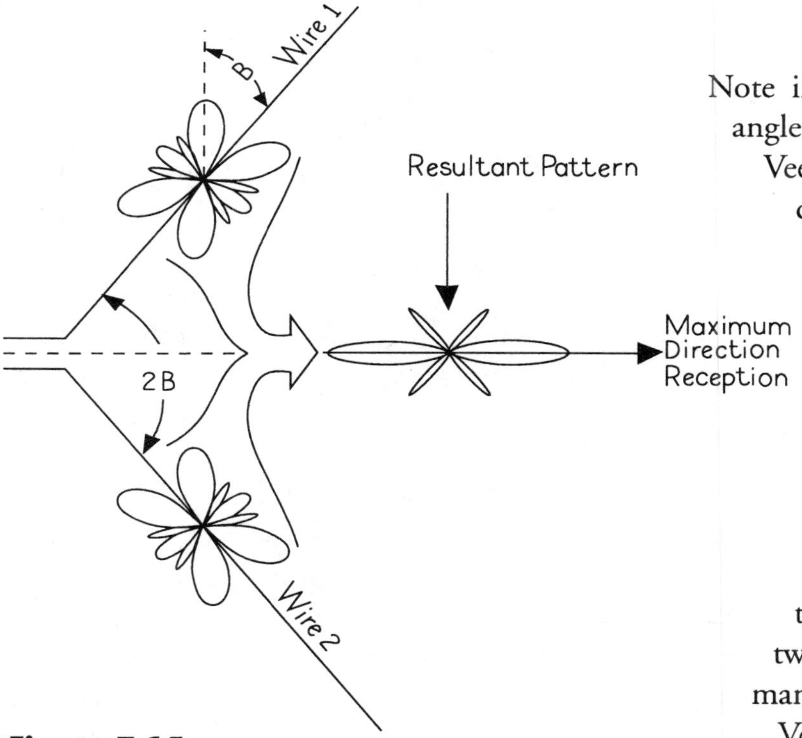

Note in the list above that the optimum angle changes on harmonically operated Vee beams. It is common practice to design a Vee beam for a low frequency (like the 60, 49, or 41-meter bands) and then use it also on higher frequencies that are harmonics of the minimum design frequency. A typical Vee beam works well over a very wide frequency range only if the included angle is adjusted to a reasonable compromise. It is common practice to use an included angle that is between 35° and 90°, depending on how many harmonic bands are required.

Vee beam patterns are based on an antenna height that is greater than a half-

Figure 7-15

wavelength from the ground. At low frequencies, such heights may not be practical, and one must expect a certain distortion of the pattern due to ground reflection effects.

Gain on a Vee beam antenna is about 3 dB higher than the gain of the single-wire longwire antenna of the same size, and is considerably higher than the gain of a dipole (see Figure 7-16). At three wavelengths, for example, the gain is 7 dB over a dipole. In addition, there may be some extra gain due to mutual impedance effects, which can be about 1 dB at 5λ and 2 dB at 8λ.

Feeding a Vee beam is similar to feeding a longwire antenna in that 600 Ω parallel wire transmission line is used. One wire of the Vee beam is connected to each conductor of the transmission line. Some books state that the two wires to the receiver are mere downloads, and need not be parallel to each other. I doubt that advice, and recommend against it. While open wire transmission line is a tad difficult to work with, it is usually worth it. Besides, there are other ways to do the job ("there's more than one way to kill a cat, ya don't gotta choke him to death on bacon fat" as a supposedly wise man once said). For example, using insulated 450 Ω twin-lead results in a slight impedance mismatch, but is entirely satisfactory for receiver use. Some people report that using 300 Ω TV-type twin lead, with an antenna tuner, as tuned feeders also works well. A 9:1 balun transformer reduces the 600 Ω impedance to about 67 Ω, so will match the feedpoint impedance to either 52 or 75 Ω coaxial cable.

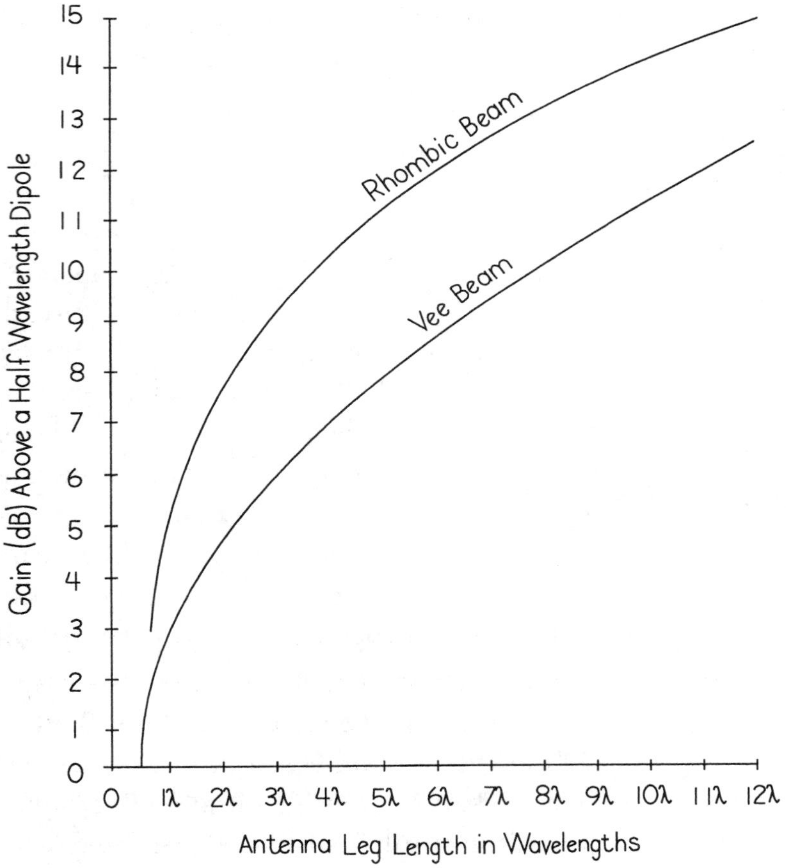

An additional 3 dB gain can be achieved by stacking two or more Vee beams together, either horizontally (Figure 7-17) or vertically (Figure 7-18).

The horizontal stacking method was popular on low-cost TV antennas for the VHF low-band channels (54 to 88 MHz). The two Vee beams are positioned approximately a quarter-wavelength apart and are connected by a quarter-wavelength section of transmission line that serves to cause a 90° phase shift between them. The bidirectional radiation and reception characteristic of normal Vee beams is replaced with a unidirectional pattern. The actual direction is a function of whether the feedline is connected across A1/A2 or B1/B2 (see arrows in Figure 7-17).

Figure 7-16

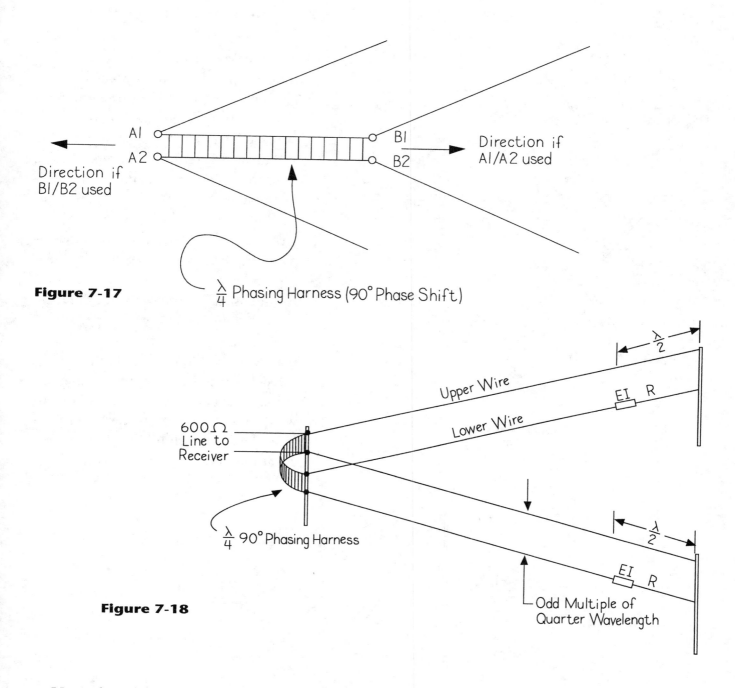

Figure 7-17

$\frac{\lambda}{4}$ Phasing Harness (90° Phase Shift)

Figure 7-18

Vertical stacking also produces a 3 dB gain, but has the additional charm of taking less space than the horizontal method. The vertically stacked Vee shown in Figure 7-18 uses two Vee beams, an upper and a lower. The upper Vee is $\lambda/2$ longer on each leg than the lower. The stacking distance between them is an odd multiple of a quarter-wavelength.

The two Vee beams of Figure 7-18 are fed 90° out of phase with each other. If a single transmission line is desired (case shown), then space the Vees $\lambda/4$ and use a $\lambda/4$ phasing harness (made of parallel transmission line) between them. Alternatively, either use two lines, with the upper being $\lambda/4$ longer than the lower, or use a 90° phase shift network in one line.

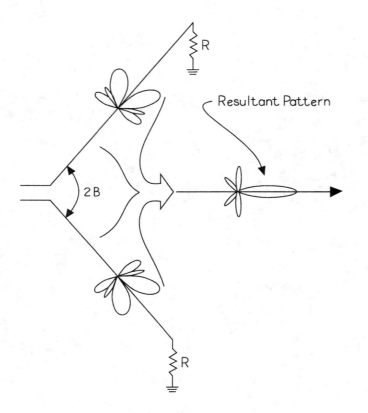

Figure 7-19

✦ *Nonresonant Vee Beams*

Like the single wire longwire antennas, the Vee beam can be made nonresonant by terminating each wire in a resistance that is equal to the antenna's characteristic impedance (Figure 7-19). While the regular Vee is a standing wave antenna, the terminated version is a traveling wave antenna and is thus unidirectional.

The same problems with practical terminated longwires also affect terminated Vee beams. As a result, some people prefer to terminate the wire in a resistor and a quarter-wavelength radial. Others prefer to use a Vee-Sloper antenna such as Figure 7-20. The supporting mast height should be about half to three-fourths of the length of either antenna leg. The legs are sloped downward to terminating resistors at ground level. Each wire should be longer than 1λ at the lowest operating frequency.

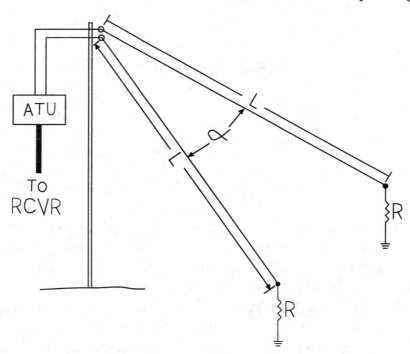

Figure 7-20

✦ *Rhombic Beams*

The rhombic beam antenna, also called the double-Vee, consists of two Vee beams positioned end-to-end with the tips connected. The bidirectional resonant (unterminated) rhombic is shown in Figure 7-21, while the unidirectional nonresonant (terminated) rhombic is shown in Figure 7-22. The resonant form gives approximately the same gain and directivity as a Vee beam of the same size. The nonresonant rhombic has a gain of about 3 dB over a Vee beam of the same size (see Figure 7-16).

There are two angles present on the rhombic antenna. Half the included angle of the two legs of one wire is the tilt angle (ϕ), while the angle between the two wires is the apex angle (Θ). A common rhombic design uses a tilt angle of 70°, a length of 6λ for each leg (two legs per side), and a height from the ground of 1.1λ.

The termination resistance for the nonresonant rhombic is 600 to 800 Ω, and must be noninductive. For transmitting rhombics, the resistor should be capable of dissipating at least one-third the average power of the transmitter. For receive-only rhombics, the termination resistor can be a 2-watt carbon composition or metal film type. Such an antenna works nicely over an octave (2:1) frequency range.

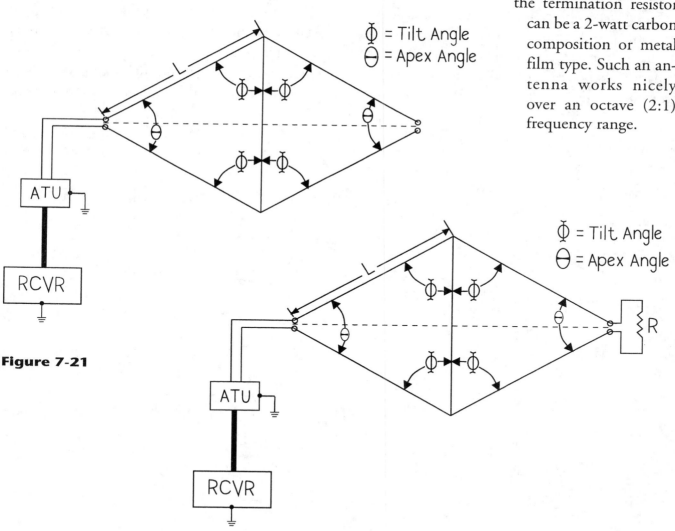

Figure 7-21

Figure 7-22

A variation on the theme is the vertically polarized rhombic of Figure 7-23. Although sometimes called an *inverted-Vee*—not to be confused with the dipole variant of the same name—this antenna is half a rhombic, with the missing half being "mirrored" in the ground (similar to a vertical). The angle at the top of the mast (Φ) is typically $\geq 90°$, while $120°$ to $145°$ is more common. Each leg should be $\geq \lambda$, with the longer being somewhat higher in gain.

Beverage or "Wave" Antennas

The *Beverage* or *Wave* antenna is considered by some people to be the best receiving antenna available for very low frequency (VLF), AM broadcast band (BCB), medium wave (MW), or tropical band (low HF region) DXing. The Beverage was used by RCA at its Riverhead, Long Island (New York) station in 1922, and a technical description by Dr. H.H. Beverage (for whom it is named) appeared in *QST* magazine for November 1922, in an article titled "The Wave Antenna for 200-Meter Reception." In 1984, an edited and updated version of the 1922 article appeared in the same magazine. In 1921, Paul Godley, under sponsorship of the American Radio Relay League (ARRL, 225 Main Street, Newington, CT 06111) journeyed to Scotland to erect a receiving station at Androssan. His mission was to listen for amateur radio signals from North America. As a result of politicking in the post-World War I era, hams were consigned to the supposedly useless short-waves ($\lambda < 200$ meters), and it was not clear that reliable international communications were possible (remember, the "200-meter and down"

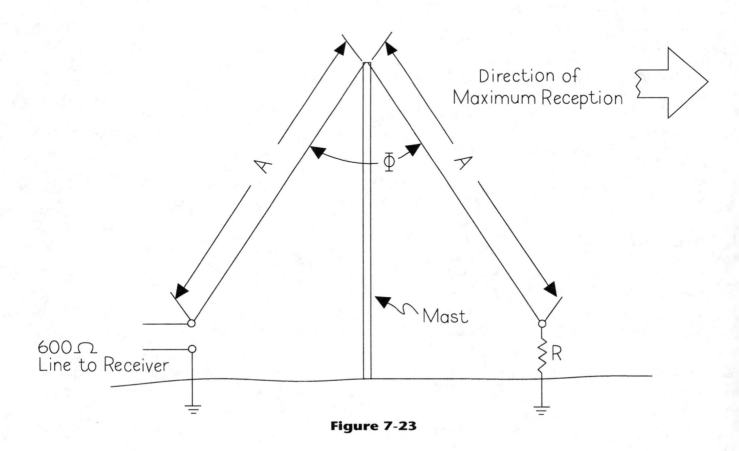

Figure 7-23

region is what we now call the MW and HF shortwave bands!). Godley went to Scotland to see if that could happen…he reportedly used a wave antenna for the task (today called the Beverage).

The Beverage antenna is a longwire of special design, more than one-wavelength (1λ) long, although some authorities maintain that > 0.5λ is minimally sufficient. The Beverage provides good directivity and good gain, but is not very efficient. As a result, it is preferred for receiving but shunned for transmitting. This is an example of how different attributes of various antennas make the Law of Reciprocity an unreliable sole guide to antenna selection. Unlike the regular longwire, which is of a different design, the Beverage is intended to be mounted close to the Earth's surface (typically < 0.1λ); heights of eight to ten feet is the usual prescription.

The Beverage works best in the low frequency bands, VLF through MW, although at least some results are reportedly relatively easy to obtain up to the 25-meter (11.5 MHz) band. Some attempts have been made at making Beverage antennas work as high as the 11-meter citizens band or the 10-meter ham band (29.7 MHz). There is a sometimes snide debate going on between those who claim good Beverage performance at higher frequencies and those who say "it t'aint so." At the risk of joining the debate—which I don't wish to do—I'll recognize that there are sound theoretical reasons to support the low frequency argument, although the high frequency adherents seem to have some impressive experimental results to show. I suspect that both sides of the argument are right, or think they are. The HF performance of Beverages to nearly 30 MHz may well be the result of regular longwire performance arising at frequencies above some unrecognized limit around 7 MHz. Either that, or particular propagation conditions made the antenna work well during

the period of the experiment. The experimental results are probably valid, but are misinterpreted. The issue can be easily resolved by a properly contrived, statistically valid, theoretically competent, side-by-side comparison experiment.

The Beverage antenna works on vertically polarized waves arriving at low angles of incidence. These conditions are normal in the AM BCB, where nearly all transmitting antennas are vertically polarized. In addition, the ground and sky wave propagation found in the VLF, AM BCB, and low MW ("tropical") bands are relatively consistent. As the frequency increases, however, two factors become increasingly dominant. First, the likelihood of horizontal polarization increases because of the size of a wavelength at those frequencies. Second, shortwave propagation becomes less consistent at higher frequencies. The polarization of the received signal not only changes in those bands, but does so constantly when conditions are unsettled. It is the strong dependence of the Beverage on relatively constant vertical polarization that makes me suspect the claims of Beverage-like performance above the 25- or even 31-meter bands.

Figure 7-24 shows the basic single wire Beverage antenna. It consists of a single conductor (#16 to #8 wire, with #14 being most common) erected about eight to ten feet above ground. Some Beverages are unterminated (and bidirectional), but most are terminated at the far end in a resistance (R) equal to the antenna's characteristic impedance (Z_o). The receiver end is also terminated in its characteristic impedance, but generally requires an impedance matching transformer to reduce the antenna impedance to the 50 Ω standard impedance used by most modern receivers (Figure 7-25).

The Beverage depends on being erected over poorly conductive soil, even though the terminating resistor needs a good ground. Thus, one source claimed that sand beaches adjacent to

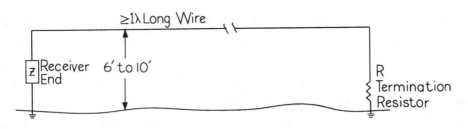

Figure 7-24

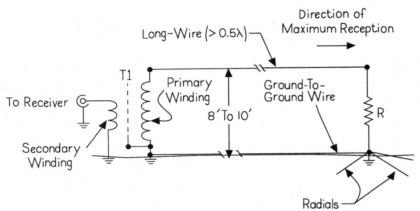

Figure 7-25

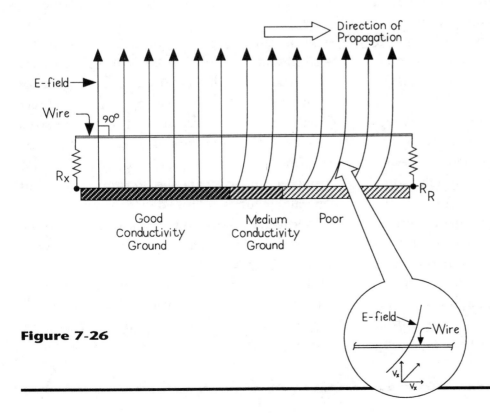

Figure 7-26

salty marshes make the best Beverage sites (a bit of overstatement). Figure 7-26 shows why poorly conductive soil is needed. The E-field vectors are launched from the transmitting antenna perpendicular to the Earth's surface. Over perfectly conducting soil, the vertical waves would remain vertical. But over imperfectly conducting soil the field lines tend to bend close to the point of contact with the ground. As shown in the inset to Figure 7-26, the bending of the wave provides a horizontal component of the E-field vector, and this provides the means of generating an RF current in the conductor wire.

Beverage directivity is an interesting phenomenon. When signals arrive from either side (perpendicular to the wire), all sections of the wire are excited in-phase with each other. When these signals propagate along the wire, they reach the receiver end essentially out of phase with each other, so they cancel. Thus, the Beverage exhibits very deep nulls off the sides at right angles to the wire.

Signals arriving from either end of the wire produce electrical situations that are similar to each other, but with opposite results. Signals from either direction set up in-phase reinforcing waves at the ends. Signals arriving from the forward direction propagate along the wire towards the receiver end, and build up a strong resultant that is heard by the receiver. Signals arriving from the rear direction also build up in-phase reinforcing electrical signals, but these propagate towards the termination resistor end, where they are absorbed by the resistor and therefore lost. If the termination resistor is matched to the characteristic impedance of the antenna ($R = Z_o$) then there will be no reflections back down the wire (which could reduce the depth of the rear null).

A good "thought model" for the Beverage is to regard it as a parallel wire transmission line with one good conductor (the wire) and one lossy, poor conductor (the soil underneath). As with any transmission line, the electrical wave in the wire has a lower velocity of propagation than the electromagnetic (EM) wave in free space. The free space EM wave travels at the speed of light (denoted by the letter c), while the electrical signal in the wire set up by the passing EM wave travels at a velocity of $0.85c$ to $0.98c$, depending on the design and installation of the antenna. The velocity factor (V) is the ratio of the actual velocity (v) to the free space velocity (c): $V = v/c$. The velocity factor is sometimes expressed as a decimal (such as 0.90) and sometimes as a percent (like 90%). The velocity factor increases with antenna height, although the rate of increase slows down above heights of ten feet or so.

As noted earlier, all transmission lines have an attribute called characteristic impedance, symbolized by Z_o. Although the rigorous definition is a bit more complex, it is possible to define Z_o in terms of what happens in practical circuits. If an electrical signal is launched onto a transmission line that is terminated at its far end by a resistance (R) equal to Z_o, then all of the forward signal power is either radiated as an electromagnetic wave or absorbed by the terminating resistor; no signal is reflected back down the line towards the source. But if $R \neq Z_o$, a reflected signal will arise, and its amplitude is proportional to the mismatch between Z_o and R. On receive antennas, a component of the signal set up in the wire by the electromagnetic wave travels towards the receiver, while another component travels towards the termination. The signal heading towards the termination is absorbed by the resistor. The value of Z_o for the single wire Beverage is:

$$Z_o = 138 \log\left(\frac{4h}{d}\right)$$

Where:

Z_o is the characteristic impedance in Ω
h is the antenna height
d is the wire diameter
[h and d must be in the same units—inches, feet, meters, etc.]

Let's look at an example. Find the characteristic impedance (Z_o) of a Beverage mounted eight feet from the ground, and made of #14 wire (diameter is 0.064 inches).

$$Z_o = 138 \log\left(\frac{(4)(8\,\text{ft})}{(0.064\,\text{in.})(1\,\text{ft}/12\,\text{in.})}\right)$$

$$Z_o = 138 \log\left(\frac{32}{0.0053}\right)$$

$$Z_o = 138 \log(6037) = (138)(3.78)$$
$$= 521\ \Omega$$

This equation is used to determine the impedance of the antenna so that a terminating resistor can be selected. Figure 7-27 shows curves of impedance vs. height for several popular wire sizes. If the calculated value of Z_o does not fall on a standard resistor value, then you can do one of three things: make a network of standard value resistors that does match Z_o, use a potentiometer (variable resistor) and set it to a value equal to Z_o, or use a compromise value fixed resistor; 600 Ω is a popular value. In any event, only noninductive resistors such as carbon composition or metal film are suitable [note: many potentiometers are wirewound]. Here are the diameters (d) of several popular U.S. wire gauges:

AWG WIRE DIAMETERS

AWG Wire Size	Outside Diameter (in.)
8	0.1285
10	0.1019
12	0.0808
14	0.0640
16	0.0508
18	0.0403

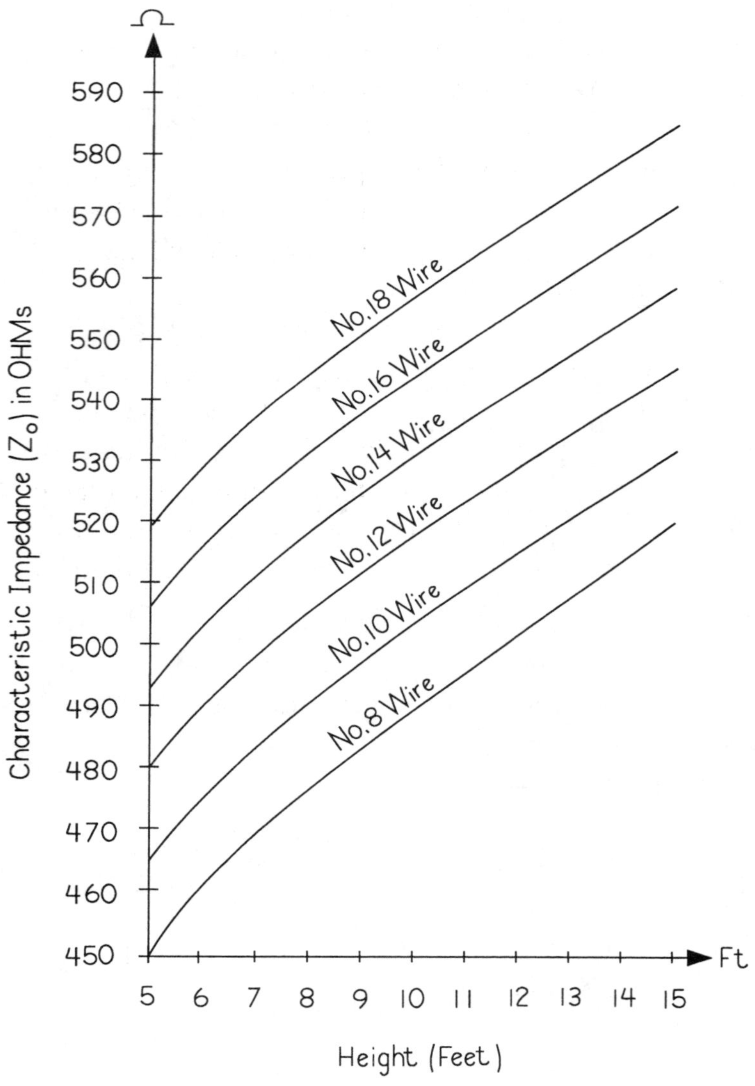

Another of the debates found among Beverage fans regards the best length for the antenna. Some sources say that the length can be anything $\geq 0.5\lambda$, while others say $\geq 1\lambda$ is the minimum size. One camp says that the length should as long as possible, while others say it should be close to a factor called the Maximum Effective Length (MEL), which is:

$$MEL = \frac{\lambda}{4}\left(\frac{100}{K-1}\right)$$

Where:

    MEL is the maximum effective length in meters (m)
    λ is the wavelength in meters (m)
    K is the velocity factor expressed as a percent

Misek, who may well be the leading exponent of the Beverage antenna, uses numbers like 1.6λ to 1.7λ over the 1.8 to 7.3 MHz region, and 0.53λ to 0.56λ on frequencies lower than 1.8 MHz. Beverage himself was once quoted as saying that the optimum length is 1λ.

Figure 7-27

Like the longwire antenna, the Beverage needs a termination resistor that is connected to a good ground. This requirement may be harder to meet on Beverage antennas because they work best over lossy ground, which doesn't make a very good ground connection. On Beverage installations, follow the same principles given earlier for grounding of nonresonant longwire terminations. As in the longwire case, insulated or bare wire a quarter-wavelength long makes the best radials. However, a substantial improvement in the ground is possible using just bare wires from 15 to 20 feet long (which is much less than λ/4), buried in the soil just below the surface far enough to prevent erosion from bringing it to the surface. Many articles and books on Beverages show ground rods of two or three feet long, which borders on the ridiculous. Poor soil requires longer ground rods, on the order of six to eight feet. As before, copperclad steel makes the best rods.

In addition to the radials and ground rod, Misek also recommends using a wire connection between the ground connection at the termination resistor and the ground connection at the receiver transformer (see again Figure 7-25). According to Misek, this wire helps stabilize the impedance variations at higher frequencies.

Installation of the Beverage antenna is not overly critical if certain rules are followed. The antenna should be installed at a height of six to ten feet off the ground, and should be level with the ground over its entire length. If the ground is not flat enough to make a level installation possible, then try to use a height that is six to ten feet above the average terrain elevation along its run.

A popular installation method is to erect 16-foot 4x4 lumber such that three to four feet are buried in a concrete filled posthole. Use lumber that is treated for outdoor use, such as lumber sold for add-on decks and porches.

The wire can be fastened to the 4x4 posts using either ceramic stand-off ("beehive") insulators or electric livestock control fence insulators (which some people deem preferable). Try to use one contiguous length of wire for the antenna, if possible, in order to avoid soldered splices and joints.

One of the Beverage installation difficulties shared with the longwire is the need to slope down to a point where a termination resistor can be easily installed close to the ground. While the longwire can be sloped over a large portion of its length, the Beverage should only be sloped downwards over the last 60 feet or so (Figure 7-28).

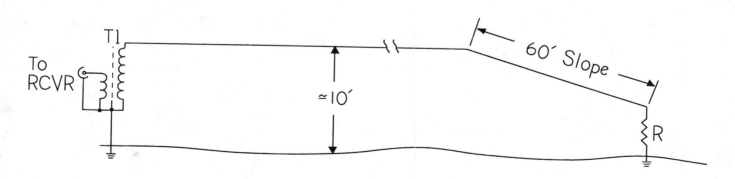

Figure 7-28

Feeding the Beverage Antenna

The Beverage antenna must be matched at both ends with terminations equal to the characteristic impedance of the antenna. At the feed end, where the receiver is connected, this requirement usually means that a transformer is needed because the usual receiver antenna connection wants to see a 50 Ω source.

A transformer consists of two or more coils of wire arranged so that the magnetic field of one coil cuts across the other. Although air transformers are common, those used with Beverage antennas tend to be either powdered iron or ferrite toroid ("doughnut" shaped) cores (see Figure 7-29). Sizes range from 0.125-inch o.d. to 5.2-inches o.d. For transmitting, size is important, but for receiving the convenience of building the transformer is more important. The cores are also classified according to material, and this attribute is frequency sensitive.

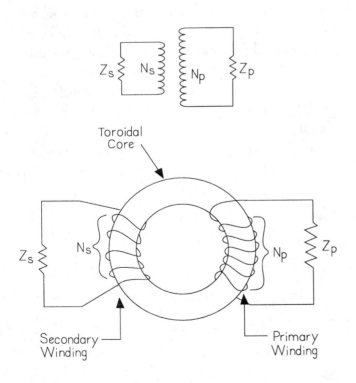

Figure 7-29

Transformers produce an impedance transformation according to the expression:

$$\frac{N_p}{N_s} = \sqrt{\frac{Z_p}{Z_s}}$$

Where:
  N_p is the number of turns in the primary winding
  N_s is the number of turns in the secondary winding
  Z_p is the impedance connected to the primary winding (in Beverage antennas it is Z_o)
  Z_s is the impedance connected to the secondary winding (typically 50 Ω).

We know the required impedance transformation (Z_p/Z_s) by comparing the value of Z_o (which connects to the primary winding), and the receiver system impedance (which connects to the secondary winding); the latter is usually 50 Ω.

The usual practice is to select an inductance for the transformer winding that is high relative to the highest impedance to be matched. Bryant and Hall-Patch recommend a reactance of 637 μH for the primary, which translates to 35 turns of wire on the Amidon FT-50-43 core ["FT" denotes ferrite material, "50" denotes a 0.50-inch o.d., and "43" is the material mixture type. The 43 mixture is nickel-zinc, works to about 50 MHz, and has a permeability μ of 850.]. To match 500 Ω to 50 Ω we need to work the following example:

$$\frac{N_p}{35 \text{ turns}} = \sqrt{\frac{50}{500}}$$

$$N_p = (35 \text{ turns}) \sqrt{0.1}$$

$$N_p = (35 \text{ turns})(0.316) = 11 \text{ turns}$$

Thus, we can select an FT-50-43 core, and then wind the primary turns of #26 enameled wire, and the secondary with 11 turns of the same wire. Other cores are also useful, and indeed may be better for the BCB. These would require different turns ratios from the example given above.

The ≈ 500 Ω impedance of the Beverage makes a reasonable match to the "Hi-Z" (high impedance) inputs of some receivers (as well as the normal impedance of older receivers), but direct connection is not recommended because of safety reasons. The Beverage is a huge static electricity generator. Static build-up on the wire can produce discharges that will destroy the RF input circuitry of solid-state receivers. As a result, even when no impedance transformation is needed, a 1:1 transformer is recommended because of the discharge path to ground through the secondary winding.

Better performance, especially noise performance, is achieved if the transformer is wound using a Faraday shield technique recommended by Misek and others. This method is shown in Figure 7-30. The primary winding is wound in the normal manner with enameled hook-up wire. The secondary, however, is made with a length of coaxial cable for the wire. Small sizes, such as RG-174/U or even RG-58/U, will suffice for medium to large size cores. One end of the wire is stripped back and the shield removed, exposing the inner insulator and conductor; remove about ¼-inch of the inner insulator to expose the conductor. The other end is trimmed

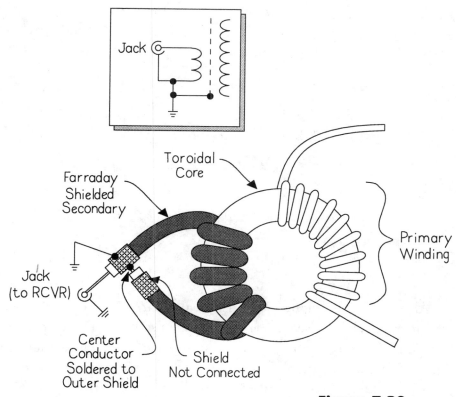

Figure 7-30

to allow ¼-inch of inner conductor to be exposed, along with ½-inch of inner insulator and ½-inch of the shielding outer conductor; solder the inner conductor of the other end to the outer conductor of this end (be sure to not use too much heat, or the inner insulator will melt).

The transformer can be mounted in either a shielded metal box, or a non-shielded box, but it must be mounted at the feed end of the wire, with no download (other than the coax). The chief requirement is that the box be weatherproofed.

Avoid mounting the transformer on the pole is possible if the Beverage wire is sloped gently from the normal height (six to ten feet) to the ground level (Figure 7-31). As in the case of the termination resistor mentioned earlier, the slope should be over about 60 feet, but not significantly more.

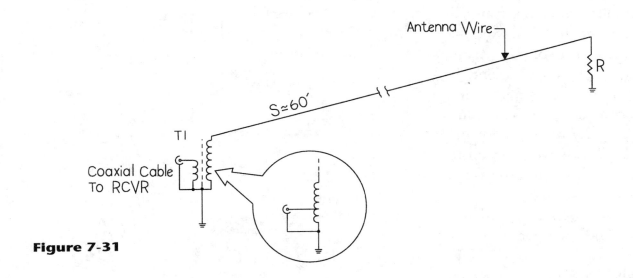

Figure 7-31

Also shown in Figure 7-31 is an alternate transformer scheme (see inset) that can be used with any Beverage, not just the sloping feed type. This transformer is called an *autotransformer* because the same winding is used for both primary and secondary. The secondary is merely tapped down on the primary at the correct impedance level. Some people use a series of taps on the primary and a switch to select one tap from the many in order to accommodate several different impedance levels.

Figure 7-32 shows a Zepp-fed Beverage antenna. A parallel transmission line is made by spacing two #14 lengths of wire, each long enough to reach the feed end of the Beverage, 12 inches apart. Use either plastic or wooden dowels to keep the wires spread apart (as many dowels as needed may be used). The feed transformer is a balanced autotransformer consisting of 36 turns of #26 enameled

wire over a suitable core (like the FT-50-43). The center tap is at 18 turns and is grounded. The center conductor of the coaxial cable to the receiver is connected to a tap on the "cold" end that matches the impedance. For 50 Ω, tap the coil six turns from the ground connection.

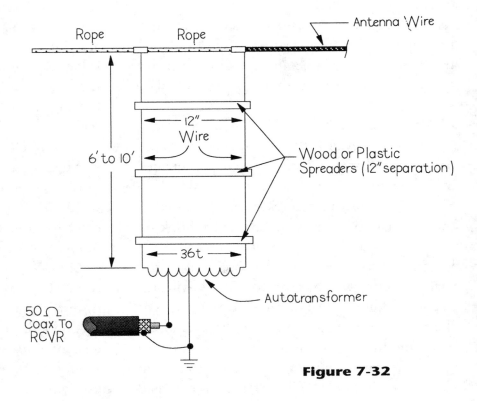

Figure 7-32

Steerable Notch Beverage Antennas

A Beverage erected with two wires—parallel to each other, at the same height, spaced about 12 inches apart, with a length that is a multiple of a half-wavelength—is capable of *null steering*. That is, the rear null in the pattern can be steered over a range of 40° to 60°. This feature allows strong off-axis signals to be reduced in amplitude so that weaker signals in the main lobe of the pattern can be received. There are at least two varieties of the *steerable wave Beverage* (SWB). One variety is shown in Figure 7-33.

The characteristic impedance (Z_o) of a two-wire Beverage antenna is calculated a little differently from that of the single wire Beverage:

$$Z_o = 69 \log \left(\frac{4h}{d} \sqrt{\frac{1+(2h)^2}{S}} \right)$$

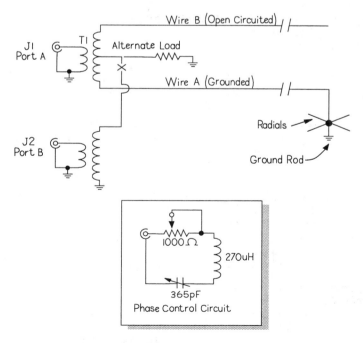

Figure 7-33

Where:

Z_o is the characteristic impedance in Ω
h is the antenna height
d is the antenna wire size diameter
S is the spacing between the wires
[h, d and S are in the same units]

The two parallel wires in Figure 7-33 are terminated differently. Wire-A is grounded in a radial and ground rod system, without a termination resistor; Wire-B is open-circuited. When a passing signal produces a signal in these wires, the results are exactly opposite. Both wires form a "transmission line" to ground, but one is open-circuited so sees an infinite load impedance, while the other is shorted so has a zero load impedance. In both wires, the traveling wave propagates to the right side end, and reflects 100% back towards the receiver. In Wire-A, however, the reflected signal reverses phase with respect to the incident forward signal, while in Wire-B the open-circuit load causes an in-phase reflection. Whether these signals cancel or add depends on the nature of the load circuit.

If the load is resistive (see "Alternate Load" in Figure 7-33) the antenna is unidirectional. If the second transformer is used as the load for T1, however, the reception is bidirectional, but only one direction at a time. A two-antenna coaxial switch can be used to select Port-A or Port-B, depending on the desired direction of reception.

If null steering behavior is desired, then a phase control circuit (abbreviated PCC—see inset to Figure 7-33) is used. It consists of a potentiometer, an inductance, and a variable capacitor in series with each other. Varying both the "pot" and the capacitor will steer the null. You can select the direction of reception, hence the direction of the null, by using a switch to swap the receiver and PCC between Port-A and Port-B.

The other variation on the theme is shown in Figure 7-34. This antenna is the same as the previous case on the receiver end (except for the PCC being hard-wired, rather than movable; both designs are acceptable). On the termination end, however, a trifilar transformer (three interleaved windings) is used to terminate the two wires.

Electrostatic Discharge (ESD) Damage Control

During my 1984 visit to Texas to see friend and antenna guru Johnnie Harper Thorne, I learned first-hand about a problem that affects all large antennas, but is especially severe on longwires of all types: electrostatic discharge (ESD) damage. Because of their very large size, longwire antennas pick up immense static electricity charges. John demonstrated to me that three series-connected NE-51 neon lamps would flash (indicating a high voltage present) when connected between the feedline of a resonant longwire and ground. Each NE-51 takes more than 65 volts to ignite so there was at least 195 volts on that line—and probably several kilovolts!

Everyone is familiar with static electricity problems from ordinary experience. Wearing certain fabrics, scuffling across certain types of rugs, or sliding across a car seat can build up a very high—many kilovolts—static charge that can cause the "bite" you receive when touching another (especially a grounded) object.

All electronic circuitry is sensitive to ESD, but the problem became more acute with the advent of solid-state circuits. These circuits are zapped into oblivion by high voltage ESD transients. While vacuum tube receivers were not immune to ESD damage, they were a lot more tolerant of ESD voltage spikes.

There are several mechanisms by which static charges build up. First, lightning storms many miles away, far out of sight, can produce electrical fields near your antenna that are intense enough to build up static charges on a long

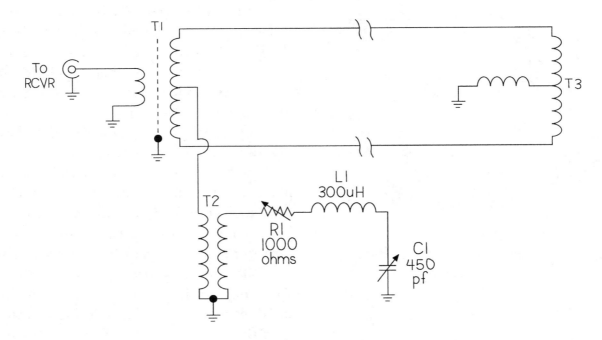

Figure 7-34

conductor. Rain, dust, snow, and even the motion of air itself across the wire is capable of building tremendous ESD potentials. Since these charges cannot be avoided, some protection is warranted.

ESD protection circuits should be added to longwire antennas in addition to, not in lieu of, lightning arrestor protection devices. Figure 7-35 shows an ESD protection module connected to the active side of the feedline, ahead of the antenna tuning unit (ATU). Several methods, or combinations of these, can be used to suppress static and transient charges. Figure 7-36A shows the use of ten 1,000,000 (1 megohm), 2-watt resistors connected in series between the antenna feedline and ground. These resistors have a high enough resistance value that they don't load down the antenna, but low enough to bleed off static charges as they develop.

The use of metal oxide varistor (MOV) transient suppressor devices is shown in Figure 7-36B. These devices offer a high resistance until the voltage exceeds a threshold level, at which

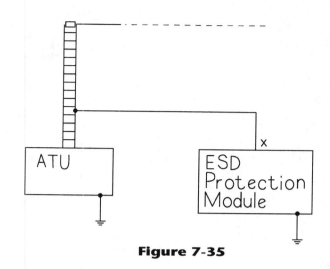

Figure 7-35

point the MOV temporarily breaks down and forms a low resistance to ground.

A combination of a resistor bank (*a la* Figure 7-36A), and neon glow lamps is shown in Figure 7-36C. The resistor bank serves its bleed-off function, while the neon lamps respond to sudden high voltage spikes. In some cases, a Siemens spark gap device is used in place of the neon lamps.

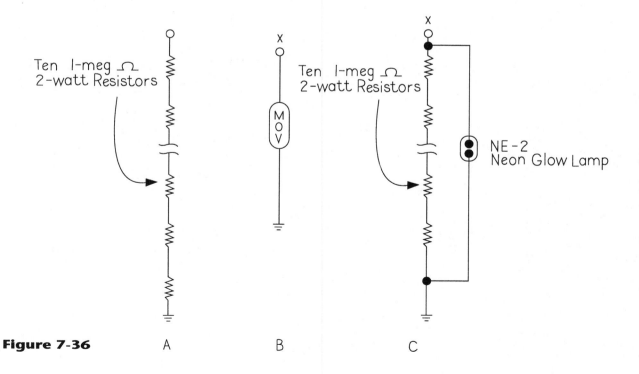

Figure 7-36   A   B   C

CHAPTER 8

Other Wire Antennas

There are a number of different wire antennas that you can easily make and might be the answer to your particular needs. However, these don't fit comfortably into any of the categories we've discussed so far. Here are those "odds and ends" that didn't fit in elsewhere…the antenna you're looking for just might be in this chapter!

G5RV Doublet

The G5RV doublet antenna (Figure 8-1) is a harmonically operated wire antenna that will operate over the entire HF spectrum—or so goes the legend. Adherents of this fine antenna sometimes claim more for it than is supported by good science. And that's too bad, because, within its constraints, the G5RV antenna is a very good shortwave antenna.

Unlike other harmonic antennas of similar appearance, the G5RV is not designed to work on the lowest operating frequency within its range, but rather on the center frequency. For example, to make an antenna for HF (3 to 30 MHz), one would split the difference to find the design frequency:

$$3 + \frac{(30-3)}{2} = 16.5 \text{ MHz}$$

[Note: Amateur radio operators would use 14.2 MHz as the design center because it is within their 20-meter band]

This type of antenna is designed to be $3\lambda/2$ at the center frequency, so each element (dimension "A" in Figure 8-1) is:

$$A_{feet} = \frac{722}{F_{MHz}}$$

Where:
A_{feet} is the length in feet (ft)
F_{MHz} is the center frequency in megahertz (MHz)
[note: at 16.5 MHz, A = 43'9"]

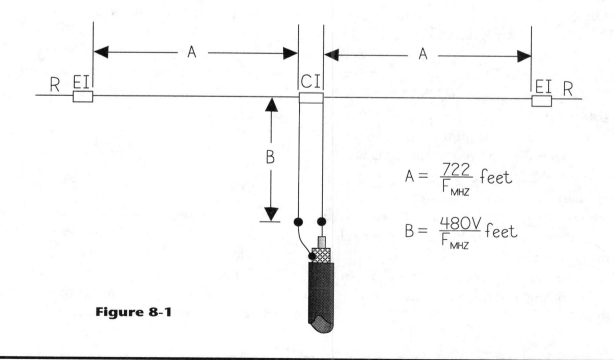

$$A = \frac{722}{F_{MHZ}} \text{ feet}$$

$$B = \frac{480V}{F_{MHZ}} \text{ feet}$$

Figure 8-1

The matching section ("B") is made from either parallel open wire transmission line, 450 Ω twin-lead, or 300 Ω television type twin-lead. It is connected at one end to the feedpoint of the antenna, and at the other end to 75 Ω coaxial cable (80 or 90 Ω cable is a better match, but harder to obtain). The length of the matching section is:

$$B_{feet} = \frac{(480\,V)}{F_{MHz}}$$

Where:

B_{feet} is the length of the matching section in feet (ft)

F_{MHz} is the operating center frequency in megahertz (MHz)

V is the transmission line velocity factor (typically 0.999 for open-wire parallel line, and 0.82 for twin-lead)

The G5RV antenna offers good performance at 16.5 MHz and 26 MHz, and at other specific points in the band. The feedpoint impedance is roughly 90 to 100 Ω at those frequencies. At other frequencies, however, it becomes highly reactive and the VSWR rises markedly. Gain also changes considerably. At 11 MHz and 23 MHz, there are sharp spikes in the VSWR that reduces the performance to that of a random length wire antenna. Because of the variation of VSWR—which ranges from 1.3:1 at 16.5 MHz to 70:1 at the "spike" frequencies—a wide impedance range antenna tuning unit should be used at the receiver end of the coaxial cable.

The G5RV antenna can be installed either horizontally as shown in Figure 8-1, or in the manner of an inverted-Vee dipole. If the Vee installation is selected, then use an apex angle at the mounting point of approximately 120°. The resonant center frequency will drop 50 to 80 kHz depending on the installation and local conditions.

Windom Antennas

The Windom antenna (as shown in Figure 8-2) dates back to the early 1920s when it was popular among hams and SWLs alike. This antenna consists of a half-wavelength wire radiator element installed (for best performance) at least λ/2 above the ground surface. The physical length of the Windom radiator element can be found from:

$$L_{feet} = \frac{470}{F_{MHz}}$$

The feedline is a single conductor insulator wire, #14 or #16, that must drop away from the antenna at a right angle (90°) for at least λ/4. The feedline connects to the radiator element at a point that is 14% off-center, or:

$$K_{feet} = \frac{66}{F_{MHz}}$$

A practical Windom for general SWL use might be cut for a low frequency, such as 4.5 MHz, so it would have an overall length (L) of 468/4.5 = 104 feet. It would be fed with a single conductor wire at 14.7 feet from the center. Because the exact center is a little harder to find than the ends, we can restate this dimension in terms of the end points. The connection point is 36% of the total length from one end of the antenna:

$$Length_{end} = \frac{168.5}{F_{MHz}}$$

The Windom antenna works well on the fundamental frequency band described by these equations as well as harmonics of the design frequency.

When designed according to the equations above, the Windom will have a single wire feeder that represents a load impedance of about 600 Ω. This impedance will not easily interface to most receivers, so an antenna tuning unit must be used. A popular form, shown in Figure 8-2, is a parallel inductor capacitor (LC) tuned circuit that resonates at the bands of interest. The coil should have an inductive reactance (X_L) of about 2000 Ω at the lowest frequency of operation. The coil is tapped at two points, "A" and "B," to work as an autotransformer to convert 800 Ω to 50 Ω.

Off-Centerfed Fullwave Doublet (OCFD) Antennas

An antenna that superficially resembles the windom is the off-centerfed doublet antenna (OCFD) of Figure 8-3. It is a single band antenna, although at harmonics it will begin to act as a resonant standing wave long wire antenna. The overall length is one wavelength long:

$$L_{feet} = \frac{936}{F_{MHz}}$$

This antenna works best at heights of at least λ/2 above ground, so practical considerations limit it to frequencies above about 11 MHz (i.e., the 25-meter band).

The feedpoint of the antenna is placed at a distance of λ/4 from one end and is a good match for 75 Ω coaxial cable. A 1:1 balun transformer at the feedpoint is highly recommended. The pattern of a 1λ antenna is a four-lobe "cloverleaf" with the major lobes being about 53° from the wire. The gain is about 1 dB.

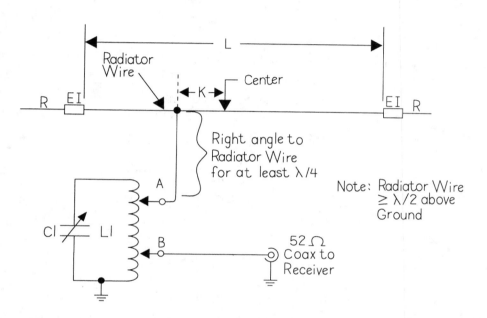

Figure 8-2

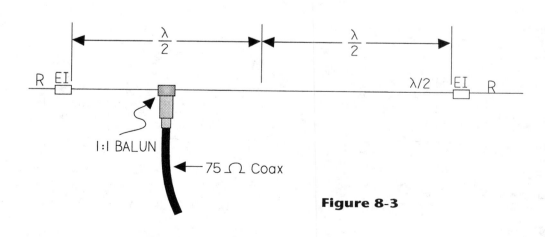

Figure 8-3

Off-Centerfed Nonresonant Sloper (OCFS)

Perhaps more viable for many SWLs is the nonresonant off-centerfed sloper (OCFS) antenna of Figure 8-4. This antenna consists of a wire radiator that is longer than $3\lambda/2$ at the lowest frequency of operation. The feedpoint is elevated at least $\lambda/4$ above ground at the lowest operating frequency. The antenna is fed with 75 Ω coaxial cable. The shield of the coax is connected to a $\lambda/4$ resonant radial (counterpoise ground). There should be at least one radial (more is better) per band of operation.

The far end of the radiator element is sloped to ground, where it is terminated in a 270 Ω noninductive resistor.

Double (Stacked) Dipole

Figure 8-5 shows a double dipole, which consists of two half-wavelength dipole antennas spaced a half-wavelength apart. The transmission lines are connected in parallel at the receiver. This antenna provides about 3 dB gain over a single dipole, plus it adds a bit of fade protection because two side-by-side antennas provide a bit of space diversity.

The two dipoles are supported by a common structure consisting of ropes (R) and end insulators (EI) to support masts on the ends. In the center, a half-wavelength space is taken up by a rope so that the structure is maintained. The space is determined by:

$$\text{Space}_\text{feet} = \frac{492}{F_\text{MHz}}$$

and, for the dipoles:

$$\text{Length}_\text{feet} = \frac{468}{F_\text{MHz}}$$

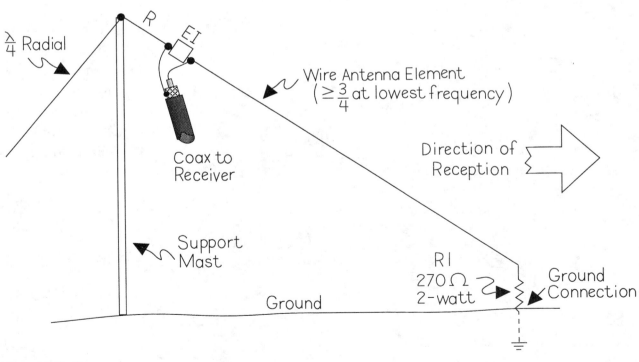

Figure 8-4

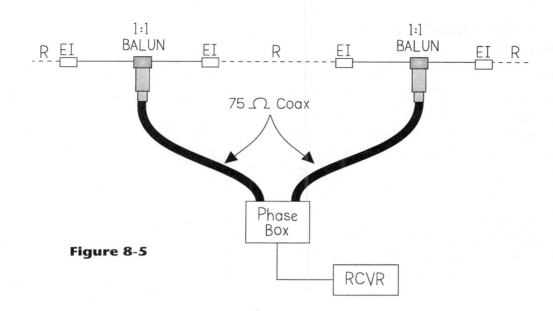

Figure 8-5

Double Extended Zepp Antenna

The *double extended Zepp* antenna (Figure 8-6) provides a gain of about 2 dB over a dipole at right angles to the antenna wire plane. It consists of two sections of wire, each one of a length of:

$$L1_{feet} = \frac{600}{F_{MHz}}$$

Typical lengths are: 27.7 feet on the 13-meter band, 51 feet on the 25-meter band, 62 feet on the 31-meter band, and 100 feet on the 49-meter band.

The double extended Zepp antenna can be fed directly with 450 Ω twin-lead (see below for supplier), especially if a balanced antenna tuner is available at the receiver, or it can be fed from a quarter-wavelength matching section made of 450 Ω twin-lead (or equivalent open air parallel line), as shown, and a balun if coax is preferred. The length of the matching section should be:

$$L2_{feet} = \frac{103}{F_{MHz}}$$

The double extended Zepp will work on a several different bands. For example, a 13-meter band double extended Zepp will work as a Zepp on the design band, a dipole on frequencies below the design band, and a four-lobed "clover-leaf" antenna on frequencies above the design band.

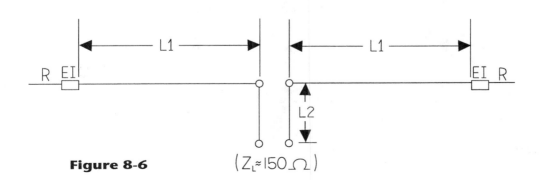

Figure 8-6

Collinear "Franklin" Array Antenna

Perhaps the cheapest approach to real serious antenna gain is the Collinear Franklin array shown in Figure 8-7. This antenna pushes the dipole and double extended Zepp concepts even further. It consists of a half-wavelength dipole that is centerfed with a 4:1 balun and 75 Ω coaxial cable. At each end of the dipole there is a quarter-wavelength *phase reversal stub* that end-feeds another half-wavelength element. Each element is a half-wavelength (λ/2) long, and its length can be calculated as follows:

$$\left(\frac{\lambda}{2}\right)=\left(\frac{492}{F_{MHz}}\right)$$

The phase reversal stubs are a quarter-wavelength long, or one-half the length calculated by the equation above.

The version of the Collinear shown in Figure 8-7 has a gain of about 3 dB. There is no theoretical reason why you can't extend the design indefinitely, but there is a practical limit set by how much wire can be held by your supports and how much real estate you own. A 4.5 dB version can be built by adding another half-wavelength section at each end, with an intervening quarter-wavelength phase reversal stub in between each new section and the preceding section. Once you get longer than five half-wavelengths—which provides the 4.5 dB gain—the physical size becomes a bit of a bother for most folks.

Lazy-H Antenna

The Lazy-H antenna (Figure 8-8) is a "stacked" antenna because it consists of two antennas, one on top of another. This antenna provides gains up 5.5 to 6 dB with just wire alone. In addition, the angle of radiation is lower than many antennas, so it's possible to put the "first hop" on shortwave a lot further out than on simple dipole antennas. The length (L1) of each element is:

$$L1_{feet}=\frac{478}{F_{MHz}}$$

While the spacing is:

$$L2_{feet}=\frac{492}{F_{MHz}}$$

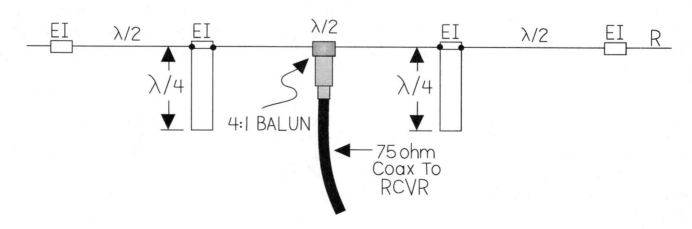

Figure 8-7

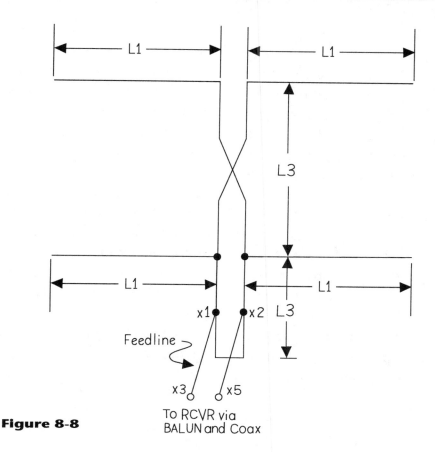

Figure 8-8

The phase reversal harness connecting the elements is made from either 450 Ω parallel transmission line, or 450 Ω twin-lead. Note that it is twisted over on itself in order to make the phase reversal happen (lack of this phase reversal is one reason why this antenna seems to "fail" when built!). The matching section is also made of 450 Ω line, and is a quarter-wavelength:

$$L3_{feet} = \frac{246}{F_{MHz}}$$

The 75 Ω coaxial cable transmission line is connected to points "X1" and "X2" through a 1:1 balun transformer. These points are found experimentally by moving the balun connection points up and down along the stub until a 1:1 impedance match is achieved.

Large Wire Loop Antennas

Antennas can be built using half- or full-wavelength pieces of wire arranged in a loop. There are two basic forms of loop antenna: small and large. These two types have different characteristics, work according to different principles, and have different purposes. Small loops are those in which the current flowing in the wire has the same phase and amplitude at every point in the loop (which fact implies a very short wire length, such as < 0.1λ). Such loops respond to the magnetic field component of the electromagnetic radio wave. We'll discuss small loops in an upcoming chapter.

A large loop antenna has a wire length > 0.1λ, with most being either λ/2, 1λ, or λ. The current in a large loop varies along the length of the wire in a manner similar to other wire antennas.

λ/2 **Large Loops**

The performance of large wire loop antennas depends in part on the size. Figure 8-9 shows a half-wavelength loop in which the four sides are each λ/8 long. There are two basic configurations for this antenna: *continuous* (S1 closed) and *open* (S1 open). In both cases, the feedpoint is at the midpoint of the side opposite the switch.

The direction of the main reception or radiation lobe—the direction of maximum reception—depends on whether S1 is open or closed. With S1 closed, the main lobe is to the right (solid arrow), and with S1 open it is to the left (broken arrow). Direction reversal can be achieved by using a switch or relay at S1, although some people opt for unidirectional operation by eliminating S1 and leaving the loop either open or closed as needed.

The feedpoint impedance is considerably different in the two configurations. In the closed loop situation (S1 closed) the antenna can be modeled as if it were a half-wavelength dipole bent into a square and fed at the ends. The feedpoint (X1-X2) impedance is on the order of 3 kilohms because it occurs at a voltage antinode (current node). The current antinode ($I \rightarrow I_{max}$) is at S1, on the side opposite the feedpoint. An antenna tuning unit or RF impedance transformer must be used to match the lower impedance of the transmission lines needed to connect to receivers.

The feedpoint impedance of the open loop configuration (S1 open) is low because the current antinode occurs at X1-X2. Some texts list the impedance as "about 50 Ω," while my own measurements on several test loops were somewhat higher (about 70 Ω). In either case, the

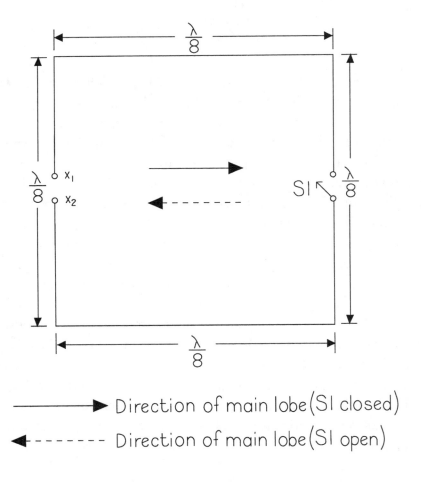

Figure 8-9

——————▶ Direction of main lobe (S1 closed)

◀- - - - - - - Direction of main lobe (S1 open)

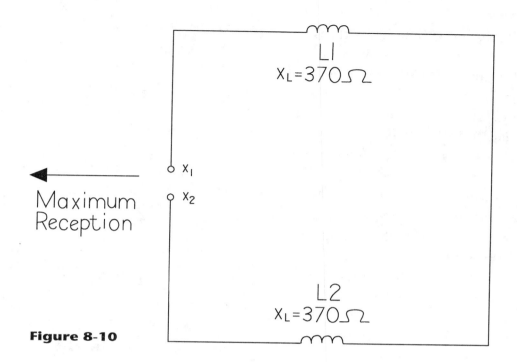

Figure 8-10

open loop is a reasonable match for either 52 Ω or 75 Ω coaxial cable.

Neither λ/2 loop configuration shows gain over a dipole. The figure usually quoted is -1 dB forward gain (a loss compared with a dipole), and about 6 dB of front-to-back ratio (FBR). Such low values of FBR indicates that there is no deep notch ("null") in the pattern.

A lossy antenna with a low FBR seems like a born loser, and in most cases it is. But the λ/2 loop finds a niche where size must be constrained for one reason or another. In those cases, the λ/2 loop may be an alternative.

A simple trick will change the gain, as well as the direction of radiation, of the closed version of the λ/2 loop. In Figure 8-10 a pair of inductors, L1 and L2, are inserted into the circuit at the midpoints of the sides adjacent to the side containing the feedpoints. These inductors should have an inductive reactance (X_L) of about 360 Ω in the center of the band of operation. The inductance of the coil is:

$$L_{\mu H} = \frac{(3.6 \times 10^8)}{(2 \pi F_{Hz})}$$

Where:

$L_{\mu H}$ is the coil inductance in microhenrys (μH)

F_{Hz} is the mid-band frequency in hertz (Hz)

Let's look at an example. Suppose we want to find the inductance for the coils in a loaded half-wavelength closed loop antenna that must operate in a band centered on 11.75 MHz. The solution would be:

$$L_{\mu H} = \frac{(3.6 \times 10^8)}{(2)(\pi)(11,750,000 \text{ Hz})} = 4.9 \, \mu H$$

The coils force the current antinodes towards the feedpoint, reversing the direction of the main lobe and creating a gain of about +1 dB over a half-wavelength dipole.

1λ **Large Loops**

If size is not forcing you to a λ/2 loop, then a 1λ loop may be just the ticket. It produces a gain of about +2 dB over a dipole in the directions that are perpendicular to the plane of the loop. The azimuth patterns formed by these antennas are similar to the "figure-8" pattern of the dipole. Three versions are shown: the *square loop* in Figure 8-11, the *diamond loop* in Figure 8-12, and the *delta loop* (a.k.a. D-loop and triangle loop) in Figure 8-13. The square and diamond loops are built with λ/4 on each side, while the delta loop is λ/3 on each side. The overall length of wire needed to build these antennas is:

$$L_{feet} = \frac{1005}{F_{MHz}}$$

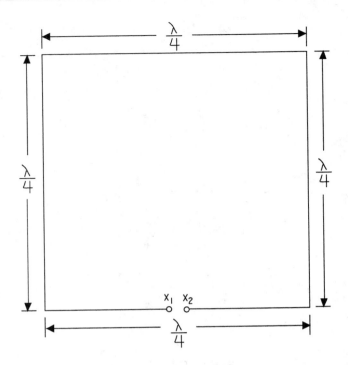

Figure 8-11

The polarization of the three loop antennas is horizontal because of the location of the feedpoints. On the square loop, moving the feedpoint to the middle of either vertical side will provide vertical polarization. Similarly, on the diamond loop vertical polarization is realized by

moving the feedpoint to either of the two adjacent apexes. On the delta loop, placing the feedpoint at either of the two other apexes produces a diagonal polarization that offers approximately equal vertical and horizontal polarization components.

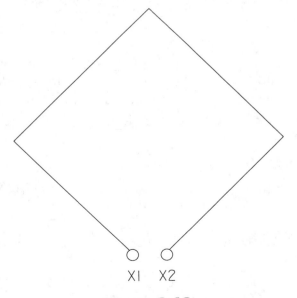

Figure 8-12

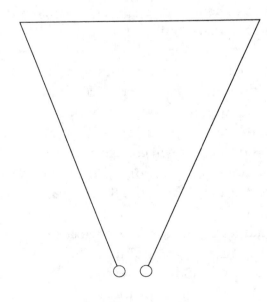

Figure 8-13

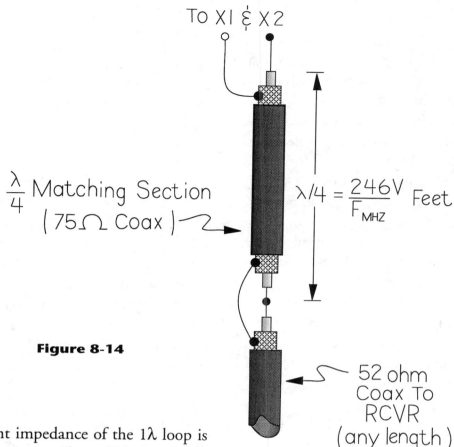

To X1 ε̇ X2

$\frac{\lambda}{4}$ Matching Section
(75Ω Coax)

$\lambda/4 = \frac{246V}{F_{MHZ}}$ Feet

Figure 8-14

52 ohm
Coax To
RCVR
(any length)

The feedpoint impedance of the 1λ loop is around 100 Ω, so it provides a slight mismatch to 75 Ω coax, and a 2:1 mismatch to 52 Ω coax. A very good match to 52 Ω coax can be produced using the scheme of Figure 8-14. Here we see a quarter-wavelength coaxial cable matching stub made of 75 Ω coaxial cable. The length of this cable should be:

$$L_{feet} = \frac{246V}{F_{MHz}}$$

Where:
 L_{feet} is the length in feet (ft)
 V is the velocity factor of the coax
 F_{MHz} is the frequency in megaHertz (MHz)

The impedance (Z_o) of the cable used for the matching section should be:

$$Z_o = \sqrt{Z_L Z_S}$$

Where:
 Z_o is the characteristic impedance of the coax used in the matching section in Ω
 Z_L is the feedpoint impedance of the antenna in Ω
 Z_S is the source impedance (the 52 Ω characteristic impedance of the line to the receiver in standard systems)

For example, where Z_S = 52 Ω and Z_L = 100 Ω:

$$Z_o = \sqrt{(100\,\Omega)(52\,\Omega)} = 72\,\Omega$$

which is a very good match to 75 Ω coaxial cable.

Half-Delta Sloper (HDS)

The half-delta sloper (HDS) shown in Figure 8-15 is similar to the full delta loop, except that (like the quarter-wavelength vertical) half of the antenna is in the form of an "image" in the ground. Gains of 1.5 to 2 dB are achievable.

The HDS antenna consists of two elements: a λ/3 wavelength sloping wire and a λ/6 vertical wire (on an insulated mast) or a λ/6 metal mast. Because the ground currents are very important, much like the vertical antenna, either an extensive radial system at both ends is needed or a base ground return wire (buried) must be provided.

The HDS will work on its design frequency plus harmonics of the design frequency. For a fundamental frequency of 5 MHz, a vertical segment of 33 feet and a sloping section of 66

feet is needed. The lengths for any frequency are found from:

$$\left(\frac{\lambda}{3}\right) = \left(\frac{328}{F_{MHz}}\right)$$

and

$$\left(\frac{\lambda}{6}\right) = \left(\frac{164}{F_{MHz}}\right)$$

The HDS is fed at one corner, close to the ground. If only the fundamental frequency is desired, then you can feed it with 52 Ω coaxial cable. But at harmonics the feedpoint impedance changes to as high as 1000 Ω. If harmonic operation is intended, then an antenna tuning unit is needed at point "A" to match these impedances.

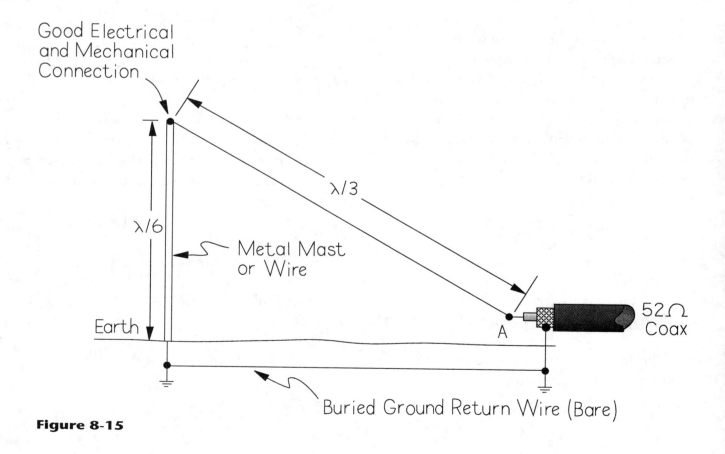

Figure 8-15

Bi-Square
Loop Antenna

The bi-square antenna, shown in Figure 8-16, is similar to the other large loops except that it is λ/2 on each side, making a total wire length of two wavelengths. This antenna is built like the diamond loop shown earlier, in that it is a large square loop fed at an apex that is set at the bottom of the assembly. In this case, the loop is fed either with an antenna tuning unit (to match a 1000 Ω impedance) or a quarter-wavelength matching section made of 300 Ω or 450 Ω twin-lead transmission line. A 1:1 balun transformer connects the 75 Ω coaxial cable to the matching section.

The bi-square antenna offers as much as 4 dB gain broadside to the plane of the antenna (in and out of the book page), in a figure-8 pattern, on the design frequency. It is horizontally polarized. When the frequency drops to one-half the design frequency, the gain drops to about 2 dB and the antenna works similarly to the diamond loop discussed above.

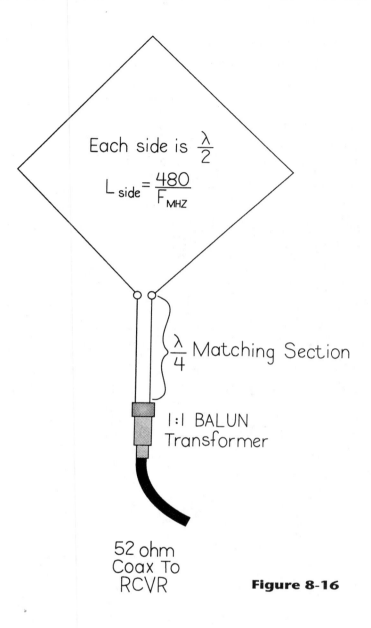

Each side is $\frac{\lambda}{2}$

$L_{side} = \frac{480}{F_{MHZ}}$

$\frac{\lambda}{4}$ Matching Section

1:1 BALUN Transformer

52 ohm Coax To RCVR

Figure 8-16

CHAPTER 9

Vertical Antennas

The vertical antenna has long been popular with hams and SWLs because of its many positive attributes. It is omnidirectional (not always a positive factor, by the way), usually quite simple to erect, is low cost, and requires only a small amount of real estate under most circumstances. The straight quarter-wavelength vertical antenna is of manageable size down to frequencies of about 5 MHz (height ≈ 50 feet), although at lower frequencies the height becomes prohibitive for most shortwave listeners. At lower frequencies (< 5 MHz), or even at higher frequencies, a vertical can be constructed with a loading coil to compensate for missing length. While not ideal (all compensation methods involve trade-offs), it is often a viable approach to making a decent antenna that is otherwise impossible. AM radio broadcasting stations and most VLF stations use vertical antennas, and there is ample evidence that they are frequently, but not always, the best engineering choice for those frequencies.

Vertical antennas can be made from either wire or piping (aluminum tubing is most often selected). In this chapter we'll take a look at antennas made from both types of construction material.

The Basic Vertical Radiator

Figure 9-1 shows the basic vertical antenna in free space (the "free space" construct is always a good place to start an antenna discussion because ground effects complicate things!). This antenna is a half-wavelength dipole antenna that is oriented with its axis perpendicular to the Earth's surface. As a theoretical "mind tool" consistent with the "free space" idea, let's use the concept of "far above the Earth's surface" for our present discussion. This idea allows us to overlook the effects of a bounced signal from the ground recombining with the principal antenna pattern. So, for the sake of our argument, this antenna is many, many wavelengths up in the air.

When the physical axis of the antenna is vertical with respect to the ground, the electromagnetic wave that it transmits is vertically polarized, meaning the electrical field is vertical with respect to the Earth's surface. On receive,

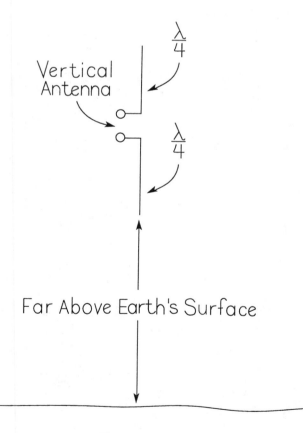

Figure 9-1

the antenna responds best to signals that are vertically polarized. In the middle and upper shortwave spectrum, the polarity of the incoming signal is messed up by ionospheric propagation problems. But on the lower shortwave, medium wave, and VLF bands, the polarity is more likely to remain consistent.

Now remember that antenna patterns are three-dimensional. They describe a solid hunk of the universe...not just vertical and horizontal planes. Figure 9-2 shows the space occupied by the antenna pattern for antennas such as Figure 9-1. The overall pattern is what the math whizzes call a "torus," but we less than brilliant types call doughnut-shaped (Figure 9-2A). When viewed from above (Figure 9-2B), and sliced horizontally, the pattern is a circle. The "omnidirectional" property of a vertical is based on this pattern; a circular pattern hears signals from

all directions (which—surprise!—is what "omnidirectional" means). The side view (Figure 9-2C) is a "figure-8" pattern with nulls projecting from the top and bottom along the antenna's physical axis. This pattern, which in practical terms is the elevation pattern, is less than omnidirectional because of the nulls. Its strongest point is perpendicular to the axis of the antenna.

Now let's get back down to Earth. Real vertical antennas are planted either on the ground or mounted a short distance above the ground, as in Figure 9-3. In this configuration, we don't need the full half-wavelength (although it could be used). When the antenna is mounted on the ground, the radiator element is a quarter-wavelength long and the other half of the antenna circuit is essentially the ground. Some books use the concept of a quarter-wavelength radiator coupled with its "image" in the ground. I've

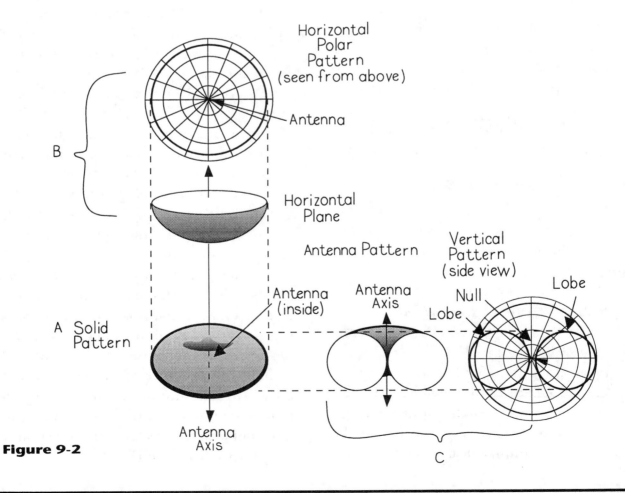

Figure 9-2

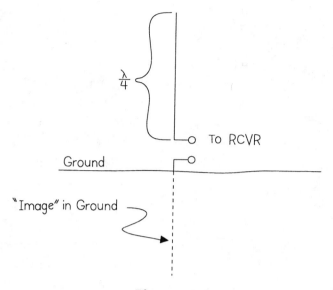

Figure 9-3A

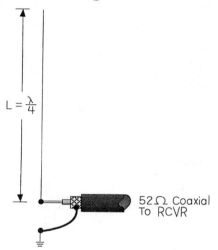

Figure 9-3B

always viewed this construct as a mite mystical, so I don't use it very often. Pretend you don't see the dotted line in Figure 9-3A. The central concept is that the antenna uses a quarter-wavelength element and is fed in an unbalanced manner by a grounded transmission line (see also Figure 9-3B).

The pattern for the ideal vertical antenna, over a perfectly conducting ground, is simply a horizontally sliced doughnut such as we saw earlier. In Figure 9-4, the solid line shows the ideal situation, i.e., the half-doughnut with the maxima positioned along the Earth's surface. Practical antennas, however, have a slightly elevated maxima (or "main lobe" if you prefer). The angle of this lobe, α, is the *angle of radiation and reception* (ADD) for the vertical. Generally, the ADD is quite low for most quarter-wavelength verticals, and this is the condition required for good DX reception. Longer verticals, such as the $5\lambda/8$ and $3\lambda/4$ verticals, tend to have lower ADDs than $\lambda/4$ models, and so are preferred for DX if the height is reasonable and impedance can be matched. The best DX reception occurs when the ADD is matched to the angle of arrival of the incoming signal. Shortening of the antenna is possible if an inductance is inserted in series with the antenna radiator element. Some people look at this type of antenna as having the coil of wire (inductor) make up for the missing length. True...but that's not quite an accurate description.

Shortened antennas tend to be *capacitive*, meaning if you measure the impedance you will find a certain amount of capacitive reactance present. The value of the inductor is selected to negate this capacitive reactance, and should have an inductive reactance equal to the value of the capacitive reactance of the antenna. A popular form of shortwave loaded vertical is the standard nine foot stainless steel mobile "whip" antenna with a base loading coil.

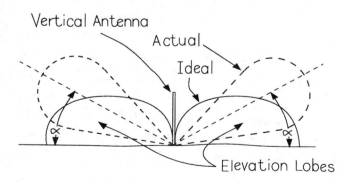

Figure 9-4

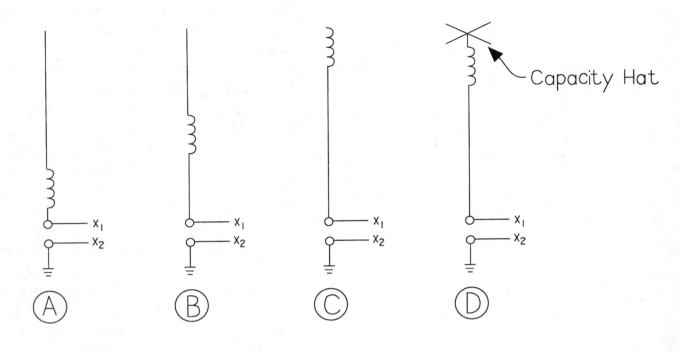

Figure 9-5

X_1,X_2: Transmission Line Connections

Figure 9-5 shows three popular coil loading schemes. The antenna in Figure 9-5A is *base loaded* because the series inductor is placed at the base right at the antenna feedpoint. A *center loaded* version is shown in Figure 9-5B, while a *top loaded* version is in Figure 9-5C. Many top loaded verticals also have a small telescoping extension above the coil to tune the antenna. Some also have a capacitive decoupling "hat," as in Figure 9-5D.

The verticals presented thus far have been insulated from ground, meaning the feedpoint is not connected to ground. Some people prefer grounded verticals for various reasons, not the least of which is possibly improved lightning protection. Figure 9-6 shows two forms of grounded vertical antenna. The version in Figure 9-6A is a base loaded vertical in which one

end of the loading coil is grounded, forming a path to ground for currents. The antenna is tuned by adjusting tap "A," while the impedance of the coaxial cable to the receiver is matched by adjusting tap "B." These taps can be adjusted with a VSWR bridge, noise bridge, or other antenna instrumentation.

A *delta fed* vertical is shown in Figure 9-6B. The basis for impedance matching in this antenna is the fact that the impedance varies along the height of the antenna, with the lowest point being the current node. In this type of antenna, the radiator element itself is directly grounded, as is one side of the coaxial cable (the shield). The center conductor of the coax is connected to a point above ground that has an impedance equal to its characteristic impedance (50 Ω, usually).

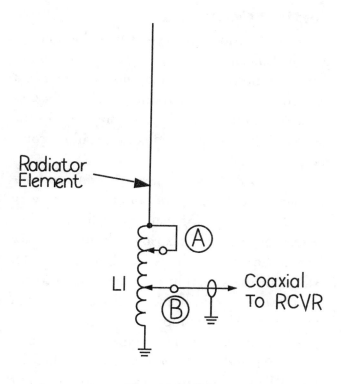

Figure 9-6A

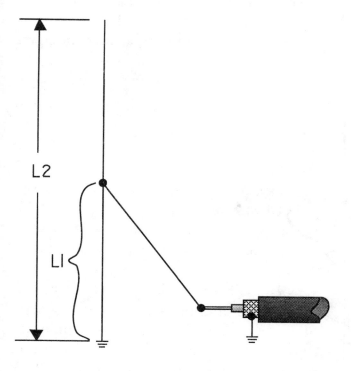

Figure 9-6B

Counterpoise Grounds, or "Radials"

There are two problems with grounding on vertical antennas. First, the Earth ground may not be all that good...and verticals require a good, low resistance ground to work properly. Second, when you elevate the vertical, which is done sometimes to adjust the elevation of the ARR, then there is no ground to connect to. Both of these situations are improved immensely by the use of quarter-wavelength *radials* (Figure 9-7) connected to the shield side of the coaxial cable. The radials form an artificial ground, also called a *counterpoise* ground. Antennas that use a counterpoise ground system are sometimes called *ground plane* antennas.

Each radial can be a half-wavelength long, but is at least a quarter-wavelength long. Its length is found from:

$$\text{Length}_{\text{feet}} = \frac{246}{\text{Frequency in MHz}}$$

The ideal number of radials is—believe it or not—120! Fortunately, as few as two will give decent results, and four will form a pretty good practical system. Even though 120 radials are ideal, there is a diminishing return above 15 or so. As a result, most books cite a number between four and 15 for the radial system. But if you can't put in four, use two...and failing two, use one. Assuming that you use the "kinda standard" four radials per band of operation, then be sure to space them equally around the antenna if at all possible.

The angle of the radials affects the feedpoint impedance. When the radials are horizontal to the ground, the feedpoint impedance will ideally be on the order of 30 to 37 Ω (it could be much lower). Drooping the radials 45° (as shown in Figure 9-7) causes the feedpoint impedance to raise to nearly 50 Ω.

When a ground plane antenna is mounted in the air, on a mast or the side of a house for example, the radials are tied to supports through end insulators and ropes (as is done in the case of the dipole and other wire antennas). If the ground plane is mounted on the ground, then the radials should be mounted a few inches above the ground. In both cases, insulated wire should be used for the radial if there is any possibility of contact with humans or animals.

A possible hazard exists with both ground mounted radials and with drooping radials that have their ends close to the ground. Pedestrian traffic could be a problem! People can trip over radials close to the ground, or run into them if they are a bit higher. A better solution is to bury the radials a few inches below the surface of the ground. In this case, a quarter-wavelength is OK, but any length is sufficient. Try to make the radials a quarter-wavelength or longer at the lowest frequency of operation. Use bare wire, not insulated. The radials can be buried in a slit trench that is made with the tip of a spade, shovel, or other gardening tool.

Vertical Construction

In this section, let's take a brief look at the principal means for installing vertical antennas. These methods may, or may not, be what you need for some specific situation, but can serve as guidelines to initiate your own thinking. In the next section we'll take a look at installing commercial vertical antennas.

Figure 9-8 shows the use of a vertical half-wavelength dipole. These antennas were very popular in Europe for many years for two simple reasons: they are cheap and take up less space than a horizontal half-wavelength dipole. (Although the situation may have changed today, most European homes didn't have enough yard space for larger "footprint" antennas.)

The support shown in Figure 9-8 is a house. The upper end of the antenna is attached by rope (R) and end insulator (EI) to the soffit underneath the roof (any other high feature could be used). The lower end, again with rope and end insulator, is attached to a long stake driven into the ground. I once used a ground rod to anchor the lower end of a 15-meter ham band vertical dipole.

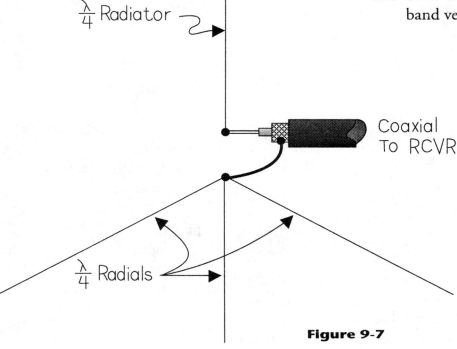

$\frac{\lambda}{4}$ Radiator

Coaxial To RCVR

$\frac{\lambda}{4}$ Radials

Figure 9-7

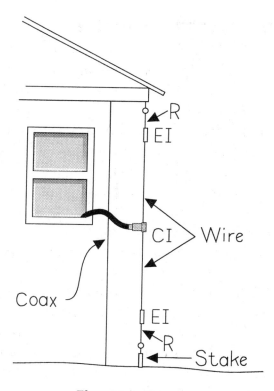

Figure 9-8

used for porch and deck construction. A six to eight foot ground rod, preferably copperclad steel, is driven into the ground next to the post. Radials are buried six or so inches below the surface, and are electrically connected to the ground rod. The shield of the coaxial cable is also connected to the ground rod. The inner conductor of the coaxial cable is connected to the antenna element, which is a copper or aluminum pipe.

The antenna radiator element is made from either copper plumbing pipe or aluminum tubing. Don't use steel, iron, or lead pipe. In Figure 9-9, the pipe is shown bolted to the wooden support with U-bolts. An alternative scheme is to use stand-off "beehive" insulators. These components, however, are becoming increasingly difficult to locate and actually have only a slight advantage over dry wood. (Of course, if the wood gets soaked there may be a considerable difference!)

I used a scheme such as Figure 9-9 for many years and never found it to be a problem.

The vertical half-wavelength dipole is built in exactly the same manner as the horizontal variety. The center insulator (CI) can be either a regular center insulator, designed for this purpose, or a 1:1 balun transformer. The coaxial cable is routed conveniently to the inside of the structure. Where possible, the coax should come away from the antenna wire at a right angle, and continue that way for a considerable distance. However, don't go overboard trying to make this ideal situation happen if it is just plain difficult.

A ground mounted vertical made from aluminum tubing is shown in Figure 9-9. The support structure is lumber, and can be a 2x4, two 2x4s planked together, or a 4x4, depending on how strong it needs to be. The wood post is anchored in the ground about three feet down. The wood should be the treated variety that is

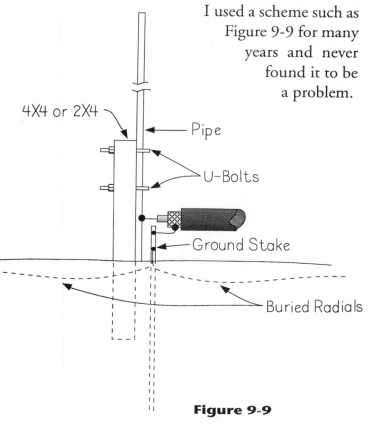

Figure 9-9

A variant using beehive stand-off insulators is shown in Figure 9-10. Depending on how high an antenna is being installed, and how robust the particular beehive insulators are, there should be at least two and as many as six insulators supporting the antenna. For most applications two, three, or four is the correct number. I can't advise which you should use because I lack specific information on your particular situation. However, use some common sense, and always opt for safety first.

Also shown in this illustration is a reasonable means for connecting the coaxial cable to the antenna radiator. If you just directly connect the cable, as might be implied from the previous illustration, then it will share a common defect with other such installations: it will break in short order. In Figure 9-10 there is an SO-239 "UHF" coaxial connector mounted on an L-bracket. The SO-239 is the standard chassis mounted coax connector used on most receivers and transmitters. A short length of wire soldered to the center conductor of the SO-239 electrically connects the coax to the antenna radiator element.

The ground wire (if ground mounted), or radial wires (which can be used on ground mounted antennas, and must be used on "up in the air" antennas), are connected to a machine screw connected to the L-bracket.

The L-bracket can be homemade from heavy metal stock or adapted from L-brackets found in hardware stores. I've done both, but find that the store-bought variety are a little better (and are at least easier).

The hardware used on the antenna should be of a type that will resist weathering. Stainless steel is a good choice for anything that must have strength; galvanized steel is a close second. For machine screws and other fasteners that don't bear weight, use brass stock hardware. I've found that most well stocked Harriet Homeowner hardware stores carry these items. Failing that, look in marine supplies stores. Boaters use brass hardware because of the inherent rusting problems they face.

The piping used for the antenna can be either copper or aluminum. While the copper solders better and is a better electrical conductor than aluminum, it's a bit less desirable for several reasons. First, copper pipe is bloody expensive! Second, it's hard to find diameters larger than ¾-inch, and the smaller diameters are only used for short heights. Third, when it weathers copper turns an icky cuprous green color that closely resembles pigeon droppings.

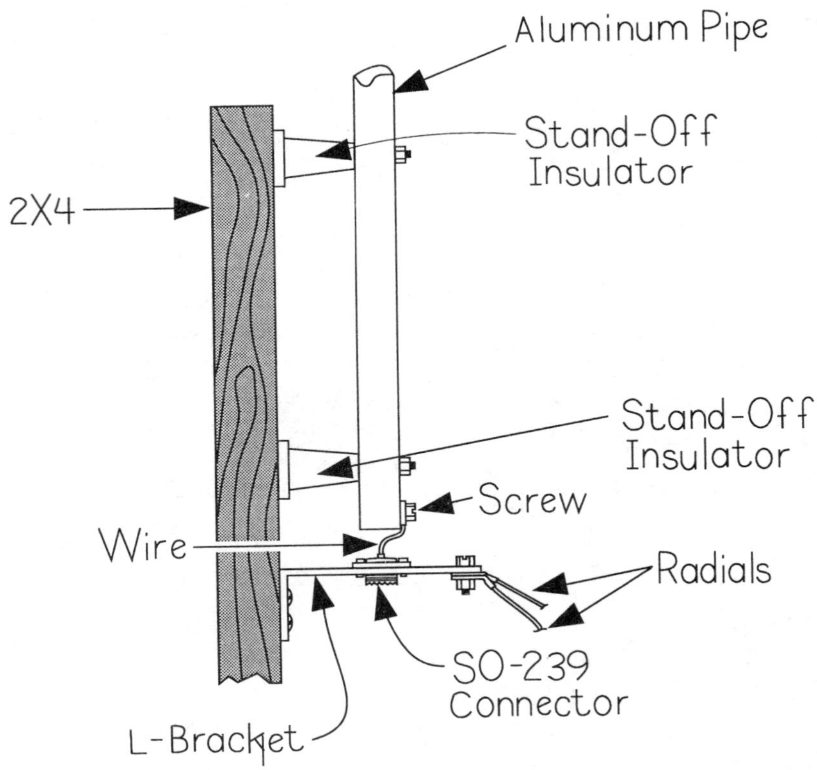

Figure 9-10

Most Harry Homeowners (notice the slick way I maintain gender neutrality) hardware stores carry displays of aluminum tubing, and metal products distributors (see Yellow Pages) carry even more types. There is a little "trade secret" that you should known about aluminum tubing: *adjacent diameters are designed so that the outside diameter (o.d.) of the smaller is a slip fit to the inside diameter (i.d.) of the larger.* This factoid means that adjacent sizes can be fitted together to form a tapered, telescoping length that can be easily assembled. In addition, the slip-fit feature makes it easy to tune the antenna. Tuning is done by adjusting the height of the vertical to resonate in the center of the band of interest.

Figure 9-11 shows one means of joining adjacent sections together. The smaller length should be slipped into the larger by at least six inches. Use two groups of three or four sheet metal screws to hold the sections. If you can get regular antenna hardware, then use clamps rather than sheet metal screws. They work better and are easier to remove (unless they are the type that "dimples" the metal).

Antenna hardware can often be salvaged from hams or bought at hamfests. It seems that there are zillions of us that have purchased verticals for the ham bands, installed the antenna, used it for several years, and then took it down. There are three reasons that I've removed verticals: I moved, the thing stopped working, and I became more enamored of another antenna (fickle, fickle). Another source of antenna hardware is a used citizens band antenna. A ⅝-wavelength CB vertical is 22.5 feet high, so can be cut down to become a quarter-wavelength on any frequency above 10.5 MHz. Of course, the radials would have to be lengthened, or wire radials adopted, but that isn't an insurmountable task. In both ham and CB antennas, the base mount, the piping, and the hardware can be pressed into service for SWL use.

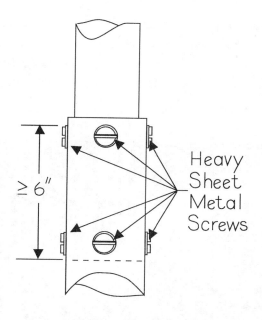

Figure 9-11

Let's take a look at some hardware salvaged from an antenna in my backyard. Figure 9-12 is a base mount assembly. It consists of a hollow section of pipe that slips over the supporting mast. A pair of heavy duty anchor rings, with associated bolt, is used to secure the assembly to the mast. The screws pass through holes in the mount and clamp the mast. A broadbanded antenna tuning circuit (Figure 9-13), mounted in a black plastic weather proof box, is used to electrically match the antenna to the coaxial cable.

Installing Store-Bought Trap and Non-Trap Verticals

Why ham antennas in a book aimed at SWLs? There are two reasons: many readers are also hams, and ham antennas are often adjustable (or modifiable) to work on nearby SWL bands. Above I described how the CB antenna can be cut down for SWL use, and the same is also true of ham antennas. A typical ham antenna, however, is used on three, four, or five bands, with LC parallel resonant frequency selective wave traps separating the sections. Most trap verticals designed for the ham bands can be tuned as much as 5% or 6% outside the ham bands, so they will work nicely for some SWL bands.

Figure 9-12

Figure 9-13

The wave traps can be treated in several ways. If you want to modify the trap to change its frequency, then connect a small value capacitor in parallel with the coil (the regular capacitor is inside and can usually be accessed). The capacitor will lower the resonant frequency. The values of capacitor vary markedly, but good trial values are 10 pF from 13 MHz and up, 33 pF from 7 to 13 MHz, and 100 pF at lower frequencies. Use a "trial and error" approach to home in on the actual capacitance.

Electrical Installation

Figure 9-14 shows the usual form of multiband trap vertical antenna. Each trap (TR1-TR3) is a parallel resonant LC tank circuit that blocks a certain frequency but passes all others. In Figure 9-14, TR1 is the 10-meter trap, TR2 is the 15-meter trap, and TR3 is the 20-meter trap. No 40-meter trap is needed because the antenna resonates the entire length of the tubing on 40-meters. Each section (except perhaps the 10-meter section) is actually a little shorter than might be expected from the standard quarter-wavelength formulas. That is because the traps tend to act inductively and lessen the length required to resonate on any given band.

The vertical manufacturer may give suggested lengths for the various segments between traps. *Do not make the mistake of assuming that these are absolute numbers!* They are only recommended starting points, even though the literature packed with the antenna may suggest otherwise. Loosely (meaning don't tighten the clamps too much) but safely install the antenna and then adjust each segment for resonance. Start with the 10-meter band, and then work each lower frequency band in succession: 10-15-20-40, etc. After each lower band is adjusted, recheck the higher bands to make sure nothing shifted because there might be a little interaction between

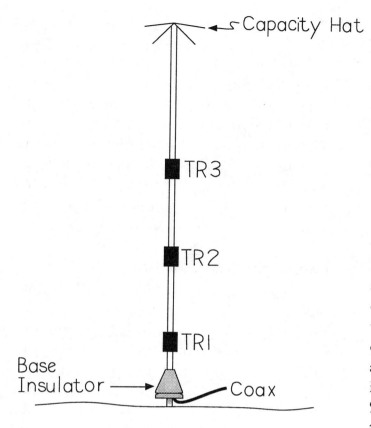

Figure 9-14

two radials per band and preferably four arranged so that they are equally spaced around the antenna. If you can't space them correctly, never fear—they'll work anyway. On a four-band antenna, that means 16 radials, which really isn't a lot.

PVC Pipe Verticals

PVC plumbing pipe is standard throughout the U.S. construction industry these days. The heavier (thick wall) grades can be used for vertical antennas with heights up to about 15 feet, especially if anchored about 12 feet high, as well as the base. The antenna radiator is one or more copper wires running the length of the PVC pipe (PVC is an insulator). It is fairly commonplace to run the wires inside the pipe, although external runs are also used if the wire is anchored properly. A loading coil (see Figure 9-15) can be used to increase the effective antenna electrical length.

bands. Once the antenna is properly resonant, tighten the clamps and make the final installation. I know this is a pain in the neck, and means putting the antenna up and taking it down a couple of times, but it pays dividends in the end. I failed to do this once, and found that the 15-meter band was useless; it resonated at 19.2 MHz.

Radials make or break a vertical antenna; they form the ground plane for the antenna. We've already noted how 120 is the optimum number of radials, but that we can get by with fewer. For our kind of work, I recommend not less than

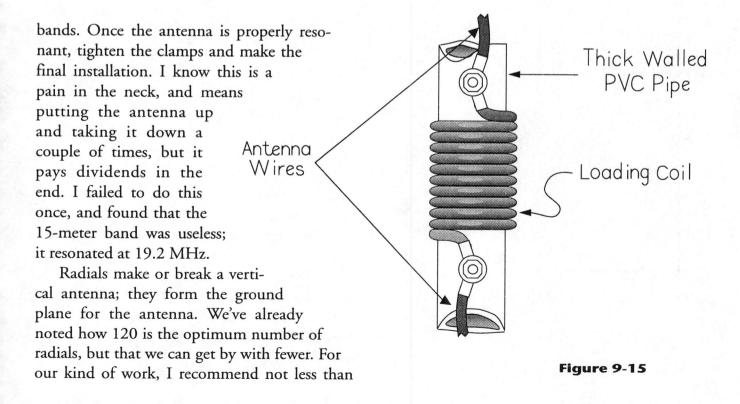

Figure 9-15

One chap I know built a multiband vertical by using separate quarter-wavelength insulated wires for each of about seven different HF shortwave bands. All of the antennas were joined together at the base in a screw connection, where they were also connected to a coaxial connector (see Figure 9-16 for detail).

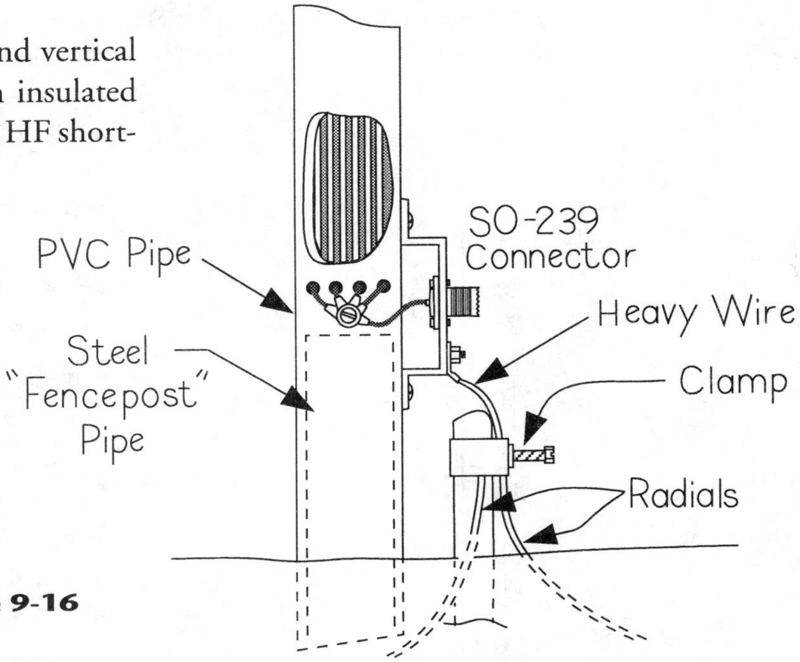

PVC Pipe

SO-239 Connector

Steel "Fencepost" Pipe

Heavy Wire

Clamp

Radials

Figure 9-16

CHAPTER 10

Directional Antennas

irectional antennas are those in which the reception pattern can be directed or steered to a specific region of the universe. The reason that we want to be able to direct the pattern is two-fold. In the main beam (or "lobe") of the antenna pattern, signals will be louder. This is because there is a gain associated with the antenna. The other reason is that a null—a point of minimum pick-up—exists in the pattern and it can be positioned towards an interfering station. In this chapter we'll take a look at several popular directional antennas.

Rotatable Dipoles

The half-wavelength dipole is probably the most popular single type of directional antenna in the shortwave bands. It has a "figure-8" directional pattern (azimuthal) consisting of two maxima at right angles to the wire, and two minima (nulls) off the ends of the wire. If the dipole can be rotated, then the nulls and the maxima can be positioned for best signal reception.

Figure 10-1 shows a rotatable half-wavelength dipole that can be built at frequencies as low as about 13 MHz, although it is probably easier to construct the antenna at the 18 MHz band and up. (At lower frequencies, the elements get too long for simple construction practices.) The antenna elements are made from ¾-inch to 1¼-inch aluminum tubing. Each element is a quarter-wavelength long. The aluminum tubing is mounted on a piece of 1x2 pressure treated lumber. A pipe floor or ceiling flange makes a

decent center mount for smaller antennas (such as for the 13-meter band) while the matching pipe serves as a mast.

Rotation of the antenna can be by either of two methods. The "Armstrong" rotor consists of a good gripping wrench or pliers and some elbow grease. Don't laugh—I've known both hams and SWLs who would open an upstairs window and use a vise grip wrench to turn the antenna mast to point the antenna in the right direction. The other method is to buy a regular antenna rotator. For lightweight antennas (above 20 MHz), an ordinary television antenna rotator will suffice, but for larger antennas a heavy duty ham radio rotator is required.

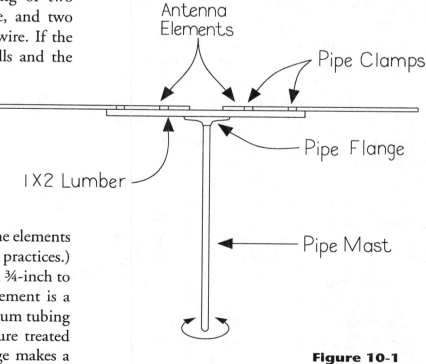

Figure 10-1

Parasitic Beam Antennas

If an array of two or more antenna elements is arranged so that only one element, such as a dipole, is connected to the receiver or transmitter, then it is called a *parasitic beam* antenna. In these antennas, the element connected to the receiver is called the *driven* element, while other—parasitic—elements are called either *reflectors* or *directors* depending on their placement. These elements are said to be parasitic to the driven element because they are not directly connected to the receiver or transmitter, but instead are electromagnetically coupled to the driven element.

The reflector elements are tuned to a slightly lower frequency than the driven element and tend to be about 4% longer than the driven element. Similarly, the director elements are tuned to a slightly higher frequency and are about 4% shorter than the driven element. There can be any number of reflectors and directors making up a parasitic beam antenna.

The radiation characteristics of the parasitic beam antenna are approximately unidirectional. The pattern is a function of the relationship between the phases and amplitudes of the currents flowing in the various elements. The pattern is altered by the tuning and position of each parasitic element. In general, the parasitic elements are located between 0.1λ and 0.26λ, with 0.15λ being very popular. There are two basic forms of parasitic antenna which we will consider: *Yagi-Uda* ("Yagi") beams and *quads*.

The Yagi antenna shown in Figure 10-2 consists of two or more half-wavelength dipoles arranged parallel to each other. The driven element is fed at the center at points X1 and X2. These antennas can be constructed of either wire or aluminum tubing, although rotatable Yagis are usually made of tubing. This type of antenna should be operated at a height of $\lambda/2$ or more above ground at the lowest frequency of operation.

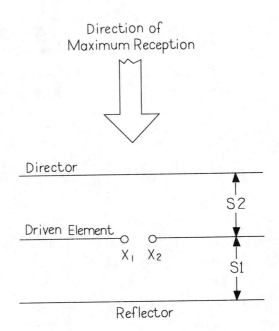

Figure 10-2

The lengths of the elements are found empirically, but the starting points are approximated by:

Driven Element:

$$L_{feet} = \frac{475}{F_{MHz}}$$

Director Element:

$$L_{feet} = \frac{456}{F_{MHz}}$$

Reflector Element:

$$L_{feet} = \frac{500}{F_{MHz}}$$

Additional directors are sized to be 4% shorter than the director one space closer to the driven element, while additional reflectors are 4% longer than the next reflector.

The direction of the maximum receive sensitivity, and maximum radiation on transmit, is in the direction away from the reflector and towards the director. The elements are spaced approximately 0.15λ apart. In this case, the gain of the Yagi will be optimized at 5.8 dB for a two element model and 7 dB for a three element model. Additional elements add gain, as does "stacking" two or more beams (about 3 dB per stack if done correctly). Yagi beam antennas can be either horizontally or vertically polarized, although the horizontal version is the most popular (except on the 11-meter citizens band).

Yagi beams can be operated on multiple bands using tuned traps, similarly to the trap dipoles discussed earlier. Amateur radio operators often use multiband, multi-element Yagi beam antennas for their operations. Yagi beam antennas can also be shortened by inserting inductors in the elements. Similarly, the inductance can be provided by helically winding the wire along the length of an insulating element. By using this method, low frequencies can be accommodated, although at the cost of lost bandwidth.

The impedance at the feedpoint of the Yagi beam antenna is lower than the 75 Ω one normally expects of dipole antennas. Values of feedpoint impedance of 12 to 60 Ω are found, depending on the number of elements and their relative spacing. This impedance can be measured, and an impedance transformer or balun provided to match it to 50 Ω coaxial cable. There are other matching methods—such as the gamma match, omega match, and hairpin stub—but these tend to get a bit dicey to build.

Quad beam antennas are full wave loops (Figure 10-3) rather than half-wavelength dipoles. The quad antenna was invented in the late 1940s by engineers for the missionary shortwave radio broadcasting station HCJB in Quito, Ecuador. HCJB was troubled by RF corona arcing of the Yagi beam antenna elements at their ends in the rarified high altitude atmosphere of Quito. By making a current mode loop antenna, the high voltages at the tips were avoided (there are no tips in a loop). The loop lengths (i.e., entire perimeter) can be found by:

Driven Element:

$$L_{feet} = \frac{1005}{F_{MHz}}$$

Director Element:

$$L_{feet} = \frac{975}{F_{MHz}}$$

Reflector Element:

$$L_{feet} = \frac{1030}{F_{MHz}}$$

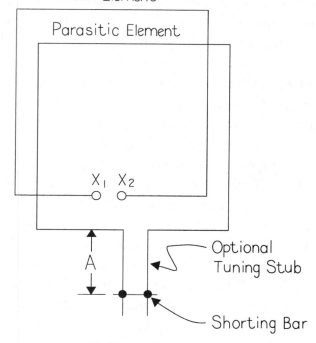

Figure 10-3

These lengths are the entire loop length, rather than each side. The length of the individual sides are one-fourth of the lengths calculated by the equations above. The antenna can be tuned by adding a quarter-wavelength tunable stub ("A") to one side of the reflector element, although this stub is considered optional by some experts.

The feedpoint impedance of the quad antenna will vary from about 40 Ω to around 90 Ω, depending on the spacing of the elements. These antennas are therefore reasonable matches to either 52 Ω or 75 Ω coaxial cable. In some cases, however, an impedance transformer or matching stub is used to improve the situation. A popular impedance matching method is to use a quarter-wavelength piece of 75 Ω coaxial

cable at the feedpoint, and then 52 Ω coaxial cable from the open end of the 75 Ω section to the receiver. The length of the 75 Ω portion is reduced by the velocity factor of the coaxial cable:

$$L_{feet} = \frac{246V}{F_{MHz}}$$

Multiband quad antennas can be built from a common mounting scheme (Figure 10-4). The wires of each band's antenna can be connected in parallel to the transmission line (points "X1" and "X2"). The spreaders are made of fiberglass, although at one time bamboo poles (used in the carpet trade) were quite popular. Unfortunately, bamboo poles are a bit hard to find these days and the cardboard rolls now used by carpet makers are not suitable. The mounting plate can be a thick piece of plywood or a fiberglass or metal plate. Check the amateur radio or SWL magazines for current suppliers of these items.

Hardware to make either Yagi or quad antennas can be obtained by salvaging parts from used amateur radio antennas. I've seen a large amount of such hardware at hamfests and other "flea market" get togethers, and the stuff is generally low cost. The elements can be either cut to SWL frequencies, or the basic hardware used to support newly constructed elements cut to SWL frequencies.

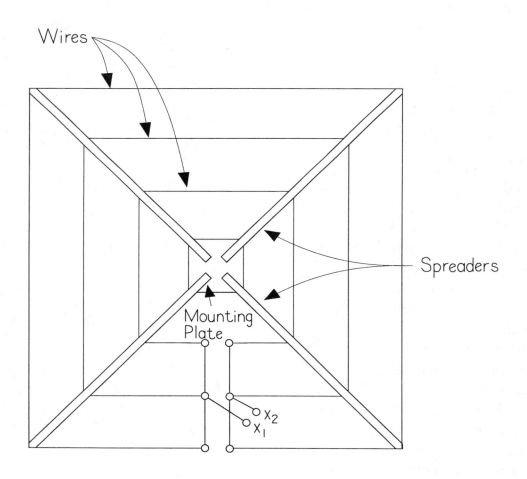

Figure 10-4

Phased Vertical Arrays

Can a vertical antenna owner get the benefit of directivity without a huge investment in a tower mounted with a Yagi beam or quad? The usual solution is to use *phased verticals*. AM broadcast stations with more than one tower are using this type of system. The idea is to place two or more antennas in close proximity and feed them with currents at specific phase angles to produce a desired radiation pattern. A lot of material is available in the literature on phased vertical antenna systems, and it is far too much to be covered here. There are "standard patterns" dating from before World War II that are created with different spacings and different phase angles of feed current. In this chapter, we will consider only one system.

Figure 10-5 shows the patterns for a pair of quarter-wavelength vertical antennas spaced a half-wavelength (180°) apart. Without getting into complex phase shifting networks, there are basically two phasings that are easily obtained: 0° (antennas in-phase) and 180° (antennas out of phase with each other). When the two antennas (P1 and P2) are fed in-phase with equal currents, the radiation pattern (shown somewhat idealized in Figure10-5A) is a bidirectional "figure-8" that is directional perpendicular to the line of centers between the two antennas. A sharp null exists along the line of centers (P1-P2). When the antennas are fed out of phase with each other by 180°, the pattern rotates 90° (quarter way around the compass) and now exhibits directivity along the line of centers (P1-P2). The interference canceling null is now perpendicular to line P1-P2.

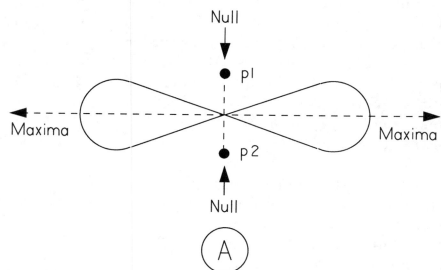

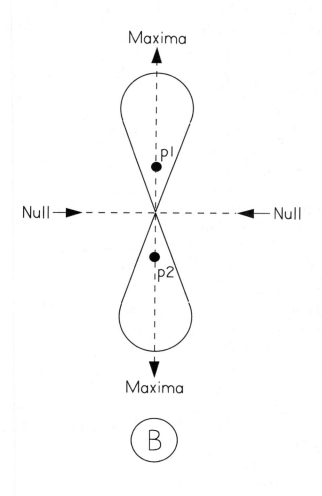

Figure 10-5

It should be apparent that we can select our directivity by selecting the phase angle of the feed currents in the two antennas. Figure 10-6 shows the two feeding systems usually cited in books for in-phase (Figure 10-6A) and out-of-phase (Figure 10-6B) systems. In Figure 10-6A, we have the coax from the transmitter coming to a coax Tee-connector. From the connector to the antenna feedpoints are two lengths of coax (A1 and A2) that are equal to each other and identical. Given the variation between coaxial cables, I suspect that it would work better if the two cables were not merely the same length (A1 = A2) but also came from the same roll!

The second variation, shown in Figure 10-6B, supposedly produces a 180° phase shift between antenna P1 and antenna P2, when the length is an electrical half-wavelength. According to much-publicized theory, the system of Figure 10-6B ought to produce the pattern of Figure 10-6B—yet experience shows "t'ain't always so." It seems that there are a couple of problems with the system in Figure 10-6B. First, remember that coax has a velocity factor (VF) which is the fraction of the speed of light at which signals in the cable propagate. The VF is a decimal fraction on the order of 0.66 to 0.82, depending

upon the type of coax used. Unfortunately, the physical spacing between P1 and P2 is a real half-wavelength (A = 492/F), while the cable length is shorter by the velocity factor (A' = ((VF) × 492)/F). Consider an example. A 13-meter band (21.65 MHz) phased vertical antenna system

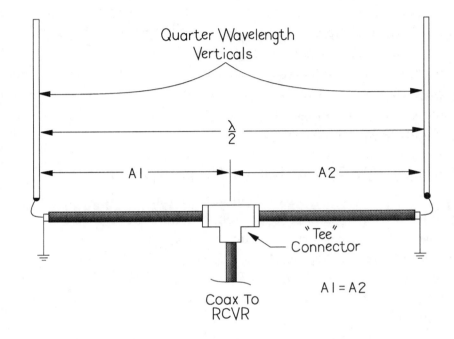

Figure 10-6   A

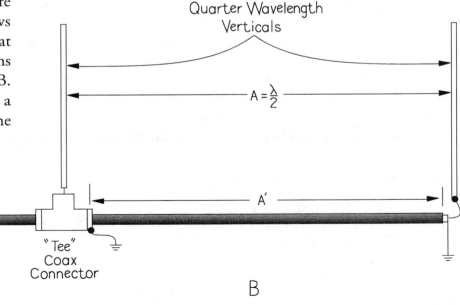

B

will have two 11.4 foot radiators spaced 22.8 feet apart (approximately, depending upon exact frequency). If we use foam coax, with VF = 0.80, the cable length is (0.8) x (22.8 feet), or 18.25 feet. In other words, despite lots of publicity, the darn cable won't fit between the towers.

Second, the patterns shown in Figure 10-5 are dependent upon one principal condition: the antenna currents are equal. If both of them are the same impedance, and are fed from the same transmitter, then it is reasonable to assume that the currents are equal—right? *Wrong!* What about coax loss? Because of normal coax loss, which is worse at higher frequencies, the power available to antenna P2 in

Figure 10-6B is less than the power available to antenna P1. Thus, the pattern will be distorted because the current produced in P2 is less than the current in P1, where they should be equal.

The first problem is sometimes fixed by using unequal lengths for cables A1 and A2 (Figure 10-7), and using it for the out of phase case. For example, if we make A1 a quarter-wavelength, and A2 a ¾-wavelength, antenna P1 is fed with a 90° phase lag (relative to the Tee connector signal), while antenna P2 is fed with a 270° phase shift. The result is still a 180° phase difference. Unfortunately, we have not only not solved the current level problem, we have actually made it worse by adding still more lossy cable to the system.

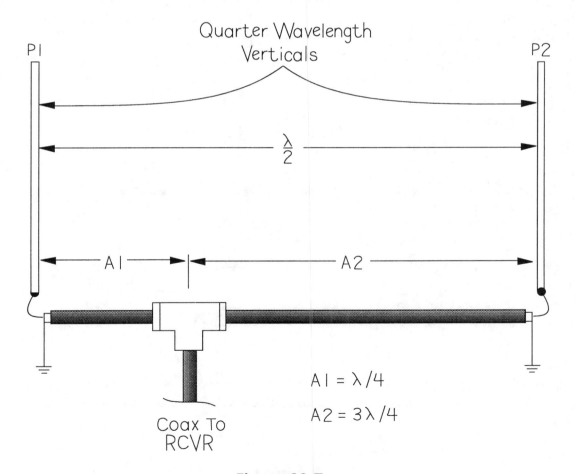

Figure 10-7

There is still another problem that is generic to the whole class of phased verticals. Once installed, the pattern is fixed. This problem doesn't bother most point-to-point commercial radio stations or broadcasters because they tend to transmit in only one direction. But we are most likely to need a rotatable antenna pattern. Neither Figure 10-5A nor Figure 10-5B is rotable without a lot of effort—like changing coax feeds around (or physically digging up the verticals and repositioning them?).

The pattern of a pair of phased vertical can be steered considerably (20 to 70°) by inserting a phase shift network in series with either antenna's coaxial cable before it inputs to the phase control box. Various RLC networks can be used for phase shifting, but the coaxial cable version of Figure 10-8 is quite simple. Cut up a half-wavelength piece of coax and fit the ends with coaxial connectors. Connect the coax junctions, via Tee connectors, to a coaxial switch (S1).

Adjustable phase control is obtained by selecting how many segments are switched into the circuit at any one time.

Bobtail Curtains

The Bobtail curtain, also called the broadside array, is shown in Figure 10-9. It is a vertically polarized array that can be made either of wire or tubing. It is blessed with a low angle of radiation and works very well for long distance DX work (over 2500 miles). The Bobtail curtain offers about 5 dB gain in a figure-8 pattern at right angles to the line connecting the three antennas (when seen from above).

The Bobtail curtain antenna consists of three quarter-wavelength vertical radiators ("A") spaced a half-wavelength apart. The center radiator element is fed between its base and ground through an antenna tuning unit (Figure 10-10). The horizontal sections ("B") act as phasing harnesses to excite the two outer radiators.

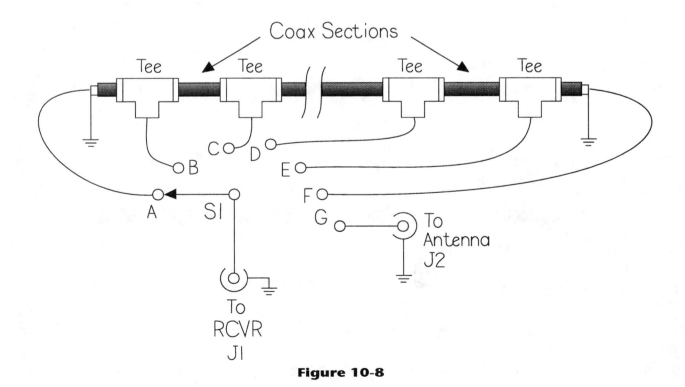

Figure 10-8

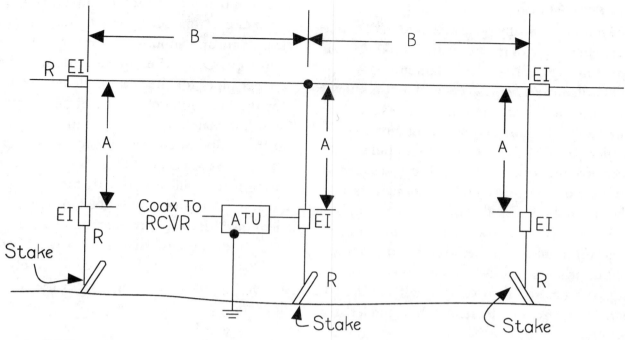

$$A = \frac{225}{F_{MHZ}} \text{ feet}$$

$$B = \frac{475}{F_{MHZ}} \text{ feet}$$

Figure 10-9

The lengths of the various elements of the Bobtail curtain are found from:

$$A_{feet} = \frac{225}{F_{MHz}}$$

and

$$B_{feet} = \frac{475}{F_{MHz}}$$

The antenna tuning unit is shown in Figure 10-10, and consists of a 140 pF capacitor and 18 µH adjustable inductor in parallel. In practice, the inductor may be set to one inductance that tunes the band when the capacitor (C1) is adjusted through its entire range.

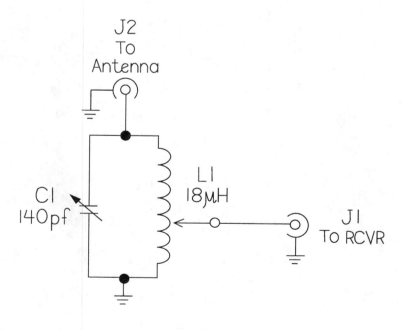

Figure 10-10

Thorne Array

Another vertically polarized antenna capable of very low angle of radiation and 5 dB of gain is shown in Figure 10-11. This antenna is sometimes called the *Thorne array*, and is also known as the inverted bobtail curtain. It is essentially a truncated version of a complex antenna called a "Sterba curtain array" (which is popular with shortwave broadcast stations), but is scaled to a size that ordinary people can sometimes use. Like the Bobtail curtain, the Thorne array antenna pattern has a low angle of radiation and reception in directions broadside to the array.

The antenna consists of three quarter-wavelength verticals ("A") spaced a half-wavelength apart by horizontal elements ("B"); the lengths are found using the same equations as in the Bobtail curtain. All three elements can be built from wire and supported from the tops with a taut rope. Otherwise, use aluminum tubing (or copper pipe) for the vertical elements and wire for the horizontal elements. Either a transmission line matching section or an antenna tuner at the feedpoint converts the feed impedance to 75 or 52 Ω as needed. The Thorne array differs from the Bobtail curtain in that it does not need an antenna tuning unit at the feedpoint. I saw a demonstration of this antenna down in Texas one time. An Australian station was very loud on this antenna, while it was considerably weaker on a dipole and a single vertical at the same location.

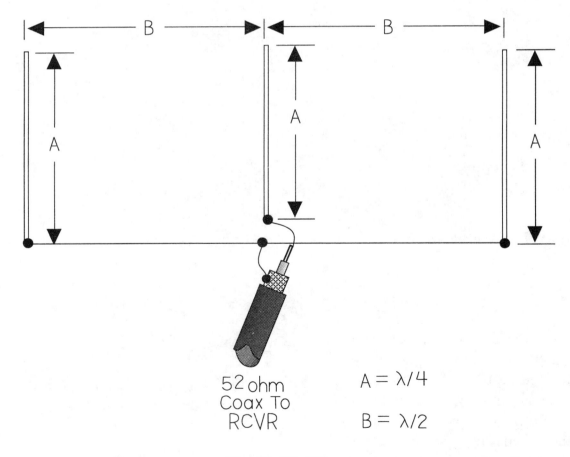

52 ohm
Coax To
RCVR

$$A = \lambda/4$$

$$B = \lambda/2$$

Figure 10-11

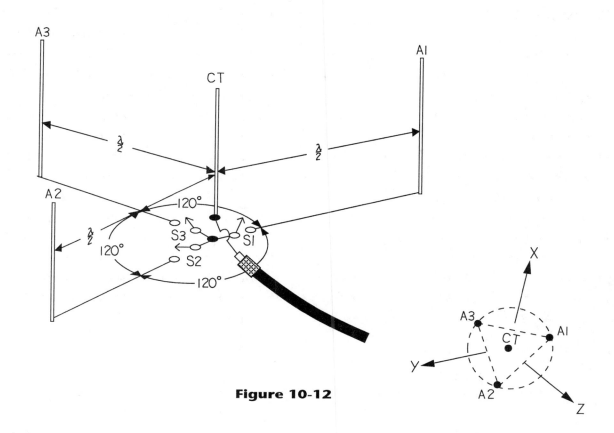

Figure 10-12

Figure 10-12 shows a multidirectional Thorne array using a center element ("CT") and three outer elements spaced at 120° intervals in a circle—with a λ/2 radius—around the center element. A set of switches (S1 through S3) allows the antenna to receive in any of three directions. For direction "X", close S1 and S3 and open S2 (that is, use elements A1 and A3). For direction "Y," close S2 and S3 and leave S1 open. For direction "Z," close S1 and S2 and leave S3 open.

The switches S1 through S3 can be either mechanical switches, or electromechanical relays. If you opt for relays, then make sure to use low current, low voltage (5 volt DC or 6 volt DC) types that are operated from a battery. *Do not use 110 volt AC relays!*

CHAPTER 11

Small Loop Receiving Antennas

If you are fond of DXing the AM broadcasting band (BCB), VLF, medium wave, or low frequency HF "tropical" bands, then this chapter was written with you in mind. In this chapter you will learn some smoke about small loop receiving antennas. These antennas are fundamentally different from the large loop types previously discussed and are very often the antenna of choice for low frequency work. Large loop antennas are 0.5λ or larger and respond to the electrical field component of the electromagnetic wave. Small loop antennas, on the other hand, are $< 0.1\lambda$ (some sources say 0.17λ and $<0.22\lambda$) and respond to the magnetic field component of the electromagnetic wave. One principal difference between the large loop and the small loop is found when examining the radio frequency current induced in the loop when a radio signal intersects it. In a large loop, the dimensions in each section are an appreciable portion of one wavelength, so the current will vary from one point in the conductor to another. But in a small loop, the current is the same throughout the entire loop.

The differences between small loops and large loops show up in some interesting ways, but perhaps the most striking is the directions of maximum response—the main lobes—and the directions of the nulls. Both types of loop produce figure-8 patterns, but in directions at right angles with respect to each other. The large loop antenna produces main lobes *orthogonal*, at right angles or "broadside" to, the plane of the loop. Nulls are off the sides of the loop. The small loop, however, is exactly the opposite: the main lobes are off the sides of the loop (in the direction of the loop plane), and the nulls are broadside to the loop plane (see Figure 11-1A). Don't confuse small loop behavior with the behavior of the loopstick antenna. Loopstick antennas are made of coils of wire wound on a ferrite or powdered iron rod. The direction of maximum response for the loopstick antenna is broadside to the rod with deep nulls off the ends (Figure 11-1B). Both loopsticks and small wire loops are used for radio direction-finding and for shortwave, low frequency medium wave, AM broadcast band, and VLF DXing.

The nulls of a loop antenna are very sharp and very deep. Small changes of pointing direction can make a profound difference in the response of the antenna. If you point a loop antenna so that its null is aimed at a strong station, the signal strength of the station appears to drop dramatically at the center of the notch. But turn the antenna only a few degrees one way or the other, and the signal strength increases sharply. The depth of the null can reach 10 to 15 dB on sloppy loops and 30 to 40 dB on well-built loops (20 dB is a very common value). I've seen claims of 60 dB nulls for some commercially available loop antennas, but until they are properly tested I discount such claims as advertising hyperbole. I would, however, like to see some scientifically valid evidence of 60 dB nulls if anyone has it available. The construction and uniformity of the loop are primary factors in the sharpness and depth of the null.

At one time, the principal use of the small loop antenna was radio direction-finding, especially in the lower frequency bands. The RDF loop is mounted with a compass rose to allow

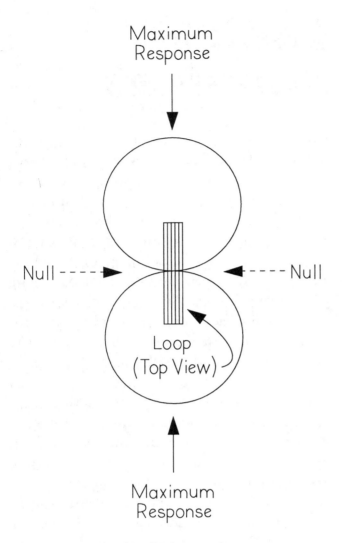

Figure 11-1A

the operator to find the direction of minimum response. The null was used, rather than the peak response point, because it is far narrower than the peak. As a result, precise determination of direction is possible. Because the null is bidirectional, ambiguity exists as to which of the two directions is the correct direction. What the direction-finder "finds" is a line along which the station exists. If the line is found from two reasonably separated locations, and the lines of direction are plotted on a map, then the two lines will cross in the area of the station. Three or more lines of direction (a process called *triangulation*) yields a pretty precise knowledge of the station's actual location.

Today, these small loops are still used for radio direction-finding, but their use has been extended into the general receiving arena, especially on the low frequencies. One of the characteristics of those bands is the possibility of strong local interference smothering weaker ground wave and sky wave stations. As a result, you can't hear co-channel signals when one of them is very strong and the other is weak. Similarly, if a co-channel station has

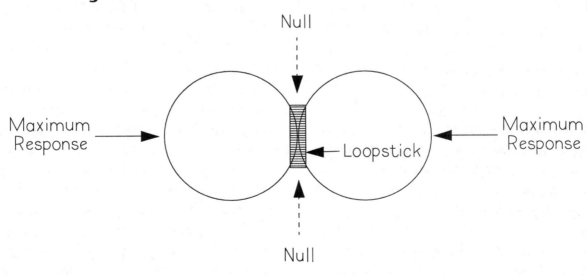

Figure 11-1B

a signal strength that is an appreciable fraction of the desired signal, and is slightly different in frequency, then the two signals will heterodyne together and form a whistling sound in the receiver output. The frequency of the whistle is an audio tone equal to the difference in frequency between the two signals. This is often the case when trying to hear foreign BCB signals on frequencies (called *split frequencies*) between the standard 10 kHz spacing used in North and South America. The directional characteristics of the loop can help if the loop null is placed in the direction of the undesired signal.

Loops are used mainly in the low frequency bands even though such loops are either physically larger than high frequency loops or require more turns of wire. Loops have been used as high as VHF and are commonly used in the 10-meter ham band for such activities as hidden transmitter hunts. The reason why low frequencies are the general preserve of loops is that those frequencies are more likely to have substantial ground wave signals. Sky wave signals lose some of their apparent directivity because of multiple reflections. Similarly, VHF and UHF waves are likely to reflect from buildings and hillsides, so will arrive at angles other than the direction of the transmitter. As a result, the loop is less useful for the purpose of radio direction-finding. If your goal is not RDF but listening to the station, that is hardly a problem. A small loop can be used in the upper shortwave bands to null a strong local ground wave station in order to hear a weaker sky wave station. Finally, loops can be useful in rejecting noise from local sources, such as a "leaky" electric power line or a neighbor's outdoor light dimmer.

Let's examine the basic theory of small loop antennas, and then take a look at some practical construction methods.

Air Core Frame Loops ("Box" Loops)

A wire loop antenna is made by winding a large coil of wire, consisting of one or more turns, on some sort of frame. The shape of the loop can be circular, square, triangular, hexagonal, or octagonal. For practical reasons, the square loop seems to be most popular. With one exception, the loops considered in this section will be square so you can easily duplicate them.

The basic form of the simplest loop is shown in Figure 11-2. This loop is square, with sides the same length "A" all around. The width of the loop ("B") is the distance from the first turn to the last turn in the loop, or the diameter of the wire if only one turn is used. The turns of the loop in Figure 11-2 are *depth wound,* meaning each turn of the loop is spaced in a slightly different parallel plane. The turns are spaced evenly across distance "B." Alternatively, the loop can be wound such that the turns are in the same plane (this is called *planar winding).* In either case, the sides of the loop ("A") should be not less than five times the width ("B"). There seems to be little difference between depth and planar wound loops. The far-field patterns of the different shape loops are nearly the same if the respective cross sectional areas (πr^2 for circular loops and A2 for square loops) are $< \lambda^2/100$.

The reason why a small loop has a null when its broadest aspect is facing the signal is simple, even though it seems counterintuitive at first blush. Take a look at Figure 11-3. Here we have two identical small loop antennas at right angles to each other. Antenna "A" is in line with the advancing radio wave, while antenna "B" is broadside to the wave. Each line in the wave represents a line where the signal strength is the same, i.e. an "isopotential line." When the loop is in line with the signal (antenna "A"), there is a difference of potential from one end of the loop to the other, so current can be induced in the wires. But when the loop is turned broadside, all points on the loop are on the same potential line, so there is no difference of potential between segments of the conductor ...thus little signal is picked up (and the antenna therefore sees a null).

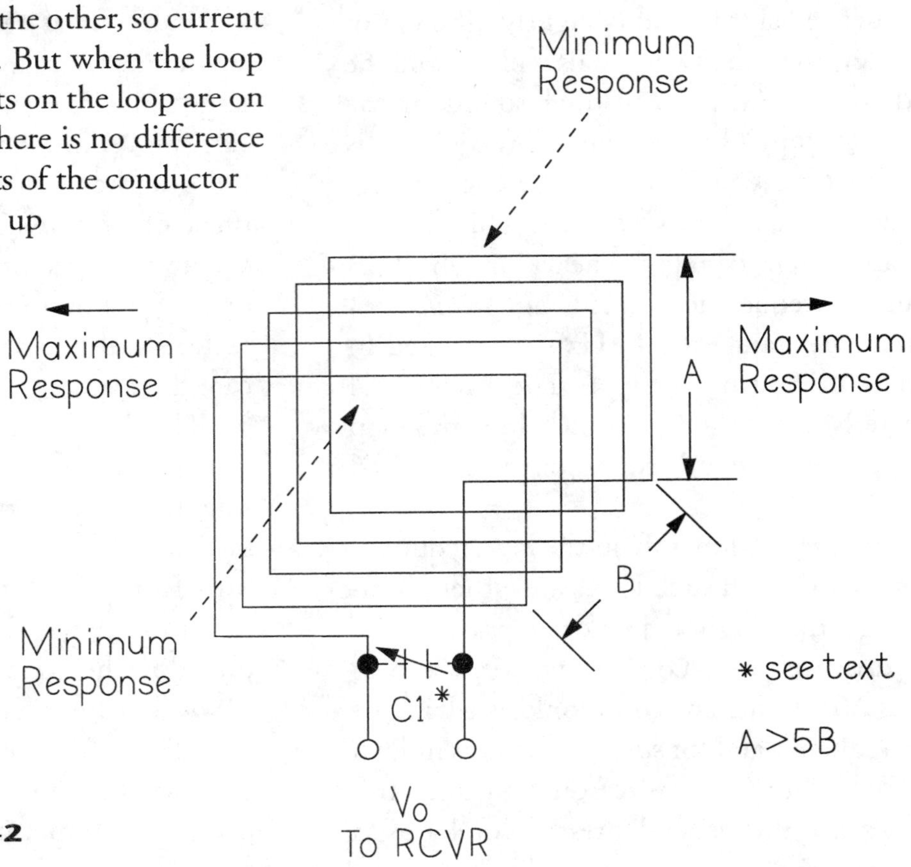

Minimum Response

Maximum Response

Maximum Response

Minimum Response

A

B

* see text

A > 5B

C1 *

V_0
To RCVR

Figure 11-2

Advancing Radio Wave

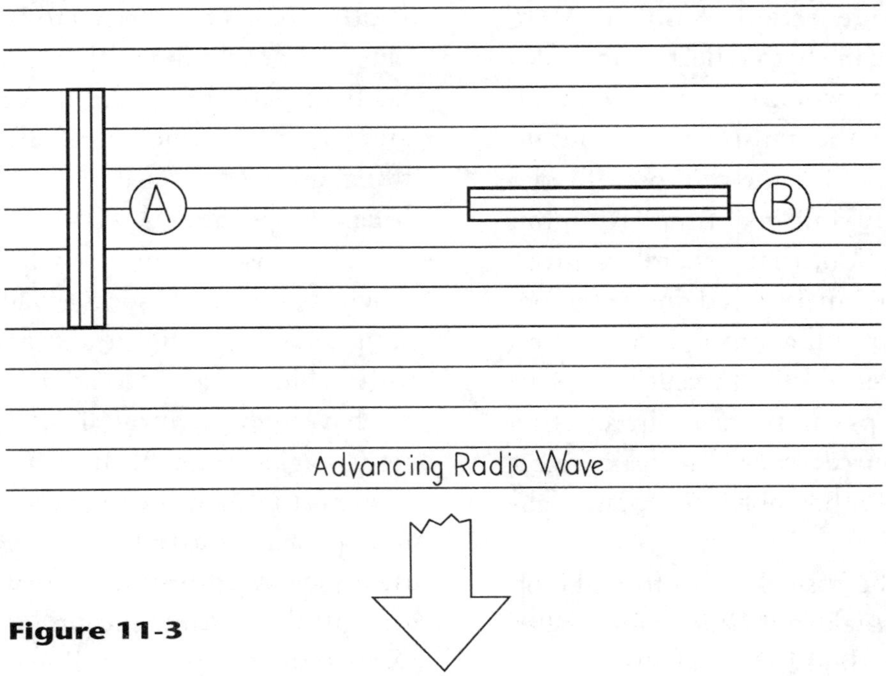

Figure 11-3

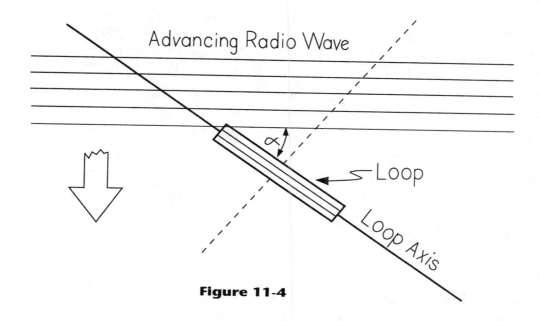

Figure 11-4

The actual voltage across the output terminals of an untuned loop is a function of the angle of arrival of the signal α (see Figure 11-4), as well as the strength of the signal and the design of the loop. The voltage V_o is given by:

$$V_o = \frac{(2\pi ANE_f \cos\alpha)}{\lambda}$$

Where:
  V_o is the output voltage of the loop
  A is the area of the loop in square meters (m2)
  N is the number of turns of wire in the loop
  E_f is the strength of the signal in volts per meter (V/m)
  α is the angle of arrival of the signal
  λ is the wavelength of the arriving signal

Loops are sometimes specified in terms of the *effective height* of the antenna. This number is a theoretical construct that compares the out-put voltage of a small loop with a vertical piece of the same kind of wire that has a height of:

$$H_{eff} = \frac{2\pi NA}{\lambda}$$

If a capacitor (such as C1 in Figure 11-2) is used to tune the loop, then the output voltage V_o will rise substantially. The output voltage found using the first equation is multiplied by the loaded Q of the tuned circuit, which can be from 10 to 100 (if the antenna is well constructed):

$$V_o = \frac{(2\pi ANE_f Q \cos\alpha)}{\lambda}$$

Even though the output signal voltage of tuned loops is higher than that of untuned loops, it is nonetheless low compared with other forms of antenna. As a result, a loop preamplifier is usually needed for best performance. More will be said about loop preamplifiers later in this chapter.

Transformer Loops

It is common practice to make a small loop antenna with two loops rather than just one. Figure 11-5 shows such a *transformer* loop antenna. The main loop is built exactly as discussed above: several turns of wire on a large frame, with a tuning capacitor to resonate it to the frequency of choice. The other loop is a one or two turn *coupling loop*. This loop is installed in very close proximity to the main loop, usually (but not necessarily) on the inside edge not more than a couple of centimeters away. The purpose of this loop is to couple signal induced from the main loop to the receiver at a more reasonable impedance match.

The coupling loop is usually untuned, but in some designs a tuning capacitor (C2) is placed in series with the coupling loop. Because there are many fewer turns on the coupling loop than the main loop, its inductance is considerably

smaller. As a result, the capacitance to resonate is usually much larger. In several loop antennas constructed for purposes of researching this chapter, I found that a 15-turn main loop resonated in the AM BCB with a standard 365 pF capacitor, but the two turn coupling loop required three sections of a ganged 3x365 pF capacitor connected in parallel to resonate at the same frequencies.

In several experiments, I used computer ribbon cable to make the loop turns. That type of cable consists of anywhere from eight to 64 parallel insulated conductors arranged in a flat ribbon shape. Properly interconnected (of which more later), the conductors of the ribbon cable form a continuous loop. It is no problem to take the outermost one or two conductors on one side of the wire array and use it for a coupling loop. In a couple of projects later in this chapter, you will see the use of both coupling loops and ribbon cable.

Tuning Schemes For Loop Antennas

Loop performance is greatly enhanced by tuning the inductance of the loop to the desired frequency. The bandwidth of the loop is reduced, which reduces front-end overload. Tuning also increases the signal level available to the receiver by a factor of 20 to 100 times. Although tuning can be a bother if the loop is installed remotely from the receiver, the benefits are well worth it in most cases.

There are several different schemes available for tuning, and these are detailed in Figure 11-6. The parallel tuning scheme, which is by far the most popular, is shown in Figure 11-6A. In this type of circuit, the capacitor (C1) is connected in parallel with the inductor, which in this case is the loop. Parallel resonant circuits have a very high impedance to signals on their resonant

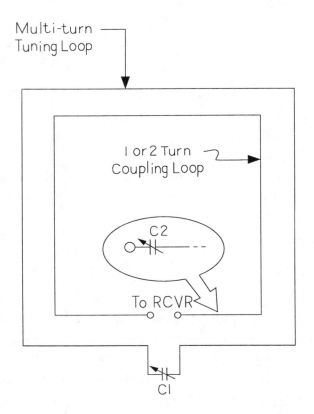

Figure 11-5

frequency, and a very low impedance to other frequencies. As a result, the voltage level of resonant signals is very much larger than the voltage level of off-frequency signals.

The series resonant scheme is shown in Figure 11-6B. In this circuit, the loop is connected in series with the capacitor. A property of series resonant circuits is that it offers a high impedance to all frequencies except the resonant frequency (exactly the opposite of the case of parallel resonant circuits). As a result, current from the signal will pass through the series resonant circuit at the resonant frequency, but off-frequency signals are blocked by the high impedance.

There is a wide margin for error in the inductance of loop antennas, and even the precise-looking equations to determine the required values of capacitance and inductance for proper tuning are actually only estimations. The exact geometry of the loop "as built" determines the actual inductance in each particular case. As a result, it is often the case that the tuning provided by the capacitor is not as exact as desired, so some form of compensation is needed. In some cases, the capacitance required for resonance is not easily available in a standard variable capacitor and some means must be provided for changing the capacitance. Figure 11-6C shows how this is done. The main tuning capacitor can be connected in either series or parallel with other capacitors to change the

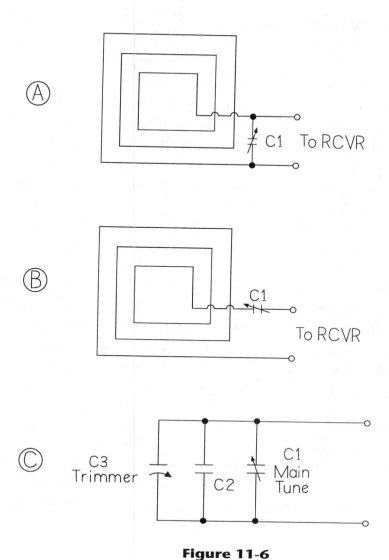

Figure 11-6

value. If the capacitors are connected in parallel, then the total capacitance is increased (all capacitances are added together). But if the extra capacitor is connected in series then the total capacitance is reduced. The extra capacitors can be switched in and out of a circuit to change frequency bands. I know one fellow who fancies listening to only two distant AM stations, one at 650 kHz and another at 780 kHz. He used screwdriver adjustable trimmer capacitors to tune the loop to those fixed frequencies. A switch selects which capacitor is in the circuit at any given time.

Tuning of a remote loop can be a bother if done by hand, so some means must be found to do it from the receiver location (unless you enjoy climbing into the attic or onto the roof). Traditional means of tuning called for using a low RPM DC motor, or stepper motor, to turn the tuning capacitor. A very popular combination was the little 1 to 12 RPM motors used to drive rotating displays in retail store show windows. But that approach is not really needed today. We can use varactor voltage variable capacitance diodes to tune the circuit.

A varactor works because the junction capacitance of the diode is a function of the applied reverse bias voltage. A high voltage (such as 30 volts) drops the capacitance while a low voltage increases it. Varactors are available with maximum capacitances of 22, 33, 60, 100, and 400 pF. The latter are of most interest to us because they have the same range as the tuning capacitors normally used with loops. Look for service shop replacement diodes intended for use in AM broadcast band radios. A good selection, which I have used, is the NTE-618 device. It produces a high capacitance > 400 pF, and a low of only a few picofarads over a range of 0 to 15 volts.

Figure 11-7 shows how a remote tuning scheme can work with loop antennas. The tuning capacitor is a combination of a varactor diode and two optional capacitors: a fixed capacitor (C1) and a trimmer (C2). The DC tuning voltage (V_t) is provided from the receiver end from a fixed DC power supply (V+). A potentiometer (R1) is used to set the voltage to the varactor, hence also to tune the loop. A DC blocking capacitor (C3) keeps the DC tuning voltage from being shorted out by the receiver input circuitry.

The "Embroiderloop"

Fashioning the loop is usually a bit of a chore, and winding even a dozen or so turns on a large form can be daunting—especially since the turns keep falling off the form. I hit upon an idea that allowed me to make a multi-turn transformer loop in which the tuned loop (L1) has 14 turns, and the receiver coupling loop is two turns. The loop is made of 16-conductor color-coded ribbon cable of the sort used by computerniks. Two wires in the center of the bundle (grey and white) are used for L2, while all the rest are used for L1. The form is a 14-inch

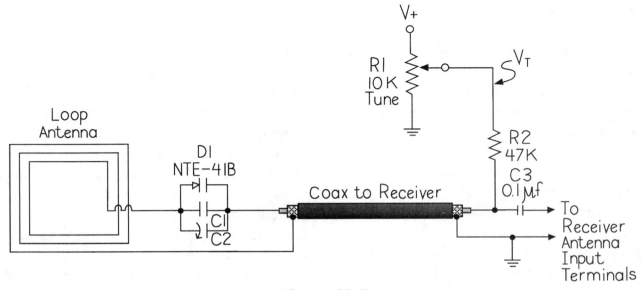

Figure 11-7

embroidery or needlepoint hoop which I bought from a craft store for $1.49. It consists of two concentric, close-fitting wooden hoops. The inner hoop is continuous, while the outer hoop is broken at one point. A screw and two tabs holds the ends together and adjust for size. In embroidery, the fabric is placed between the two hoops and secured with the screw; in our loop antenna, the 16-conductor ribbon cable is sandwiched into the space between inner and outer hoops as shown in Figure 11-8. The conductors of the cable are cross-connected in the manner shown in Figure 11-9 to form one continuous coil.

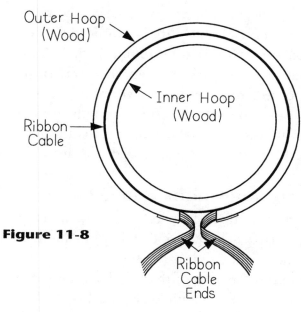

Figure 11-8

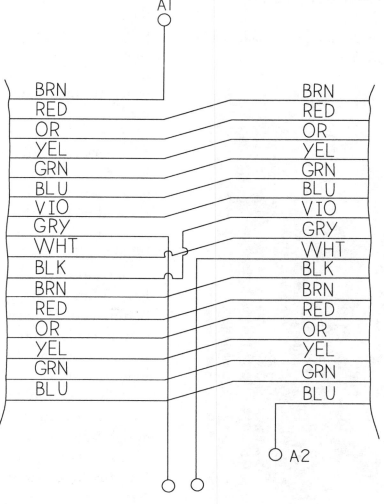

Figure 11-9   To RCVR

The inner loop is connected to a length of coaxial cable, which carries signal to the radio receiver. The outer loop is connected to a variable tuning capacitor. I found that a 365 pF "broadcast band variable" capacitor was sufficient to tune the loop in all sections of the AM band. But two or three 365 pF sections may be needed in some cases where fewer turns are used. Figure 11-10 shows the completed loop antenna.

The Square Hobby Board Loop

A very common way to build a square loop antenna is to take two pieces of thin lumber, place them in a cross shape, and then wind the wire around the ends of the wooden arms. This type of antenna is shown in Figure 11-11. The wooden supports can be made of 1x2 lumber, or some other stock. A test loop made while researching this book was made with two

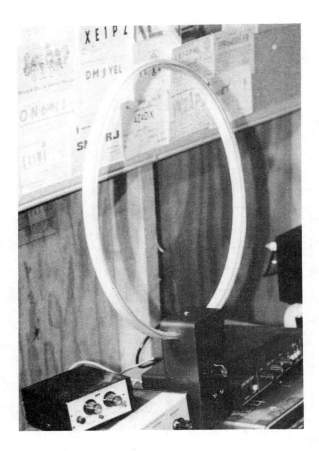

⅛x3x24-inch Bass wood "hobby board" stock acquired from a local hobby shop. Model builders use this wood as a stronger alternative to balsa wood.

The electrical circuit of the Hobby Board Loop shown in Figure 11-11 is a transformer loop design. The main tuned loop is on the outside and consists of ten turns of #26 enameled wire. It is tuned by a 365 pF capacitor. The inner loop is used for coupling to the receiver and consists of a single turn of #22 insulated solid hook-up wire.

The mechanical fit between the vertical and horizontal wooden pieces is shown in Figure 11-12. Note that four ½-inch wooden blocks (also obtained at the hobby shop) are glued to the junction of the two cross pieces in order to stiffen the joint. Details for the boards are shown in Figure 11-13. Each board is 24 inches long. At the mid-point (12"), there is a ⅛-inch wide, 1½-inch long slot cut. These slots are used to mate the two boards together.

At each end there are ten tiny slits made by a jeweler's saw (also called a "jig saw" in hobbyist circles) with a thin blade. These slits are just wide enough to allow a single #26 wire to be inserted without slipping. The slits are ¼-inch long, start ½-inch from one edge, and are ⅛-inch apart. There are ten slits on both ends of the horizontal piece while the vertical piece has ten slits on the top end and 11 slits on the bottom end. The reason for offsetting the wire slits is to allow room on the other side of the 3-inch width of the vertical member for a mounting stick.

When assembling the antenna, use wood glue on the mating surfaces, square them to be at right angles to each other, and clamp the two pieces in a vice or with C-clamps for 30 minutes (or longer if the glue maker specifies). Next, glue the support blocks into place and clamp them for a similar period.

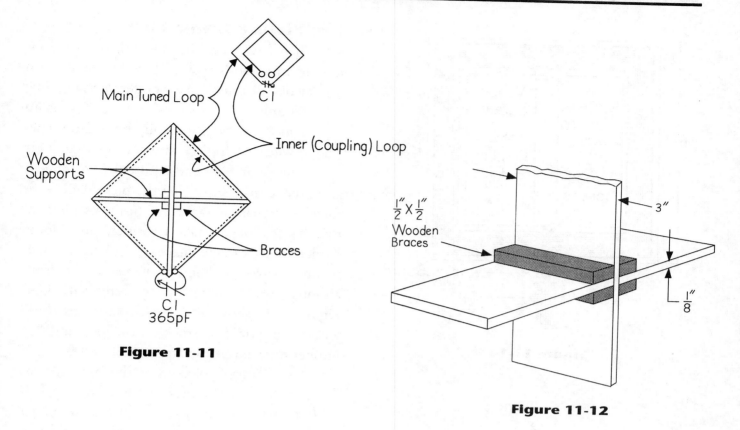

Main Tuned Loop

Inner (Coupling) Loop

Wooden Supports

Braces

C1
365pF

Figure 11-11

$\frac{1}{2}'' \times \frac{1}{2}''$ Wooden Braces

3"

$\frac{1}{8}''$

Figure 11-12

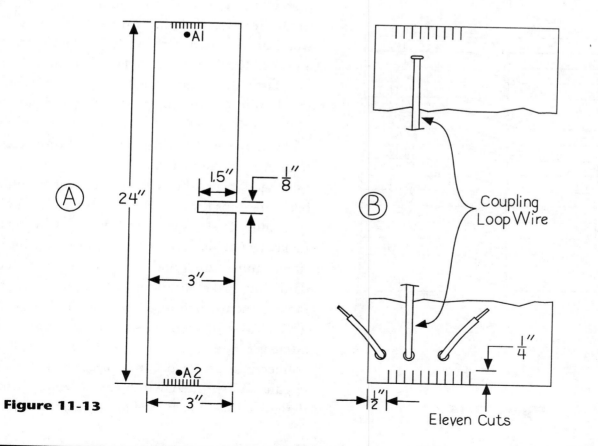

(A)

•A1

24"

1.5"

$\frac{1}{8}''$

3"

•A2

3"

Figure 11-13

(B)

Coupling Loop Wire

$\frac{1}{4}''$

$\frac{1}{2}''$

Eleven Cuts

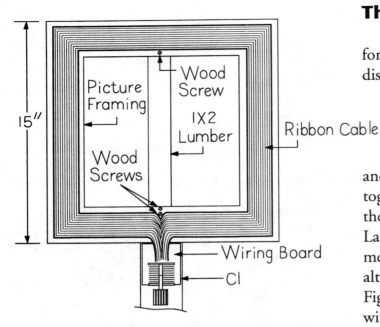

Figure 11-14

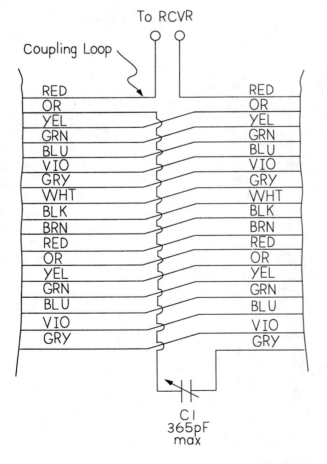

Figure 11-15

The Picture Frame Loop

When I went to buy the embroidery loops for the antenna discussed above, I ran across a display of raw, unfinished wooden picture frame lumber. These sticks came in lengths up to 15 inches long and about 2½ inches wide. Each piece of wood is cut at a 45° angle at each end, and cut in a tongue-and-groove manner so that the pieces can be fit together to make a frame. If four pieces are used, then it's possible to make a 15-inch square loop. Larger loops can be made (in 15-inch increments) by connecting the pieces end-to-end, although the 15-inch variety seems sufficient. Figure 11-14 shows a square loop antenna made with picture framing stock for the loop and 1x2 lumber for the vertical support.

The antenna is made using the same kind of color-coded 16-conductor computer ribbon cable that was used in the Embroiderloop. 15 turns were used as the multi-turn loop while one turn was used as a coupling loop to carry signal to the receiver. The flat ribbon cable and the wood are smeared with wood contact cement, and then the cable is pressed onto the wood and held fast with clamps. The first loop of this type that I built used ordinary wood glue and did not hold the wire well. As a substitute, I held the cable to the wood with ordinary thumb tacks (one every three inches or so). The types that I used had a plastic body, which reduces coupling between loops through the tack head.

Figure 11-15 shows the wiring scheme to make the parallel ribbon cable conductors into a single, multi-turn loop. The color scheme is standard, but make sure that your cable is of the same standard before relying on the diagram. The idea is to connect each conductor to its adjacent conductor at the feedpoint. The connections are made on a piece of integrated circuit (IC) printed wiring prototyping board designed for DIP ICs. This comes in several

Figure 11-16

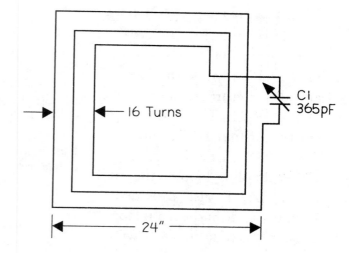

Figure 11-17

varieties, most of which are suitable.

Details of the connections board, less a shielded enclosure, are shown in Figure 11-16.

The Sports Fan's Loop

OK, sports fans, what do you do when the best game of the week is broadcast only on a low-powered AM station…and you live at the outer edge of their service area where the signal strength leaves much to be desired? You use the Sports Fan's Loop antenna, that's what! I first learned of this antenna from a friend of mine, a professional broadcast engineer, who worked at a religious radio station that had a pipsqueek signal but lots of fans. It really works…*one might say it's a miracle.*

The basic idea is to build a 16-turn, 24-inch square tuned loop (Figure 11-17) and then place the AM portable radio at the center (Figure 11-18) so that its loopstick is aimed so that its null end is broadside of the loop (Figure 11-19). When you do so, the nulls of both the loop and the loopstick are in the same direction. The signal will be picked up by the loop and then coupled to the radio's loopstick antenna. Sixteen-conductor ribbon cable can be used for making the loop. For an extra touch of class,

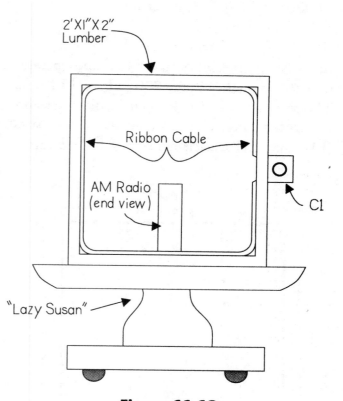

Figure 11-18

place the antenna and radio assembly on a dining room table "Lazy Susan" to make rotation easier. A 365 pF tuning capacitor is used to resonate the loop. If you listen to only one station, then this capacitor can be a trimmer type.

The FerriLoop Antenna

The circuit for the Ferri-Loop antenna is shown in Figure 11-20, while the mechanical structure is shown in Figure 11-21. The main loop consists of four ferrite core inductors, L1A/L1B, L2, L3, and L4. A coupling loop to the receiver (L5) is also provided. Each inductor in the main loop consists of ten turns of #24 wire wound over a section of ¾-inch PVC plumbing that contains an Amidon R61-050-750 ferrite rod. The rod is made of nickel-zinc "type-61" ferrite material that has a permeability (μ) of 125, and operates over the frequency range 200 kHz to 15 MHz. The size of the rod is ½ inch in diameter and 7½ inches long. Coil L1 consists of two parts (L1A and L1B), each consisting of five turns,

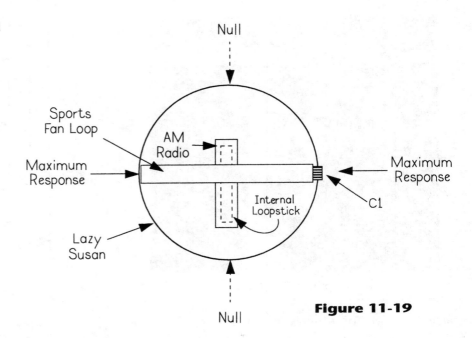

Figure 11-19

spaced apart sufficiently to insert the "Tee" connector (see Figure 11-21).

Note the coupling scheme. This allows us to couple the antenna to the receiver or a preamplifier without additional external circuitry.

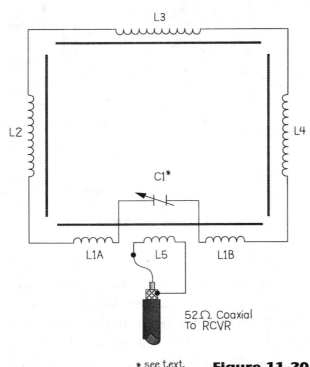

* see text   **Figure 11-20**

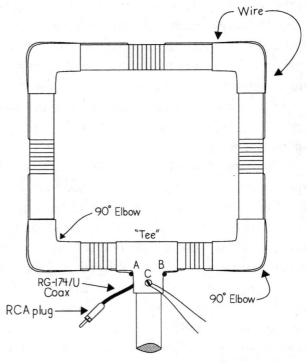

Figure 11-21

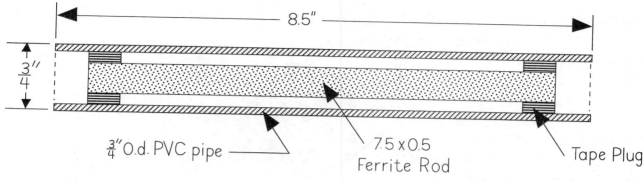

8.5"

3/4"

3/4" O.d. PVC pipe

7.5 x 0.5
Ferrite Rod

Tape Plug

Figure 11-22

Coil L5 acts as a transformer secondary to the main loop, and it supplies the output signal from the loop. It worked well directly to a receiver through 52 Ω coaxial cable, but a pre-amplifier is nonetheless highly recommended.

Construction of the FerriLoop

The construction of three of the arms of the FerriLoop antenna is shown in Figure 11-22. An 8½-inch long section of ¾-inch PVC plumbing pipe is cut and the burrs trimmed off the ends. The ferrite rod will not fit snugly inside the pipe, so the ends must be built up with masking or electrical tape to form a tape plug. How many turns of tape are required depends on the thickness of the tape you use. With the 3M brand black electrical tape that I used, 13 turns were sufficient to allow a snug slip-fit that held the rod but did not require excess force to insert it. You might find it advisable to plug the ends of the PVC pipe with wood glue or some other substance to further improve the stability of the rod inside the loop.

The section containing the Tee piece (refer again to Figure 11-21) is broken into two segments of PVC pipe, each 3½ inches long, placed on either side of the Tee piece. Four small holes (I used a 3/16-inch bit) are drilled into the Tee at the points shown in Figure 11-21 (holes A, B and C are shown; D is at the same point as C on the opposite side of the Tee).

Before assembling the Tee piece segment, it is necessary to wind the coupling loop (L5). This coil is wound directly on the ferrite rod and not on the PVC pipe (Figure 11-23). It consists of four turns of #24 wire in the center of the ferrite rod. Before winding L5, place a single layer of electrical tape at the point on the rod where the coil will be wound and for a distance about one inch either side. Anchor one end of the wire (with a second piece of tape) at the point where the coil will start, and then wind four turns. The turns are wound so that each wire touches its neighbor. When the four turns are wound, anchor the other end of the wire with another piece of electrical tape.

Next, prepare a length of RG-174/U coaxial cable. This cable is 52 Ω coax, but is about half the size of RG-58/U so is easy to use in applications such as this antenna. Strip off the outer insulation and unbraid the shield. Then twist the unbraided shield tightly, and tin with solder to keep the strands from straying. Strip off about a ¼-inch of the inner insulator to expose the inner conductor. Tin the inner conductor and then solder it to one end of coil L5; solder the other end of L5 to the shield of the coaxial cable. After the entire assembly is finished, place a single turn of electrical tape over all connections to further secure them. Be careful not to build up the layer so much that it won't slip into the Tee junction.

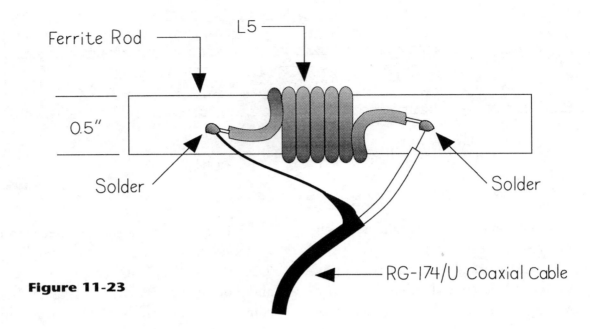

Figure 11-23

To assemble the bottom portion of the antenna, gather together the two 3½-inch sections of PVC pipe, the Tee junction, and the ferrite rod. Insert one end of the ferrite rod into one of the PVC pipe pieces until it is about ½-inch from the far end. Next, insert the coaxial cable through hole "D" in the Tee junction and then pull some cable through to the outside (*gently!*). As you do this operation, slide the Tee over the ferrite rod until L5 is centered inside the Tee. Pull all of the excess coax out so that only enough is left to prevent strain on the electrical connections. Finally, place the other piece of PVC pipe over the ferrite rod and secure both ends of the assembly with wood glue or other "potting" substance.

At this point, you should have three arms containing rods 2, 3, and 4 plus a bottom section containing rod 1 and the Tee section. These sections are assembled into a square by using 90° PVC elbow junctions at the corners (refer again to Figure 11-21). Each elbow is scored from one end to the other on the outer surface, with a triangle or flat file to form a "Vee" shaped wire groove.

The loop will tend to flex and become misshapen unless the pieces are glued together. After you assemble the unit to make sure all sizes are correct and it will actually fit together properly, disassemble each joint and coat the ¾-inch PVC pipe ends with wood glue. You should use a glue that takes a few minutes to set up (I used Elmer's wood glue) so that the antenna can be adjusted. Lay the glued assembly on a flat surface and square the corners in all planes. Leave it sitting there undisturbed until the glue is cured.

Now it's time to add the main loop. For this operation we need about ten feet of #24 wire. I used regular solid insulated hook-up wire, but you might want to use enameled magnet wire instead. Pass one end of the wire through hole "A" from the outside towards the inside, and then pass it out the bottom of the Tee so that there is about eight inches of free wire. Anchor this wire temporarily with electrical tape. Next, wind coil L1A, securing it on either end with electrical tape. Pass the far end of the wire over the first elbow joint (so that the wire lays in the vee groove), anchoring either end with tape, and then wind L2. Similarly, pass it over each elbow in succession, and wind each coil in a similar manner. Always anchor each end of each coil with tape to keep the thing all together. Finally, wind L1B and pass the loose end of the wire through hole "B" and trim to the same size as the other end.

Figure 11-24 shows the detail of the lower end of the loop and its wiring, while Figure 11-25 shows the completed loop. Note that the rest of the PVC pipe was used as a handle and mount for the tuning capacitor. (Not shown in this view is the small aluminum shielded box that I used for the preamplifier that I eventually added to the circuit.)

The main loop is resonated by capacitor C1. I found that the antenna would resonate in the bands just below the 80-meter ham band when a 365 pF variable capacitor was used for C1. To resonate in the AM broadcast band (550 to 1600 kHz), it was necessary to use a three-section variable, where each section was 365 pF, and all three sections were connected in parallel. It is reasonable to experiment with the number of turns needed in each coil to change the resonance scheme. Fewer turns will raise the resonant frequency while more turns reduce it for any given capacitance. If you are inclined to experiment, then try as few as two turns per coil and as many as you like.

The resonant frequency of the loop antenna can be checked either on-the-air with a receiver equipped with an S-meter or by using a signal generator (the best approach). Temporarily wrap about four turns of hook-up wire around one arm of the loop to form a "gimmick" for the signal generator. The output cable of an RF signal generator is connected to the gimmick. I found that just connecting the "hot" lead alligator clip to one end of the gimmick gave enough signal, but if not then connect both the hot and ground clips to opposite ends of the gimmick. An oscilloscope or receiver connected across

Figure 11-24

Figure 11-25

L5 will show the RF signal output. With an ordinary "service-grade" RF signal generator running at about half the maximum output level, I found signal levels of more than 100 mV at 550 kHz across L5 with my oscilloscope.

Shielded Loop Antennas

The loop antennas discussed thus far in this chapter have all been unshielded types. Unshielded loops work well under most circumstances, but in some cases their pattern is distorted by interaction with the ground and nearby structures (trees, buildings, etc.). In my own tests, trips to a nearby field proved necessary to measure the depth of the null because of interaction with the aluminum siding on my house. Figure 11-26 shows two situations. In Figure 11-26A, we see the pattern of the normal "free-space" loop, i.e., a perfect figure-8 pattern. But when the loop interacts with the nearby environment, the pattern distorts. In Figure 11-26B we see some filling of the notch for a moderately distorted pattern. Some interactions are so severe that the pattern is distorted beyond all recognition.

The solution to the problem is to reduce interaction by shielding the loop, as in Figure 11-27. Loop antennas operate on the magnetic component of the electromagnetic wave, so the loop can be shielded against voltage signals and electrostatic interactions. In order to prevent harming the ability to pick up the magnetic field, a gap is left in the shield at one point.

There are several ways to shield a loop. You can, for example, wrap the loop in adhesive-backed copper foil tape. Alternatively, you can wrap the loop in aluminum foil and hold it together with tape. Another method is to insert the loop inside a copper or aluminum tubing frame. Or…the list seems endless. Perhaps one of the most popular methods is to use coaxial cable to make a large single turn loop. Figure 11-28 shows this type of loop made with RG-8/U

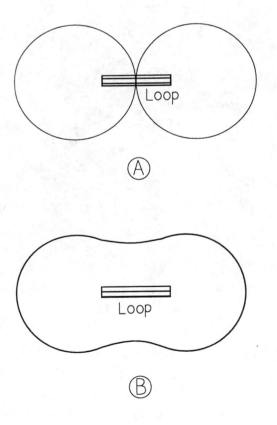

Figure 11-26

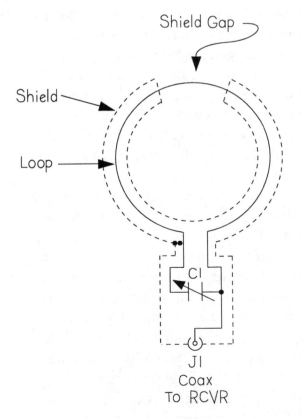

Figure 11-27

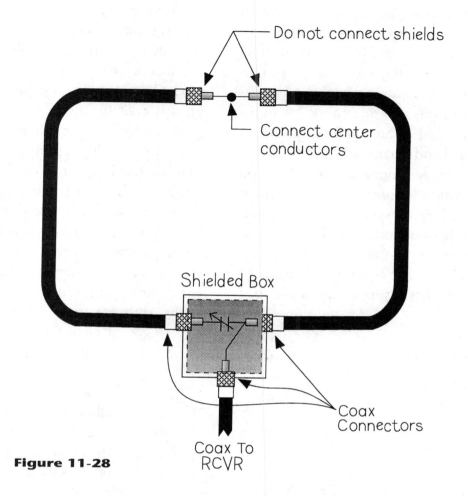

Figure 11-28

or RG-11/U coaxial cable. The cable is normally supported by wooden cross arms, as in the other forms of loop, but they are not shown here for sake of simplicity. Note that, at the upper end, the coaxial cable shields are not connected.

Shortwave Performance Enhancer Loop Antennas

Small portable shortwave radios are not always the best performers, although they work better today than ever in the past. Nevertheless, they are severely "antenna limited." In most cases, the only antenna is a small telescoping whip extending from the case of the radio. Attempts to put up random length wire antennas of large size will help, but will destroy all of the porta-

bility and may cause overload of the receiver front-end circuitry.

Another problem with shortwave reception, whether using a portable radio or a AC powered radio, is due to the nature of ionospheric shortwave propagation. When signals are refracted in the ionosphere, their components tend to spread out, causing the signal to arrive at different angles of arrival at different times. As the dynamic ionosphere changes, the angle of arrival changes. These changes can occur over the course of a few minutes. Common loop antennas aimed at the desired station are reasonably insensitive to changes of elevation angle of arrival, but their null is essentially a point-source notch. The solution to the problem is to build antennas with a fan-shaped, adjustable null with reasonable insensitivity to the vertical angle. This class of antenna, popularized by Villard, includes the single-turn, low-inductance wide loop. This trick is seen in a lot of antenna books and magazine articles, and was also told to me by a missionary who worked in Sudan. This guy was a Swedish national and a ham radio operator, and in the course of a three hour evening at Wheaton College taught me a lot of smoke about "antennaing" under bad circumstances and at low budget. Some of his antennas are found in the emergency antennas chapter of my other antlers book, *Radio Antenna Handbook* published by TAB/McGraw-Hill. (Buy two copies please, I need the money.)

A clever and simple-to-build antenna of this class is shown in Figure 11-29. This loop antenna calls for a 30-inch single turn square loop antenna made from three-inch wide sheet metal stock. The metal can be copper, aluminum, or brass as available (not aluminum if you want to solder to it). A gap is left at one end to accommodate the tuning capacitor, C1. This capacitor must be relatively large, on the order of 750 to 1200 pF. This capacitance can be accommodated by two-section and three-section AM broadcast band variable capacitors of 365 pF per section (some capacitors, intended for superheterodyne radios, have two sections that are different capacitances). On the same side of the loop as the gap there are four 5/32-inch holes (A, B, C, and D) drilled to accommodate mounting the loop to a 1x2 wooden piece or other suitable support. A wire that is equipped with an alligator clip is attached to the loop, and this clip will be connected to the telescopic antenna on the portable radio. In operation, the loop can be oriented for best reception.

Another example is the antenna designed by Villard as shown in Figure 11-30. This antenna is made of wide metal conductors. Examples include the same type of hobbyist's brass stock as used above. It can also be copper foil or some other stock that can be soldered. Some electronic parts stores sell adhesive backed foil stock used for making printed circuit boards. The foil can be glued to some flat insulating surface. Although ⅜-inch plywood springs to mind immediately, another alternative is found in artists' supplies stores. Ordinary poster board is too floppy to stand up, but poster board

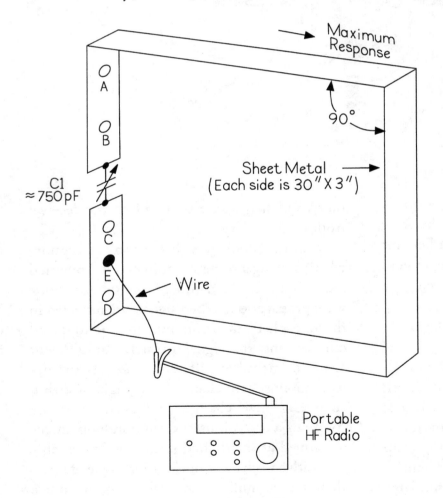

Figure 11-29

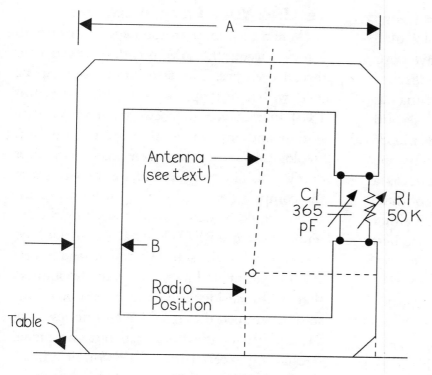

Figure 11-30

(four inches), then the inductance increases and only 28 pF are needed at 15 MHz. The larger size loop can be used at lower frequencies as well. For example, the 91 cm loop will resonate at 6 MHz with 177 pF.

To use this antenna, position the radio's telescopic antenna close and adjacent to the loop *but not touching it.* The loop antenna can be rotated to find the best position to either null or enhance a particular station. The "Lazy Susan" idea will work well in this case.

A traditional method is shown in Figure 11-31. These antennas consist of two small loops spaced d < λ/4 apart, but not too close. The version in Figure 11-32A consists of two

glued to a Styrofoam backing can be used. It is extremely easy to work with using X-acto knives and other common household tools.

Two controls are used on this antenna. Capacitor C1 tunes the loop to the resonant frequency of the desired station. Potentiometer R1 is used as a phasing control. The dimensions of the antenna are not terribly critical, although some guidelines are in order. In the Villard article, he recommended a 40 cm (15.75-inch) square loop ("A"). If the loop is 7.62 cm (three inches) wide, the antenna will resonate at 15 MHz with around 33 pF of capacitance. If the dimensions are increased to A = 91 cm (36 inches) and B = 10.16 cm

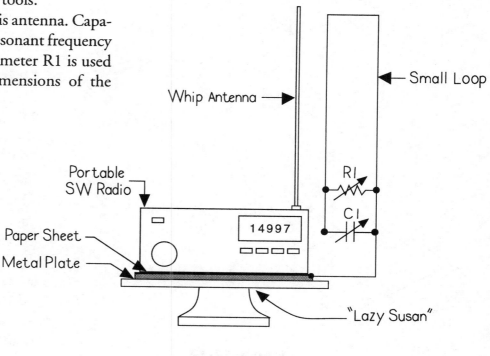

Figure 11-31

vertical coaxial loops (the loops are on the same axis, not that they are made of coaxial cable). This antenna is less sensitive to skywave error than single loops, but at the expense of changing the pattern. This style of antenna has a four lobe "cloverleaf" pattern. The second class of antenna is the horizontal coplanar loops of Figure 11-32B. This antenna retains the figure-8 pattern for $d < \lambda/4$, and produces a minimal elevation skywave error. Both of these antennas can be mechanically rotated in either azimuth or elevation in order to find the best reception conditions.

Testing Your Loop Antenna

When each loop prototype was completed, I tested it on the AM broadcast band over several evenings. The same procedure can be used with any loop. A strong local signal at 1310 kHz served to check the pattern. The station and my home were located on U.S. Geological Survey 7.5-minute quadrangle maps of my area. The maps had adjacent coverage, so the compass bearing from my location to the station could be determined. Checking the antenna showed an S7/S8 signal when the loop was endwise to the station—that is, the station was in one of its lobes. Rotating the loop so that its broadside faced the direction of the station dropped the signal strength to less than S1, and frequently bottomed out the meter. Because my receiver has a 3-dB/S-unit calibration on the S-meter, I figured the null to be more than 20 dB, although it will take a bit more experimentation to find the actual depth.

This test is best done during daylight hours, I found out, because there is always a residual sky wave cacophony on the AM band that raises the S-meter "floor" in the null.

Using a Loop Antenna

Most readers will use a loop for DXing rather than hidden transmitter hunting, navigation, or other RDF purposes. For the DXer, there are actually two uses for the loop. One is when you are a renter or live in a community that has routine covenants against outdoor antennas. In this situation, the loop will serve as an active antenna for receiving AM BCB and other low frequency signals without the neighbors or landlord becoming PFJs (purple-faced jerks).

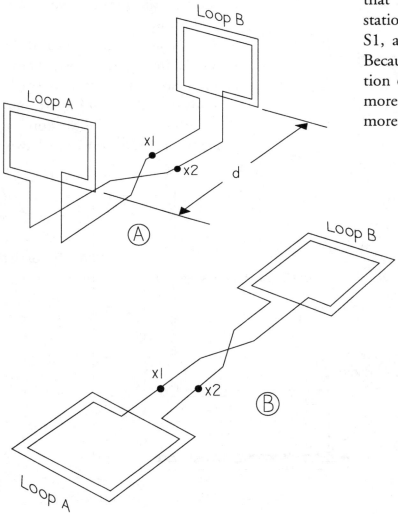

Figure 11-32

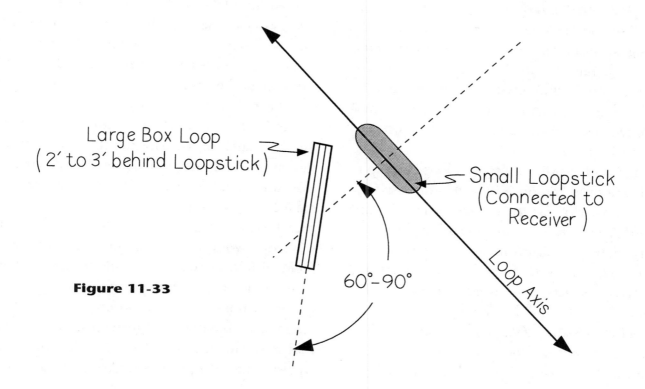

Large Box Loop
(2' to 3' behind Loopstick)

Small Loopstick
(Connected to
Receiver)

Loop Axis

60°–90°

Figure 11-33

The other use is illustrated by the case of a friend of mine. He regularly tunes in clear channel WSM (650 kHz, Nashville) in the wee hours between Saturday evening ("Grand Ole Opry" time) and dawn. However, that "clear" channel of WSM isn't really so clear, especially without a narrow filter in the receiver. He uses a loop antenna to null out a nearby 630 kHz signal that made listening a bit dicey, and can now tape his 1940s/1950s vintage country music.

It isn't necessary to place the desired station directly in the main lobes off the ends of the antenna, but rather place the nulls (broadside) in the direction of the offending station that you want to eliminate. So what happens if the offending station and the desired station are in a direct line with each other with your receiving location in the middle between them? Both nulls and lobes on a loop antenna are bidirectional, so a null on the offending station will

also null the desired station in the opposite direction.

One method is to use a sense antenna to spoil the pattern of the loop to a cardioid shape. Another method is to use a spoiler loop to null the undesired signal. The spoiler loop is a large box loop placed one to three feet (found experimentally) behind the reception loop in the direction of the offending signal. This method was first described by Levintow and is detailed in Figure 11-33. The small loopstick may be the antenna inside the receiver, while the large loop is a box loop such as the Sports Fan's Loop. The large box loop is placed about one to three feet behind the loopstick and in the direction of the offending station. The angle with respect to the line of centers should be 60° to 90°, which is also found experimentally. It's also possible to use two air core loops, such as those in Figures 11-8 and 11-14, to produce an *asymmetrical* receiving pattern.

Loop Preamplifiers

All small loop antennas produce a weak output signal, so a loop preamplifier is indicated for all but the most sensitive receivers. The preamplifier can be mounted either at the receiver or the antenna, but it is most effective when mounted at the antenna (unless the coax to the receiver is short).

Figure 11-34 shows a typical loop preamplifier based on common NPN silicon transistors. The transistor for this application is the 2N5179, but they are a bit hard to locate at many hobbyist electronic parts distributors. There are, however, suitable substitutes from the service replacement transistor manufacturers such as ECG and NTE. The direct crossover is the NTE-316 and ECG-316 devices. I had to order these from my local distributor, so in the meantime I successfully used the NTE-108

(similar to ECG-108) device which they did have in stock. The amplifier produced an average gain of about 15 dB across the AM broadcast band, although it had higher gain at the upper end than at the lower end.

The circuit for the preamplifier shown in Figure 11-34 is relatively straightforward, except for the matching transformer T1. This transformer is a balun device that you wind yourself. Use Amidon TF-37-61 or TF-50-61 ferrite toroidal cores. The winding is bifilar #26 enameled wire. I used 12 turns on a TF-37-61 form, which seemed to work well. You might want to experiment with this circuit by varying the number of turns with changes of frequency.

Balun transformers are wound in the bifilar manner, as mentioned above. Just what does that mean in this case? It means that the two wires used for the primary and secondary wind-

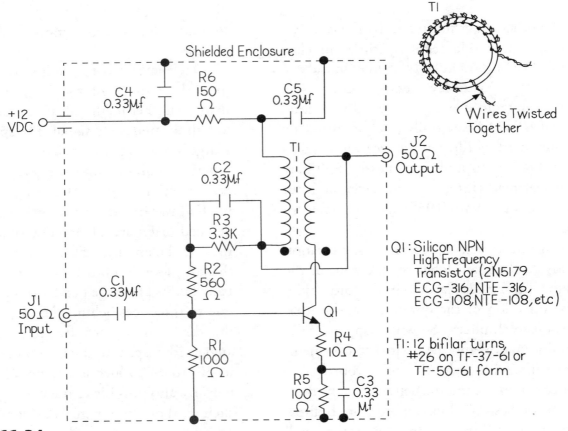

Figure 11-34

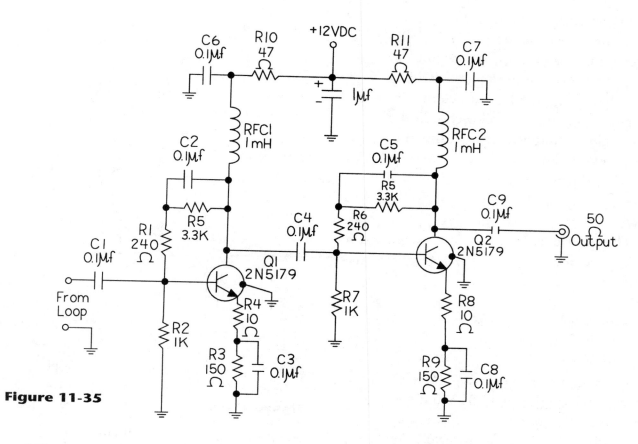

Figure 11-35

ings of T1 are twisted together, about eight twists to the inch, and then wound over the form as if they were a single wire. I make twisted enameled wire for baluns by taking a length of #26 enamel insulated wire, folding it back on itself, and then chucking it up in a hand drill. Anchor the far end in a vise, and then turn the crank on the drill to twist the wire. This operation can be done on an electrical drill, if the drill has a gentle trigger and speed control, but can be <u>DANGEROUS</u>. If you do this operation, then wear safety goggles or glasses to protect your eyesight. If that wire comes loose and starts whipping around, it could damage your eyes.

A related amplifier circuit is shown in Figure 11-35. This circuit also uses the 2N5179 transistor, or its service grade replacements. The amplifier consists of two identical stages, each of which provides 10 dB of gain. Up to four

stages can be cascaded for 40 dB of gain, although one must be cautious to observe good layout practices in such a case (inadvertent feedback can cause oscillation when gains are high).

The amplifier of Figure 11-35 is useful at full specification gain from about 1 MHz throughout the shortwave bands. At lower frequencies, gain will drop off somewhat, but that doesn't necessarily mean that it becomes useless. Besides, you can make certain modifications that will coax (that's "coax," not "co-ax" like the transmission line!) a little more gain out of the circuit at VLF frequencies. For example, all of the coupling and decoupling capacitors (that is, every one but C2 and C5) can be increased in value to accommodate lower frequencies. I noticed a bit more gain by using 0.47 μF instead of 0.1 μF for those capacitors. You can also increase the values of the RF chokes (RFC1 and RFC2) from 1 mH to 2.5 mH.

The circuits of Figures 11-36 and 11-37 are based on the junction field effect transistor (JFET); the circuit of Figure 11-36 is a common gate design, while that of Figure 11-37 is a common drain design (a "source follower"). Both are broadband amplifier circuits and can be used throughout the HF spectrum as well as VLF and MW.

The particular JFET specified for these circuits is the MPF-102, a device that works well into the VHF region. Suitable replacements from the service shop lines of devices include the ECG-312 and the NTE-312. Because the application is not terribly critical, and the devices are not expensive, it is reasonable to experiment with other JFET devices if they are more readily available than those selected here.

All of the preamplifier circuits in this section can be used with either tuned or untuned loops, although neither the loop nor the tuning capacitor are shown in all cases.

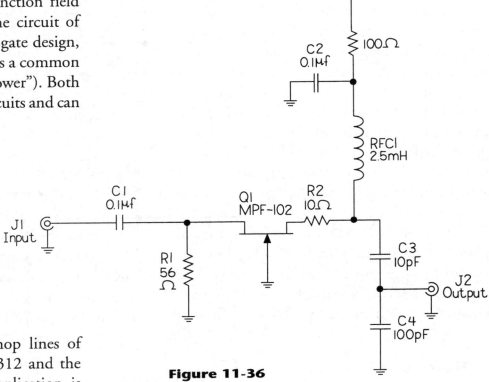

Figure 11-36

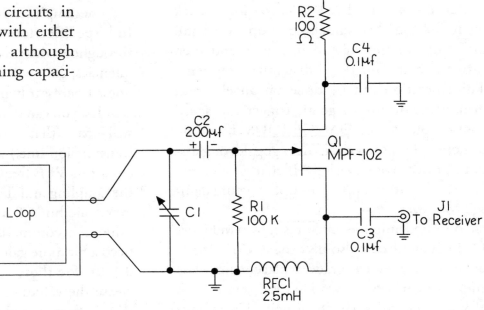

Figure 11-37

Sharpening the Loop

Many years ago the *Q-multiplier* was a popular add-on accessory for a communications receiver. These devices were sold as Heathkits and many construction projects were seen in magazines and amateur radio books. The Q-multiplier has the effect of seeming to greatly increase the sensitivity of a receiver, as well as greatly reducing the bandwidth of the front-end. Thus, it allows better reception of some stations because of increased sensitivity and narrowed bandwidth.

A Q-multiplier is an active electronic circuit placed at the antenna input of a receiver. It is essentially an Armstrong oscillator, as shown in Figure 11-38, that doesn't quite oscillate. These circuits have a tuned circuit (L1/C1) at the input of an amplifier stage, and a feedback coupling loop (L3). The degree of feedback is controlled by the coupling between L1 and L3. The coupling is varied both by varying how close the two coils are, and their relative orientation with respect to each other. Certain other circuits use a series potentiometer in the L3 side that controls the amount of feedback.

The Q-multiplier is adjusted to the point that the circuit is just on the verge of oscillating, but not quite. As the feedback is backed away from the threshold of oscillation, but not too far, the narrowing of bandwidth occurs as does the increase in sensitivity. It takes some skill to operate a Q-multiplier, but it is easy to use once you get the hang of it and is a terrific accessory for any loop antenna.

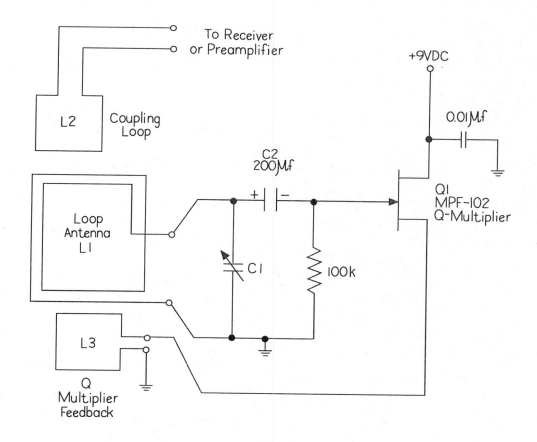

Figure 11-38

CHAPTER 12

Low Frequency Antennas

The low frequency (below 6 MHz) antenna is a Particularly Perplexing Problem (dare we call it a "P³"???) for most people. There is a large amount of interesting DX on the low frequencies (which we'll define as near DC to about 6 MHz or so). Unfortunately, many of the wonderful antennas that I've discussed in this book are "as useless as teats on a boar hog…" (to coin a phrase) on low frequencies because of one little problem: they're too darn big. The size of resonant antennas varies inversely with frequency, so we can expect low frequency antlers to be a mighty assemblies indeed. Consider the ubiquitous (that's a fancy word for "seen everywhere") half-wavelength dipole. A 6 MHz dipole is a reasonable 78 feet long. But in the marine radiotelephone band (e.g., 2182 kHz), the dipole antenna becomes 215 feet long, and in the middle of the AM broadcast band (1 MHz or 1000 kHz) it becomes 468 feet long. On 1600 kHz, at the top end of the AM broadcast band, the dipole is 293 feet long and wants to be at least as high. On the low end of the AM band—550 kHz—the dipole becomes 850 feet long and its ideal $\lambda/2$ mounting height would look down on the Washington Monument (555 feet tall, provided it has stopped sinking like the dollar) from a height of nearly 300 feet.

The dipole antenna should be installed half-wavelength above the ground, or about as high as it is long. An AM broadcast band dipole, cut for midband, would require two Washington Monuments, spaced their own height apart, to support the optimal half-wavelength dipole. Or maybe two hot air balloons could be used to support the dipole (properly connected to a herd of cows to supply the methane needed for the burner, of course). And a vertical antenna is no less problematic. Quarter-wavelength vertical antennas would rapidly become too high for easy or economical construction, and would be illegal under existing zoning and engineering regulations in most locations. And while the Beverage is always a good bet if you own a farm or have some mighty tolerant neighbors, its 600 to 1500 foot length reduces its appeal and practicality for most people.

There are any number of other reasons why conventional half- and quarter-wavelength antennas become less and less practical as the operating frequency decreases, but those given above are probably sufficiently depressing to render you senseless. Let's press on and prevent a generalized *weltschmertz* from setting in. It is, after all, somewhat more rewarding to dwell on possibilities than on what can't be done.

Low frequency receiving systems depend in part on the propagation phenomena applicable to those frequencies and also to the practices of radio stations operating there. As the frequency drops, there is an increased tendency to see both a ground wave and a sky wave. In some situations, both may arrive at a distant receive site (although that is rare) and interfere with each other. When DXing the AM broadcast band, signals, especially on ground wave, tend to be vertically polarized. This is in contrast to higher frequencies where the polarization may be skewed by propagation conditions even though the signal started out as either horizontal or vertical.

Obvious Solutions

There are, fortunately, several obvious solutions that lend themselves well to the low frequency antenna problem. For SWLs, there are more solutions than for ham operators because some antennas, such as the small loop, are very good on receive but work poorly on transmit. Indeed, some ham operators operating on the 80- and 160-meter bands will use a small loop antenna on their receiver, mostly to null out interfering signals, and a dipole or other full sized antenna on transmit.

You might be well advised to consider a loop antenna because they work very well for low frequency reception while offering very deep nulls (for removing interference) that would otherwise require large—very large at low frequencies—arrays to otherwise achieve.

Another approach is to use a *loaded* antenna of one sort or another. These antennas are physically shorter than the full sized quarter-wave or half-wave antenna, and perform well enough to be quite useful. Do they perform as well as the full sized antennas? In a word: *heckno*. But when the decision is optimum performance versus any performance at all, then you might be enticed to try one of these compensation antennas. Besides, the correct comparison is between the compensation antenna and a random length wire of convenient size rather than an optimal antenna. The random length wire is, after all, the option that most people will otherwise select.

Loaded "Plumber's Delight" Vertical

We've seen in a previous chapter how vertical antennas can be constructed using PVC pipe to support the antenna wiring. The same technique can be used when building a low frequency antenna.

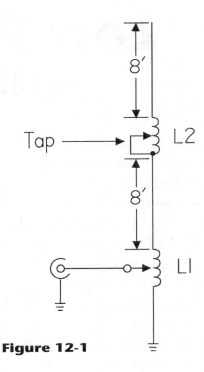

Figure 12-1

Figure 12-1 shows a typical low frequency antenna made from either a single 16-foot long thickwall section of PVC pipe, or two eight-foot sections coupled at the middle. There are two coils used in this antenna. Inductor L1 is used to impedance match the feedpoint of the antenna to the 50 Ω system impedance used by the receiver; a length of 52 Ω coaxial cable is used to connect the tap on this coil to the receiver. The other coil in Figure 12-1, L2, is a loading coil. Its use is to increase the effective length of the antenna. All antennas that are used on frequencies lower than their natural resonant frequency exhibit a capacitance, and this capacitance has a capacitive reactance. Inductive reactance will cancel capacitive reactance, so coil L2 is needed to "tune" the antenna to the operating frequency. For practical use in the 2 to 7 MHz band—assuming a two to three inch PVC pipe and two vertical runs of wire (#12, #14, or #16), each eight feet long—we can make L2 of 30 turns of #16 enameled wire closely wound. Tap the coil every five turns or so in order to find the exact inductance needed, and to accommodate different bands. A tap is made by scraping the enameled insulation off the wire at the correct point, and soldering the tap wire to it. Some authorities actually made a little loop of the wire used for the coil at that point to facilitate tapping.

Tuning the loaded vertical can be a little tricky if you are not equipped with proper instrumentation. The best way is to use a VSWR meter, dipper, a noise bridge, or some other instrument that is legal for SWLs to use (that is, it doesn't require a ham transmitter for RF excitation). Another way that's a little flaky but often works is to pick a strong station at a distance, on a frequency where you want to listen, and then find the correct tap by looking at the S-meter of the receiver. The maximum signal strength is theoretically found when the tap is correctly set. The reason this method is a bit flaky is that the changes are going to be very subtle—so subtle, in fact, that ordinary fading (and other variation) in the signal strength may easily be mistaken for the correct setting (or obscure the correct setting). For this reason, I recommend using an instrumentation approach. After all, if you're going to be active in the shortwave hobby, the price of the instrument will be justified over time.

Figure 12-2

Using a CB Whip On The Low Frequencies

Figure 12-2 shows two ways to use a nine foot CB whip antenna on low frequencies. One method is to treat it as a very short random length wire antenna, albeit in the vertical position, and use a reverse L-section antenna tuner to match the impedance to the 50 Ω used by the receiver. Typical values for the components will be 140 pF for the capacitor (C1) and 28 μH for the inductor (L1). These values can be increased or decreased if it is found that they are insufficient for any particular installation. If you buy an antenna tuner for this application, then select one that will match a high impedance to a low impedance, rather than a mere "line flattener" (typical of coax-to-coax tuners).

The method of Figure 12-2 does not actually resonate the antenna, but rather it matches the high impedance to the receiver system impedance. An alternative is to use a loading coil (see inset for Figure 12-2) to bring the antenna to resonance.

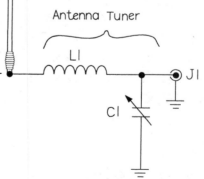

The coil can be mounted anywhere in the antenna, but typically it is located at either the base or in the middle (the latter position involves some mechanical problems that must be solved).

The value of the loading coil required varies somewhat depending on the details of the local environment where the antenna is installed, but a reasonable approximation is found from the curves in Figure 12-3. Two curves are shown, one each for base mounting and center mounting of the loading coil.

One of the nice features of this antenna is that it can be an indoor antenna, even in the attic of some houses, for those SWLs who live in neighborhoods with restrictions on building antennas.

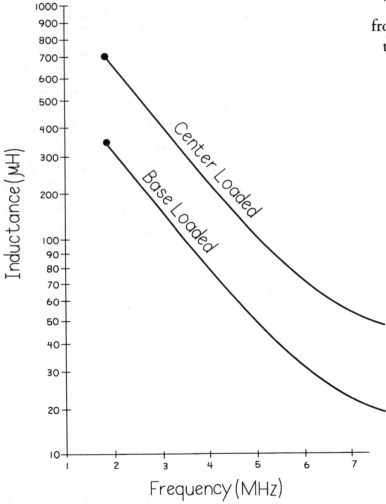

Loading Coil Inductance (μH) for 8' Whip

Figure 12-3

All-Band (More or Less) Shortwave/Low Frequency Antenna

Figure 12-4 shows a vertical antenna that can be used for nearly the entire shortwave spectrum from 2 to 30 MHz depending on the components selected. The 16-foot to 18-foot radiator element is either aluminum tubing, or PVC pipe fitted with wire (as described above). The entire length of the antenna should be vertical, although a single conductor "down-lead" to an antenna tuning unit close to the receiver can become part of its overall length.

The versatility of this antenna is derived from the tuning network at the base. This tuner can be placed at the receiver location, if a single wire feedline is used, but that is not the best solution "antenna wise" (even though it might be as a practical consideration).

The inductor should have a maximum value of 25 to 40 μH, and is tapped twice. One tap provides an impedance match to the receiver (50 Ω), while the other provides the correct loading inductance to make the antenna resonant on a low frequency. At these low frequencies, the switch is closed so the "cold" end of the coil is grounded. At higher frequencies, where the antenna length is close to or more than a quarter-wavelength, the switch is opened and the capacitor used to counteract some of the inductive reactance of the antenna and loading coil, effectively shortening the antenna. In those cases, the loading coil tap and the impedance matching tap may nearly or actually coincide.

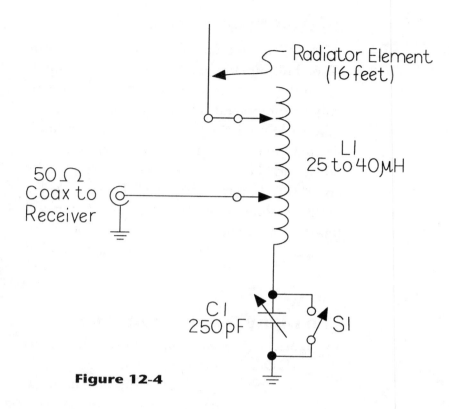

Figure 12-4

lead transmission line. Horizontal section "A" has a length of:

$$A = \frac{270}{F_{MHz}}$$

While length "B" is "A" multiplied by the velocity factor ("V") of the transmission line, which is typically 0.82 for 300 Ω twin-lead. The "B" section should be brought away from "A" at a right angle for as long a distance as possible. If the entire length cannot be accommodated at a right angle, then slope away the portion that cannot as gently as possible.

Note the arrangement of the feedpoint. One conductor of the "B" twin-lead is connected to 52 Ω coaxial cable to the receiver, while the other conductor is connected to ground.

The Twin-Lead Tee Antenna (TLTA)

Figure 12-5 shows a reasonably well performing antenna that is used typically in the 1 to 7 MHz region, although it will work at higher frequencies as well. The TLTA has been used by hams for dual coverage of either 160- and 80-meter bands, or the 80- and 40-meter bands. The TLTA antenna works on a design band where dimension "A" is approximately a quarter-wavelength and on a band that is one-half that frequency.

This antenna is made from 300 Ω television antenna twin-

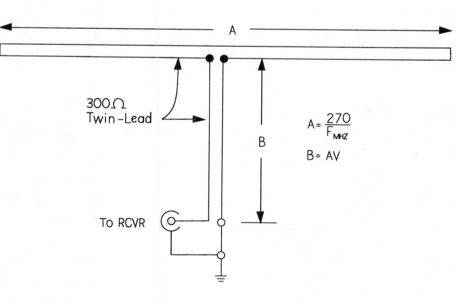

Figure 12-5

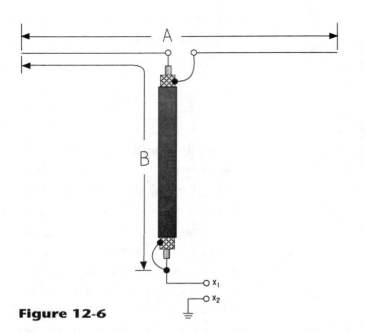

Figure 12-6

Coaxial "Tee" Antenna

A coaxial Tee antenna is shown in Figure 12-6. This antenna can be built from a dipole cut to the lowest frequency that you can physically accommodate at your location. For operation on lower frequencies, the coaxial cable is shorted (shield to inner conductor) at the receiver end. The cable then acts as a single wire downlead. At certain frequencies, however, the cable acts something like a "bazooka" balun and transforms a higher impedance to a lower impedance, making the antenna work somewhat better.

The Dippy Discone Antenna

Figure 12-7 shows a Dippy Discone Antenna (DDA; "dippy" because it's not quite as good as a full-sized discone antenna) that uses loading coils to make the different wire elements look longer than they really are.

The values of L1 through L4 are found experimentally, but the starting point is the loaded dipole inductance for the 50% point. Adjustment is difficult without a transmitter, but VSWR or feedpoint impedance is a good way to proceed.

An advantage of the DDA is that it provides an impedance transformation *upwards*—the feedpoint impedance is higher than the impedance of each individual element. The impedance transformation is equal to the square of the number of elements (N^2). In the configuration shown, there are five elements so the impedance transformation is 25:1. Thus, relatively short antennas (relative to received wavelength) can be accommodated without an antenna tuning unit.

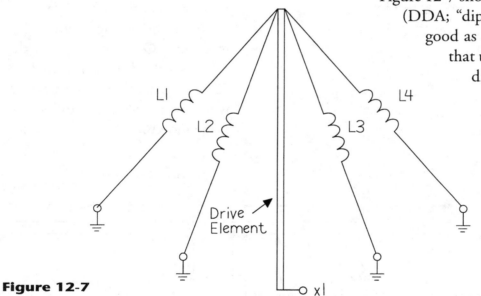

Figure 12-7

Helically Wound Verticals

An old friend of mine, who was something of a cracker barrel (actually it was an old oil drum) philosopher, was fond of claiming "there's more than one way to kill a cat, ya don't gotta choke him to death on butter." (Or something like that…) Likewise with antennas for low frequencies. Vertical antennas for low frequency operation tend to be too high for practical applications. Of course, if you have a 50 to 100 foot tower for a ham or SWL beam antenna for higher frequencies, the tower itself can be used as a low frequency antenna as well as a support structure. There is another way.

Short vertical low frequency antennas can be built from wood or from PVC pipes helically wound with wire. For example, at 2 MHz we could use a 25-foot insulated support wound with wire. There are two wire wrapping schemes. The first, shown in Figure 12-8, is the slow pitch method. In this method, a bit more than a quarter-wavelength of wire is wound over the entire length of the support. It is assumed here that the support is quite high (0.1λ to 0.2λ) so that the wire turns are made at a slow pitch.

For very short helically wound antennas ($> 0.05\lambda$) we can use the fast pitch method shown in Figure 12-9. This method can be used when the diameter of the winding (which is essentially the diameter of the PVC pipe) must be very small compared with the wavelength of the received signal. Practically speaking, this means anything up to about ten inches diameter is acceptable, although two to four inches is most commonly used.

In these helically wound vertical antennas, about a half-wavelength of wire is linearly wound and spaced so that the entire available length of the support is evenly covered. A 16-foot PVC pipe is 0.05λ at 3 MHz, while a 20-foot PVC pipe is 0.05λ at 2.46 MHz. As an example, consider a 16-foot PVC pipe designed to operate

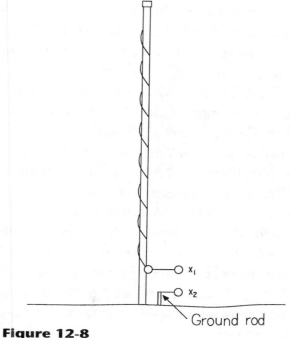

Figure 12-8

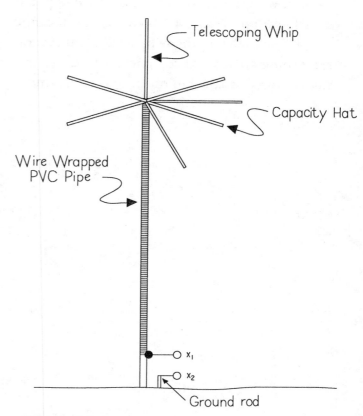

Figure 12-9

at 5 MHz. A half-wavelength of wire at this frequency is about 100 feet. To make the helically wound vertical, then, 100 feet of insulated wire (any type) is wound so that it is evenly spaced over the entire 16 feet of length.

The helically wound antenna simulates a quarter-wavelength vertical, but typically is much higher "Q" than a full-sized vertical. As a result, the helically wound antenna is much narrower in bandwidth than the full-sized version. In order to alleviate that problem, it is common to use a capacity hat made from four to six rods measuring eight to 12 inches (brazing rods or hobby brass rod stock are popular) arranged evenly spaced around the antenna at the top end. Some people report that a ten to 12 inch aluminum pie pan works just as well, although it tends to look a bit tacky.

The actual length required of the antenna is found experimentally. The interaction of the turns of wire change the physical length required to achieve an electrical half-wavelength. Some people use a telescoping whip antenna at the top for tuning to resonance. These whips are salvaged from portable radios (or new replacement antennas for same) or from car radio antennas.

Adjustment of the helically wound antenna is done similarly to any other antenna. The correct wire length is found experimentally by using a grid dip meter, impedance meter, SWR meter, or noise bridge. The feedpoint impedance tends to be very low, about 4 Ω, so either a broadband impedance transformer or an antenna tuning unit is needed.

Ground Systems for Low Frequency Antennas

A good ground is important for all antennas, especially unbalanced types, but it is even more critical in the low frequency bands. Whenever you see the ground symbol in the illustrations in this chapter, assume that it refers to a very good Earth ground or to at least a multiple radial counterpoise ground. Such a counterpoise need not have straight radials, but they at least should be resonant. Keep in mind that the efficiency of a compensation antenna is poorer than full-sized antennas at best, so we don't want to burn up any more signal in losses than is absolutely necessary. Get a good ground!

CHAPTER 13

Odds & Ends

In previous chapters, we've often referred to *antenna tuning units* (ATUs), also known as antenna tuners. These devices take the impedance of an antenna as an input and "transform" it to a 50 Ω output. ATUs do this by a network of variable inductors and capacitors. Since the impedance of an antenna will vary with frequency, you'll have to readjust the settings of the inductors and capacitors as you change the receiver's frequency.

While it's possible to build your own ATU, they are also available from several radio equipment manufacturers at reasonable cost. Deluxe units are able to accept three different types of antenna inputs, namely random wire, parallel line (such as 300 Ω twin-lead), and coaxial cable. Simpler antenna tuning units only have a coaxial input and output, but these can be used with random wire inputs simply by inserting the random wire lead into the SO-239 coaxial input jack. (You might have better results by attaching the random wire leading to a "banana" plug so that it will fit more snugly into the SO-239 connector.) These simpler ATUs are sometimes known as "random wire" tuners, and most were originally designed for use with low power ham transmitters. A typical random wire tuner manufactured by MFJ is shown in Figure 13-1. This type of unit will give satisfactory performance as the ATU specified in some antennas covered in earlier chapters.

Preamplifiers

RF *preamplifiers* or *preselectors* are used ahead of the receiver to boost weak antenna signals to a level where they can be received better. Most incorporate a gain control to allow you to select the desired degree of amplification. A growing trend is to combine an antenna tuning unit and preamplifier in the same unit, as shown in Figure 13-2. The unit in Figure 13-2 is the MFJ-959B. This unit lets users select between two different antennas, and can operate as an antenna tuning unit only, as a preamplifier/ATU combination, or it can feed either antenna directly to the receiver.

Preamplifiers can be useful in many situations, such as when chasing weak DX signals that are just barely above the atmospheric noise level or when using less-than-optimum antennas (indoor antennas, shortened antennas, etc.). However, they must be used carefully. If their gain is set too high, the receiver may be "overloaded," producing cross-modulation and spurious signals in the receiver. If your listening is

Figure 13-1

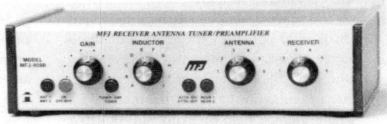

Figure 13-2

restricted to powerful, well-heard stations, or if you're using a "full size" antenna, odds are that you will seldom need to use a preamplifier.

Active Antennas

Active antennas are very short (two to six feet) antennas that include a built-in preamplifier. They are used to replace longer antennas in places where a longer antenna is not viable, such as when you're an apartment dweller, townhouse or rowhouse dweller, or live in a single family house with a lot too small to support even a limited space antenna. You might also be a listener who lives in a rented house owned by a landlord with no sympathy for the shortwave listening hobby.

Unfortunately, the active antenna has been touted perhaps a little too much by advertisers in the shortwave industry. I don't believe that, when all factors are considered, an active antenna will actually work as well overall as a 50 to 100 foot random length wire antenna. However, there are situations where they are very useful, especially when living under some of the constraints noted above. Don't expect a miracle, however. Try an active antenna, if you must, but expect to have to live with the defects.

Some of the defects are those that also afflict a preamplifier: strong signals will overload some active antennas. If there is no filtering in the front-end, then you will find that local AM stations tend to "swamp" an active antenna badly. Also, the electrical noise inside a building tends to become worse when an active antenna is used because the antenna amplifies noise as much as it does real signals. Various electrical noises are all seen as valid signals by the active antenna—and are amplified. The noise also afflicts regular wire antennas (they are real signals, after all) but the wire antennas don't amplify the mess.

A false premise held by many fans of active antennas is that they will magically pick up signals. In fact, they can't receive signals that aren't present. An active antenna used inside a metal frame structure, such as a high rise apartment building, or one with aluminum siding such as my house, will not pick up signals that are shielded by the metal building…and most will be. If some signal is present, and the electrical noise is not too high, then the active antenna will work reasonably well if the signal's strength is not too low.

It is also possible to build your own active antenna by using a preamplifier with a physically shortened antenna, a length of aluminum tubing, or random length of wire. This can be a versatile solution and less expensive than many active antennas.

Indoor Antennas

Indoor antennas are relatively easy to install, and except for certain circumstances work quite well. Indoor antennas typically don't work as well as the same antenna outdoors, but in some cases the differences aren't profound.

Several problems insinuate themselves into the indoor antenna installation. Perhaps the most important is the matter of safety. You don't want to install the wire where humans or pets can tangle with it. It can be quite dangerous to be trotting towards what the British call the "loo" and get decapitated by a wire antenna. Place the wire where it can't be a hazard.

The attic or loft probably represents the best alternative for indoor antennas. In the attic or loft, the antenna is well hidden. Besides, it is also above most of the effects of siding, wiring, and plumbing so it will probably work better than most other indoor antennas. To support antennas in the attic, you can use television antenna wire stand-off insulators screwed into a roof rafter or truss. Don't screw these into the roof itself, especially if it penetrates to the outside—the screw threads can serve as a "wick" to draw water into the attic, rotting the wood around the screw.

The random length wire is probably the most common attic antenna. It can be installed out of the way to prevent interference from people trying to stuff stuff into the attic, or balancing precariously on the rafters trying desperately not to get fiberglass on your skin.

Be careful in the attic, by the way. Most attics are not finished, and the only thing between you and the floor below is a bit of half-inch dry wall and a coating of paint. If there is no floor in the attic, then stay on the wooden joists...or you might accidentally drop into the loo while someone...errr...*looses,* so to speak.

Attic antenna feed lines can be routed through the walls to your receiver if the correct path can be found. Avoid paths that also include the electrical wires. Not only is there a potential electrical hazard, but the power wires sometimes carry loads of noise signals, and they can couple into the receiver through the antenna line. In cases where the receiver is on the floor below the

attic, then a route through the ceiling of a closet is an unobtrusive way to run the coax or down-lead.

Another popular form of attic antenna is the mobile antenna. For years, hams have done this trick. A pair of loaded whips, fed back to back, become a decent replacement for a short, loaded dipole. Adjusting the coil values will make such antennas work on the shortwave broadcasting bands as well.

Clandestine, Stealth, and Disguised Antennas

Some people are in a seemingly intractable situation regarding receiving antennas. The home-owners association, the landlord, or some other Person of Higher Authority just simply won't (*won't won't won't*) let you put up an antenna. There are several approaches that can be taken:

1. Hire a witch doctor to stick pins in a little doll that has a photo print of the offender's face pasted on it.

2. Wish fervently (the ferventer the better) that they be visited by a thousand cockroaches, all of them the size of ducks.

3. Cheat. Put up an antenna that no one knows is an antenna.

Of these, option number three seems to be the most viable. It is quite possible to make an antenna that either doesn't look like an antenna, isn't easily seen, or is only used intermittently and is retracted at other times.

One method for making a clandestine-sorta-stealthy antenna is the old flagpole trick as shown in Figure 13-3. A flagpole is a delightful vertical and can even be tuned at the base if the tuning unit is unobtrusive. In some cases, the flag pole is metal, so you can either shunt feed the pole or insulate it from ground and feed it the regular way. If the flagpole is fiberglass (or other insulating material), then pass a wire up through the center of it (see Figure 13-3 inset).

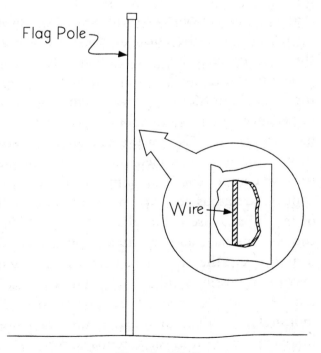

Figure 13-3

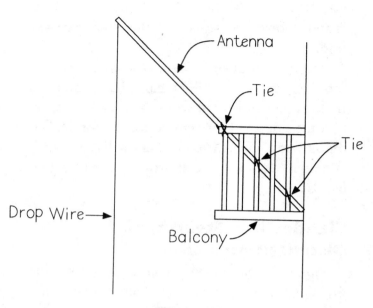

Figure 13-4

Another neat job is the ol' fishing pole trick (Figure 13-4), which is popular with high-rise apartment dwellers. Drop a thin (repeat—*thin*) wire out the window, or from the balcony, while you are listening to the shortwave radio. When you are finished, then reel it in and stow it in the closet. Why not? After all military and civilian aircraft have been trailing HF wires for years.

One caution, however. Whatever you do, DON'T place a weight on the end of the wire. I know that the weight will make the antenna wire hang straighter, but there are at least two dangers that I see from the practice. First, when the wind blows the weight and wire become a pendulum and will sway back and forth, picking up distance on every gust, and then *SMASSSSHHHH!!!* right through the window on a floor below. Second, even a small weight can badly injure or even kill if a pedestrian on the street if it falls far enough, and will make a real mess out of car roofs and windshields. *Safety first!*

Another neat trick involves flower pots. Some developments allow tall flowers and plants—even artificial—on the balcony or patio. Some people make it a rather tall artificial plant, maybe six or eight feet high. A thin wire woven into the foliage can make a reasonable (not good, but OK) antenna for shortwave receivers. Alternatively, wrap the fake stalk with a long length of wire. It will work similarly to a helical wound vertical at some frequencies.

Noise Bridges

One of the most useful instruments in adjusting antennas is the *noise bridge*. It is a combination of an *impedance bridge* with a wideband gaussian *noise generator*. An impedance bridge is a device that allows you to measure the impedance of the antenna, and the noise generator supplies a signal to excite the impedance bridge so an impedance measurement can be made.

Figure 13-5 shows how a noise bridge is connected into an antenna circuit. To use the noise bridge, you first tune the receiver to a frequency in the center of the desired band of operation. Next, the noise generator section of the noise bridge is turned on. When the noise generator is on, you'll hear a "hiss" sound ranging from about S6 to S9 from the receiver. The impedance bridge section of the noise bridge has two controls, "X" for the reactance component of the antenna impedance and "R" for the resistive component of the impedance. The two controls are adjusted until the best overall null of the "hiss" noise is found. The "X" and "R" controls interact, so some twiddling back and forth between the two will be necessary until the maximum possible null is found. The setting of the "R" and "X" controls at maximum null indicates the values of resistive and reactance impedance present in the antenna circuit.

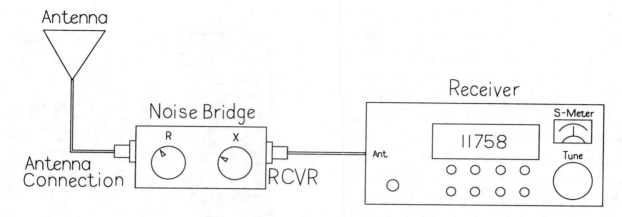

Figure 13-5

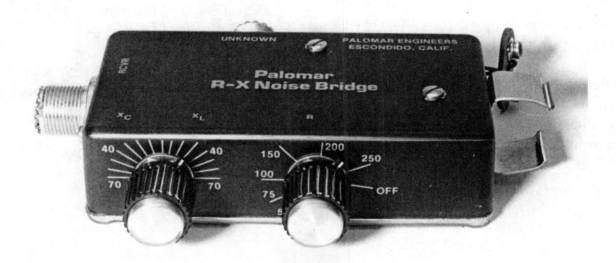

Figure 13-6

Figure 13-6 shows the "R–X Noise Bridge" from Palomar Engineers. This is a low cost noise bridge that I've used for several years and have found quite competent for its intended applications. Other manufacturers offer noise bridges as well. If antenna building becomes your thing and you want to know just what the impedance of an antenna is, then you'll need to add a noise bridge to your set of tools.

An "SWL-Legal" VSWR Analyzer

Measuring VSWR is relatively easy for amateur radio operators: they excite the antenna with their transmitters and then measure the forward and reflected power levels. They can either calculate the VSWR from a standard formula (or look it up on a nonomograph), or they can use a RF power meter calibrated for VSWR as well as in watts. But SWLs have a problem. They are not allowed to use transmitters, and most signal generators don't have sufficient output to drive most VSWR or RF power meters. Luckily for SWLs, there are instruments available, known as *SWR analyzers,* that combine a VSWR meter with a signal source. Figure 13-7 shows two available from MFJ Enterprises. The unit on the left, the MFJ-207, is used on frequencies below 30 MHz while the unit on the right, the MFJ-208 is intended for use above 30 MHz.

Determining SWR with such units is a snap. The idea is to adjust the frequency knob on the analyzer until the SWR meter hits bottom (or *nulls).* The meter reading is directly in terms of SWR, so nothing further is needed. This tells you the resonant frequency of the antenna and the VSWR at that frequency. The antenna and/ or its tuner can then be adjusted to bring the antenna to a point that is useful to you.

After having spent a few weekends using these units, I am convinced that no SWL who is serious about antenna experimentation can get along without one of these instruments.

Figure 13-7

Bibliography and Further Reading

American Radio Relay League, *ARRL Antenna Handbook*. American Radio Relay League (multiple editions).

Bryant, John, "Beverage Antennas" in *Fine Tuning Proceedings 1989* (available from Fine Tuning Special Publications, c/o John Bryant, Route 5, Box 14, Stillwater, OK, 74074).

Carr, Joseph J., *Practical Antenna Handbook*. TAB/McGraw-Hill, 1991.

Eldridge, Bob, "The Wave (Beverage) Antenna: Design and Operation," in *Fine Tuning Proceedings 1991* (available from Fine Tuning Special Publications, c/o John Bryant, Route 5, Box 14, Stillwater, OK, 74074).

Jasik, Henry, *Antenna Engineering Handbook*, McGraw-Hill, 1961.

Levintow, Mike, "Using Two Loop Antennas to Generate Asymmetrical Receiving Patterns," National Radio Club reprint #13. Available from National Radio Club Publications Center, P. O. Box 164, Mannsville, NY, 13661.

Marris, Richard Q., "Experimental Quadraform Ferrite Transmit/Receive Antenna" in *Elektor Electronics USA*, November, 1991.
— "Improving Portable Radio Performance" in *Elektor Electronics USA*, February, 1992.

Misek, Victor, *The Beverage Antenna Handbook*. Published by the author; 142 Wason Road, Hudson, NH, 03051.

National Radio Club, *Beverage and Longwire Antennas: Design and Theory*. Available from National Radio Club Publications Center, P. O. Box 164, Mannsville, NY, 13661.

National Radio Club, *Loop Antennas: Design and Theory*. Available from National Radio Club Publications Center, P. O. Box 164, Mannsville, NY, 13661.

Orr, William I., *Radio Handbook*. Howard W. Sams & Co., Inc. (multiple editions).
— *Wire Antennas for Radio Amateurs*. Radio Publications, Inc., 1972.

Somerfield, A., *Electrodynamics*. Academic Press, 1952.

Villard, O. G., "Indoor Interference-Reducing Antennas for Shortwave Listening" in *Newsletter of the Association of North American Radio Clubs*, January, 1990.
— "Miniature Indoor Directional Antennas for Reducing Sky-Wave and Ground-Wave Interference in the Shortwave Bands" in *Newsletter of the Association of North American Radio Clubs*, March, 1990.
— "Combating Interference in Shortwave Reception with Compact Indoor Directive Antennas" in *World Radio-Television Handbook*, 1990.

Index